The Basque Series

N
W
E
S
Luzon Strait
Batan Islands
20°N
Pacific
Ocean
Babuyan Islands
Luzon
Sea
Luzon
15°N
Philippine
Sea
Manila
South China
Sea
Visayas
Samar
Palawan
Cebu
10°N
Sulu Sea
Davao
Zamboanga
Mindanao
Celebes
(Mindanao)
Sea
5°N
120°E
125°E
0
100
200
mi
0
200
400
km
Cam Sutherland

MARCIANO R. DE BORJA

Basques in the Philippines

FOREWORD BY WILLIAM A. DOUGLASS

University of Nevada Press ▲▲ Reno, Las Vegas

The Basque Series
Series Editor: William A. Douglass
University of Nevada Press,
Reno, Nevada 89557 USA

Library of Congress
Cataloging-in-Publication Data
De Borja, Marciano R., 1966–
Basques in the Philippines / Marciano R. de Borja ; foreword by William A. Douglass. — 1st ed.
p. cm. — (The Basque series)
Includes bibliographical references and index.
ISBN 0-87417-590-9 (hardcover : alk. paper)
1. Basques—Philippines—History. I. Title. II. Series.
DS666.B33D4 2005
959.9′0049992—dc22 2004018176

The paper used in this book is a recycled stock made from 30 percent post-consumer waste materials, certified by FSC, and meets the requirements of American National Standard for Information Sciences—Permanence of Paper for Printed Library Materials, ANSI/NISO Z39.48-1992 (R2002). Binding materials were selected for strength and durability.

University of Nevada Press
Paperback Edition, 2012
21 20 19 18 17 16 15 14 13 12
5 4 3 2 1

ISBN-13: 978-0-87417-590-5
(cloth: alk. paper)
ISBN-13: 978-0-87417-883-8
(pbk. : alk. paper)
ISBN-13: 978-0-87417-891-3
(ebook)

For Atoy, Angel, and Agatha

Contents

Illustrations

Foreword

As quintessential medieval shipbuilders and mariners, Basques played a key role in Spain's expeditionary voyages of discovery and conquest—beginning with those of Christopher Columbus. It is equally documented that Basque mariners, mercenaries, missionaries, and merchants were represented disproportionately (with regards to Iberian regional demography) in the annals of Spanish colonial history. Furthermore, in disparate times and places throughout the empire, and particularly in several Latin American colonies, Basques displayed a propensity to act as a self-aware and mutually supporting ethnic group whose interests could diverge from those of distant Madrid and non-Basque locals alike. In sixteenth-century Potosí and eighteenth-century Caracas this engendered resentment that culminated in violent anti-Basque backlashes. In sum, whether Basques acted as handmaidens of empire or its subverter, the contributions of the Basque diaspora in many parts of the globe are now reasonably well documented.

This scholarly awareness includes the Philippines. However, until the present study by Marciano R. de Borja, our understanding of the island nation's Basque presence has been fragmentary and focused largely on the larger-than-life figures of a few personages. This is ironic since it might be argued that in no other destination has the influence of Basque immigration been greater and more sustained. It is a history initiated by Europe's first contact with the Philippines as personified in Juan Sebastián Elcano (from the Gipuzkoan coastal village of Getaria) and reflected in the continuing importance within Philippine society of the influential Ayala, Elizalde, and Aboitiz families (among others). The importance of the story is further underscored by the uniqueness of the area within Spanish colonial history. In the aftermath of the successful independence movement in continental Latin America, for the remainder of the nineteenth century the Philippines (along with Cuba and Puerto Rico) provided the only "internal" overseas destination for Spanish citizens. Consequently, it remained an outpost for the continuing flow of Iberian-based administrators, clerics, and businessmen. Since rural Basques were on the losing side in Spain's Carlist wars, the Philippines also attracted some Basque political refugees.

In sum, within Basque diasporic history the Philippine experience exhibits certain particularities that can only be understood in their own terms. The present excellent work represents the first comprehensive overview of a heretofore missing chapter.

WILLIAM A. DOUGLASS

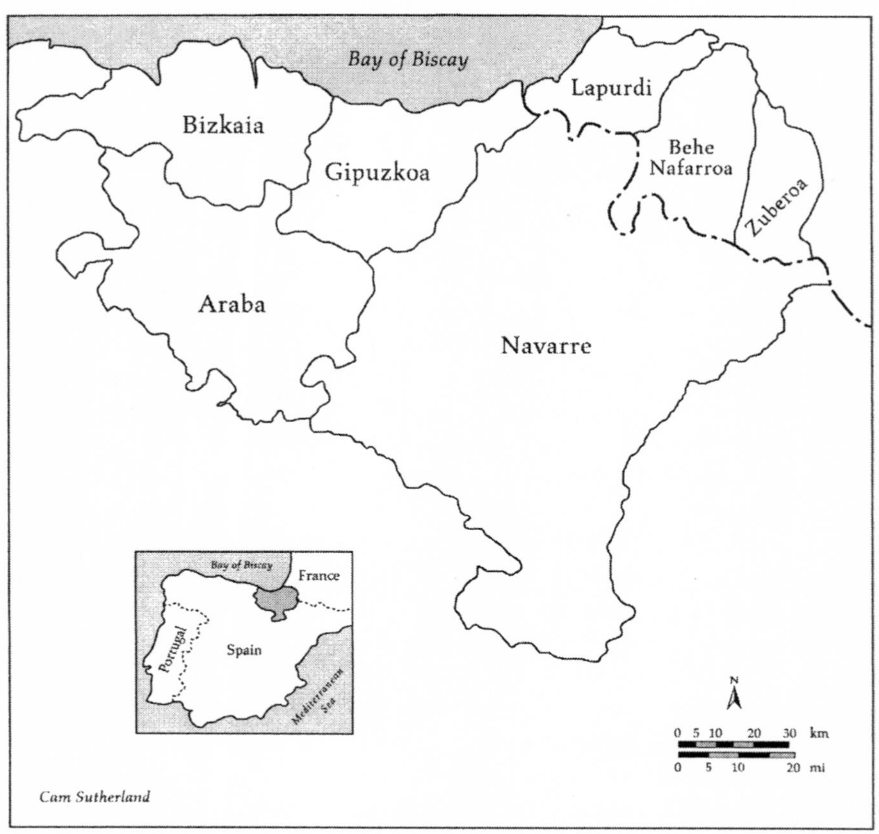

The Basque Country

Preface

This work is an initial attempt to reconstruct the story of the Basques in the Philippines from the arrival of the first Basques in the archipelago in 1521 with the Magellan expedition to the present Basque descendants. It is a study of Basque immigrants in the Philippines and an acknowledgment of their contribution to Philippine nationhood—a significant but unexplored topic in Philippine society and culture.

Most of the people who spearheaded and monopolized the expeditions and the colonization of the New World and the Philippines came from the Kingdom of Castille. Thus, in the Philippines the Spaniards are generally called "Kastila" without distinguishing their regional origin. In truth, regional identities are well delineated in Spain. Apart from the *castellanos,* other groups participated actively in the enterprise of discovering, colonizing, evangelizing, and finally settling the vast Spanish possessions overseas. There were the *gallegos* from Galicia, the *catalanes* from Catalonia, the *andaluces* from Andalucia, and, of course, the *vascos,* or *euskaldunak,* from the Basque Country.

The incorporation of the Basque provinces of Araba, Gipuzkoa, and Bizkaia into the Kingdom of Castille during the thirteenth and fourteenth centuries allowed the Basques to participate later in the colonial undertakings of the Spanish crown. The discovery of the New World by Christopher Columbus in 1492 had a great impact on the Basque economy and later on the emigrant spirit of the Basques. There was a great demand for iron from the Basque foundries. The majority of the ships destined to ply the commercial sea routes of the Spanish colonies were also constructed in Basque shipyards.

During the rise and fall of the Spanish Empire, the Basques played a decisive role in the conquest of the Americas and also of the Philippines. They supplied the Spanish monarchy with soldiers, navigators, merchants, bureaucrats, and missionaries. Some of their descendants heroically defended the interests of the Spanish crown and fended off the encroachment of foreign powers. Others like Simón Bolívar would lead the South American colonies to independence.

If we examine the pages of Philippine history books that recount the Spanish maritime expeditions and colonial regime (1521–1898), we find that the Basques played a leading role in the colonization, evangelization, and administration of the archipelago. Men like Juan Sebastián Elcano, Andrés de Urdaneta, Miguel López de Legazpi, Juan de Salcedo, Martín de Goiti, and Guido de Lavezares represented the

Basque energy, industry, and audacity that laid the foundation of Spanish sovereignty in the Philippines.

The first bishop of Manila, Domingo de Salazar, was a Basque. Other distinguished missionaries during the early years of Spanish evangelization of the Philippines were Basques, including Andrés de Aguirre, Diego de Herrera, Martín de Rada, and Pedro Arce. Basque merchants and capitalists actively participated in the Manila-Acapulco galleon trade. Some of them would form the nucleus of the Royal Economic Society of the Friends of the Country during the latter part of the eighteenth century. The Royal Philippine Company, a state trading company founded in 1785, was actually a successor of the Royal Guizpuzcoan Company of Caracas, a Basque trading company that monopolized colonial trade in Venezuela.

During the British invasion of Manila in 1762, a Basque stood out in resisting the British forces even as the Spaniards surrendered the city. He was Simón de Anda, a native of Araba. He would later be appointed as governor-general of the Philippines after the return of the archipelago to the Spanish crown.

The first bank in the Philippines and Southeast Asia, the Banco Español-Filipino de Isabel II, now known as the Bank of the Philippine Islands, the biggest private bank in the country, was established by the Basque governor-general Antonio de Urbiztondo in 1851. The biggest commercial and trading firm in the Philippines during the second half of the nineteenth century was Ynchausti y Compañía, owned by the Basque Joaquín José de Ynchausti. During the 1870s, international shipping in the Philippines was dominated by the Olano, Larrinaga y Compañía, a Basque shipping firm based in Liverpool, England.

In the two immortal novels of Philippine national hero José Rizal (1861–1896)—*Noli Me Tangere* and *El Filibusterismo* (works that inspired the Philippine revolution against Spain in 1896 and 1898)—the leading character, Crisóstomo Ibarra, is of Basque ancestry. This is probably a tribute to Basque ubiquitousness within the Philippine society during his time. During World War II, some Basques such as Higinio de Uriarte joined the guerrilla movement against the Japanese imperial forces and provided the Allied forces with valuable intelligence.

Looking at the present, we cannot but marvel at the continuity in leadership provided by Basque descendants in various aspects of Philippine life, particularly in economic and political spheres. The Aboitiz, Araneta, Arrespacochaga, Ayala, Bilbao, Eizmendi, Elizalde, Garchitorena, Isasi, Loyzaga, Luzuriaga, Moraza, Uriarte, Ynchausti, Yulo, Zubiri, and Zuluaga families, among others, continue to occupy privileged positions in contemporary Philippine society.

The Ayalas, for example, own a chain of blue chip companies with headquarters in Makati, Manila's financial center, whose famous avenue bears the name of the family. The Aboitizes, on the other hand, are a dominating presence in the inter-island shipping, energy, and telecommunication sectors. For their part, the Luzuriagas founded Victorias Milling Corporation, during the American period the largest producer of refined sugar in the Philippines. It also became one of the biggest sugar companies in the world during the American regime.

Jai alai, which literally means "happy feast" in Euskara and is the name of a variant of Basque pelota, was for a long time a popular betting game in the Philippines. The Manila fronton closed in 1986 and reopened briefly in 1998 only to be padlocked again a year and a half later. Despite a massive effort and protest to save it, the building was ordered demolished by the Manila city government in September 2000. The controversial Basque sport may still stage a comeback.

Contemplating the current Philippine map, one will be surprised by the number of Basque place-names. There are provinces, towns, and cities called Anda, Garchitorena, Lavezares, Legazpi, Mondragon, Nueva Vizcaya, Pamplona, Urdaneta, and Zumarraga. Many of Manila's streets also carry Basque names. Among them are Ayala, Arlegui, Barrengoa, Bilbao, Durango, Echague, Elizondo, Gaztambide, Goiti, Guernica, Mendiola, Oscariz, and many more. They are only some of the visible manifestations of the Basque presence in the country. How can we ignore the contribution of this group who exerted tremendous influence in the political, economic, religious, and social development of the Philippines?

The process of singling out the Basques' achievements or failures among the several ethnic groups that make up the Spanish population in the Philippines is not a simple task inasmuch as their actions and interests were intertwined with the general colonial activity and policy of the Spanish crown. Still, their exploits and outlook differentiated them from other Spanish settlers. Despite their small number, they maintained their strong ethnic identity and never fully assimilated themselves with others from the Iberian Peninsula. Such aloof and reticent behavior sometimes facilitated my research.

I wish to clarify from the outset that this book deals mainly with the Basques from the Spanish side of the Basque Country, covering the four provinces of Araba, Gipuzkoa, Bizkaia, and Navarre, although there is a sporadic mention of French Basques and those who came to the Philippines from the Spanish colonies in the New World. Lastly, aside from learning about the Basques' presence in the Philippines, it is also interesting to find out how many Filipinos today can trace their roots to an immigrant Basque ancestor and how many Basques can still identify their own families' or their relatives' descendants in the Philippines.

Acknowledgments

I could have not written this book if not for the valuable assistance of various institutions and people. I wish therefore to thank the Agencia Española de Cooperación Internacional of the Spanish Ministry of Foreign Affairs and the Fundación General Mediterránea for the scholarships granted to me so that I could undertake graduate studies at the University of Navarra. Others in Spain to whom I am grateful include the late Ronald Escobedo Mancilla, my thesis adviser; José Luis Illueca, then vice president of Philip Morris (España); my relatives Danny and Ester Pascual, for allowing me to stay with them while I did my research in Madrid; Ramón Herrando, who provided me with moral support and fraternal guidance during my whole stay in Spain; and Vice Consul Iric Arribas of the Philippine Embassy in Madrid.

I am grateful to several people in Chile, including Rodolfo A. Arizala, former Philippine ambassador to Chile; Pedro Aretxabala, former delegate of the Basque Country in Chile; Pedro Oyanguren, director of the Basque-Chilean Foundation for Development; and Juan Mendicute of the Eusko Etxea (Basque Center) in Santiago. All of them provided me with useful information, encouragement, and advice.

In the Philippines, I was assisted by Antonio M. de Ynchausti and Andoni F. Aboitiz, who generously shared information about their families and gave me a general view of the Basque descendants in contemporary Philippine society. Special thanks to Maritoni C. Ortigas and the Filipinas Heritage Library in Makati City (Philippines) for providing me with various references and photos that make up most of the pictorial section of this book.

I am especially indebted to William A. Douglass, former coordinator of the Basque Studies Program (now Center for Basque Studies) of the University of Nevada, Reno, in the United States, for writing the foreword for this book and for providing me with relevant documents and materials. Needless to say, any errors in and shortcomings of this book are solely mine.

Last, I wish to thank my wife, Espie, for her love and for patiently listening to my stories about the Basques for years and perhaps for many more years to come.

Basques in the Philippines

Chapter One

The Basque People

> To be an authentic Basque, there are three requirements: to carry a sonorous name that indicates the origin; to speak the language of the sons of Aitor, and . . . to have an uncle in the Americas.
>
> Pierre Lhande, S.J., *L'Emigration basque*, 1909

To Lhande's description of the past emigrant vocation of the Basques, we can add "to have an uncle in the Philippines," since the Basque diaspora was not limited to the Americas. A handful of Basques also migrated to, settled in, and left their indelible mark on Philippine society. The saga of the Basques in the Philippines is by no means negligible and is perhaps even more compelling and colorful than that of their brethren and cousins who settled in Latin America and the American West.

In the Philippines the Basques played a decisive role in the establishment and maintenance of Spanish sovereignty from 1565 to 1898. They stayed even after Spain ceded the islands to the United States in December 1898. Even at present, Basque descendants, while maintaining a low profile, still play a prominent role in Philippine society. We cannot therefore thoroughly appreciate contemporary Philippine history and society without discussing the role of the Basques. Although they formed part of the Spanish contingent that colonized the archipelago, the Basques had a distinct character and remained outside the mainstream. They exhibited a brand of heroism and ambition, sometimes bordering on the bizarre. Who are the Basques? What is their character as a people? What makes them different from the other Spaniards or French? What was their role in the creation of the Spanish Empire?

The Basques refer to themselves as *euskaldunak*, which means "speakers of Euskara," the Basque language. They call their homeland Euskal Herria, although they have never had their own nation-state. They live in the seven traditional Basque territories of Araba, Gipuzkoa, Bizkaia, and Navarre, which belong to Spain, while Behe Nafarroa, Lapurdi, and Zuberoa are part of France. Together the Basque Country has a total land area of 20,864 square kilometers. In the Basque context, the territories located in Spain are known as Hegoalde (Land of the South), while those situated in France are called Iparralde (Land of the North), or what the Anglophones refer to as French Basque Country.

For centuries, the Basque people have been the object of numerous ethnographic, historical, and linguistic studies. Some scholars claim that they were the first inhabitants of the Iberian Peninsula and even the oldest surviving ethnic group in Europe. But the Basques' first claim to uniqueness is their language, Euskara, whose origin is shrouded in mystery. Linguists are baffled by the fact that it is not related to the Indo-European linguistic family or to any known language at all, though there were serious attempts to compare it with such diverse tongues as Hungarian and Japanese. No linguistic affinities have yet been established. Remarkably, Euskara has survived and even thrived, notwithstanding the strong influences of Latin, Spanish, and French.

In addition, the Basque language has always been famed for its difficulty. The Basques say that the Devil came to their country to learn it, but after seven years, having got no further than *bai* (yes) and *ez* (no), he gave it up in disgust. They add that he forgot even these two words as he was departing.[1] Referring to the Basques' pride in their language, the French *writer* Victor Hugo said, "The Basque language is not just the nation, it is almost a religion."[2]

Basques are normally identifiable by their sonorous surnames, which often refer to places, such as Bilbao, Elizondo, Loyola, and Zumarraga. Although this kind of surname formation is not unique to the Basques, what is surprising is that a great number of Basque surnames are related to the homestead (*eche*, or *etxe*): Echeverria, Echegoyen, Echegaray, Etcheverri, Echezarra, Echenique, Echeandia, and so forth; and names of trees: for example, *areitz*, or *aretx* (oak), from which hundreds of Basque surnames are derived: Areizaga, Aretxaga, Aresti, Arismendi, Aritegui, and so on. Other surnames are rooted in geographical features—mountain (*mendi*), valley (*ibar*), prairie (*larre*), and valley (*aran*), to name just a few. Prominent examples are Mendiburu, Ibarra, Larreta, and Arana. Basque surnames can also be a combination of the preceding.

Another distinctive trait of the Basques is the unusually high proportion of blood type O (57 percent) and blood type A (41 percent), higher than in any European population, as well as an almost complete absence of blood type B (1 percent) and AB (nearly 0 percent). The Basques also manifest the highest occurrence of Rh negative factor (about 42 percent) of any population in the world. Rh negative O blood, which occurs frequently among Basques, is in high demand since it can be donated to any individual. Many Basques therefore are in theory "universal blood donors."

The Basques also exhibit physical features that differentiate them from other Europeans. They have good height, a strong body, large legs, a wide back, fair skin, brown eyes and hair, an oval face, aquiline nose, narrow jaw, bad teeth, small chin, and a large temple behind the forehead. The Basques' propensity for hard, manual work and athletic abilities in sports and dances can be partly explained by these physical attributes. Basques are also widely known for being independent-minded, stubborn, adventurous, opportunistic, indomitable, and strongly attached to their traditions. Other traits that could be added are hardworking, loyal, religious, courageous, persevering, and cheerful.

Basque culture has survived despite centuries of foreign influence, be it Roman, Frank, Visigoth, Moor, Spanish, or French. After incorporation of the Basque Country within Spain during the thirteenth and fourteenth centuries (although Navarre remained an independent kingdom until 1512 when it succumbed to Castille), Basques have continuously enjoyed autonomy for centuries in exchange for loyalty to the Spanish crown. This arrangement was codified in the *fueros* (charter of local laws and privileges). The *fueros* enabled the Basques to be subjects of imperial Spain without altering their political system and cultural norms. By tradition, each ascending Spanish monarch had to travel to the Bizkaian city of Gernika and swear his obedience to the fueros beneath the famous oak tree of the city, before his sovereignty extended to Bizkaia. Inhabitants of other Spanish Basque provinces expected similar demonstrations of loyalty from the monarch.[3]

A nation's character and identity is greatly influenced by geography and historical circumstances. The Basques are no exception. The Basque Country lies in between two great European states with equally glorious imperial pasts. Bounded by the Bay of Biscay in the northwest, the great mountains of the Pyrenees in the northeast, and the rugged plains of Castille in the south, the Basques live in a small, but diverse territory that played a key role in the imperial designs of both Spain and France.

According to Julio Caro Baroja, the great Basque anthropologist, the smallness and narrowness of the Basque Country, its rich mineral resources, particularly iron, its abundant forests in the past, and its access to the sea have made the Basques, from the Middle Ages up to the present, ironsmiths, fishermen on the high seas, skilled navigators, shipbuilders, and industrialists.[4]

The Basques contributed immensely to the conquest of Seville and southern Spain during the time of King Ferdinand II (1452–1516). They also intervened decisively in the reconquest of the kingdom of Granada, and some Basque sea captains were charged with transporting to Africa the Moors who chose not to accept the yoke of the Christian victors. There were also Basque mariners and mercenaries fighting in France in the service of the English or French during the wars of the fourteenth and fifteenth centuries. The French Basques sided with the English, while the Spanish Basques supported the French. There were also Basque merchant ships trading in the Scandinavian countries and the eastern Mediterranean. And side by side with the mariners and merchants were the Basque corsairs who raided the English and French coasts and prowled the waters of the Mediterranean and North Seas.[5] The Basques were also intrepid whalers and were said to have reached the coast of North America long before the Columbus expedition.

Gipuzkoa and Bizkaia produced arms and supplies for Spain during the fifteenth century. Later, when swords and crossbows became obsolete because of the introduction of harquebuses, the Basques were quick to manufacture the new weapon, and, by the seventeenth century, their firearms had gained wide recognition.[6]

The initial maritime expeditions aimed at reaching the Indies by sailing west gave Basque navigation a great impetus. By the end of the fifteenth century, Basques and Sevillians had participated in the first reconnaissance of the Canary Islands, which eventually became a springboard for future expeditions to the Americas. Soon Seville and the Basque Country became the main axis of the Spanish Empire. When the Great Armada of Philip II attacked England, the Basques were counted on to provide a considerable number of ships.[7]

The Basques' participation in Spain's maritime expedition dates back to the voyage of Christopher Columbus to the New World in 1492. They became fixtures of succeeding enterprises. The Basques often formed the expeditionary and religious contingent. Their involvement in the commercial traffic was significant throughout the colonial period. Thus, the Basque Country was considered the cradle of Spanish navigators, providing in great part the manpower for the conquest of the Americas.[8]

The participation of Basque sailors in maritime expeditions can be partly explained by the strong Basque influence in their preparation. Many of those occupying important positions in the Casa de Contratación (clearing house for maritime ventures) in Seville were Basques who engaged in all aspects of maritime and commercial enterprises. The Basque participation in the Spanish maritime expeditions and conquests was crucial. Basques were often at the vanguard of these daring enterprises at a time when they were considered "missions with no return."

The maritime discoveries stimulated the emigrant spirit of the Basque people and had a great impact on the Basque economy. The demand for iron from Basque foundries trebled during the first decades of the sixteenth century following the Spanish advances to the New World, and Basque shipyards almost monopolized the construction of vessels that plied the commercial routes to Spanish overseas possessions. Traveling to the Basque Country in 1572, the Italian Venturino remarked, "Here, more ships are built than in the rest of Spain and the people are the most skillful in the art of navigation. They are very tough and expert seafarers and better than all other mariners."[9]

Although the Basque Country, despite being a region of Spain and France, only belatedly converted to Catholicism, the Basque embraced the religion with great zeal and vigor. A Gipuzkoan, Ignatius Loyola (1491–1556), founded the Society of Jesus. Later, Francis Xavier (1506–1552), a Navarrese Jesuit and a disciple of Ignatius, would be known as the "Apostle of the Indies." Thousands of Basque missionaries and clerics would propagate the Catholic faith worldwide, particularly in the Spanish colonies in the New World and the Philippines.

Basques were also famed calligraphers and amanuenses, at a time when printing was not yet widely available. The Spanish monarchs Charles I and Philip II, the Habsburg and Bourbon kings, as well as the nobility, employed personal Basque writers. Aside from their handwriting skills, the Basques were sought after as trusted and loyal secretaries.[10]

Furthermore, the Basques have always been famous as stonecutters and were so employed by Philip II in the construction of the Escorial (a sumptuous palace outside of Madrid). On one occasion when they struck for better pay, the king was forced to grant their demands, for both he and they knew that nowhere else could he find such skilled workmen.[11] In short, Basques were the pivotal agents of the imperial enterprise.

During the second half of the eighteenth century, the twilight years of the Spanish Empire, the expanded role of the Basques in Spanish administrative and commercial circles was uniquely imbued with the philosophical influences of the Enlightenment. Thus an ethnic network was established that not only pervaded the totality of the Hispanic world but infused its highest levels of social, political, and economic life.[12] This network was typified by the Royal Basque Society, which inspired, among others, the creation of the Royal Economic Society of the Friends of the Country in the Philippines toward the end of the eighteenth century.

Economics must have been the overriding consideration of emigrants leaving the Basque Country. Before the rise of Spain as a world power in the sixteenth century, there were few choices for young male Basques aside from becoming a "soldier, priest, or poet." The standard of living was low and even much lower in the countryside. Basque soil is not fertile, and the iron mines were not fully exploited until the nineteenth century. For many Basques at the time the future lay beyond the high seas, particularly in the North Atlantic fisheries and whaling. The newly established Spanish colonies in the New World and, much later, in the Philippines would provide economic opportunities for the adventurous and daring.

Before the age of discovery, San Sebastian and Bilbao, the two prosperous cities of Gipuzkoa and Bizkaia today, were small and backward settlements that were still nurturing an incipient bourgeoisie. They subsisted through maritime trade, construction, iron foundries, arms production, and metal works. Basque families were large. Ignatius Loyola, the founder of the Society of Jesus, was the youngest of thirteen brothers. Juan Sebastián Elcano, the first circumnavigator of the world, was the eldest of nine.[13]

Therefore, another key factor to consider in understanding Basque emigration is the rule of inheritance. In rural Basque society the practice was to select a single heir(ess) for the family patrimony. The remaining offspring were dowered but then forced to fend for themselves. Many of these *segundones* left in search of fame and fortune in the far-flung colonies of the Spanish Empire. In later centuries, some left their homeland to escape military conscription during times of civil wars and international conflicts; some left because of political persecution; while others fled prosecution for criminal and civil offenses.

It is not my intention here to enumerate in detail the causes of Basque emigration, since the topic is treated more exhaustively in other works. For present purposes what is important to highlight is the background of the Basques, who would later play a crucial role in the establishment of Spanish hegemony in the Philippines and its subsequent development.

Chapter Two

Initial Contacts

> The Islands of the eastern ocean of the Spanish Crown, adjacent to outer Asia, are commonly called Western Islands (Islas del Poniente) by those who sail there; by the demarcation of Castille, and its seas and lands of the Americas, because one sails from Spain by following the movement of the sun, from East to West. And by the same reason, they are called Eastern Islands by those who navigate to India from Portugal, from West to East; making round trips until reaching these islands, which are numerous, big and small, that are aptly called the Philippines.
>
> Antonio de Morga, *Sucesos de las Islas Filipinas,* 1609

September 6, 1522. San Lúcar de Barrameda.

Three years after leaving Spain, the ship *Victoria* docked once again in the bustling port in Seville carrying the remaining crew of Ferdinand Magellan's expedition. The *Victoria* was one of five ships that in 1519 had embarked westward with the goal of reaching the Indies and laying claim to the coveted Spice Islands. Only the *Victoria,* living up to its name, returned. Of the 275 men who made up the original crew, only 18 survived the expedition.[1] Four of them were Basques, including the last skipper of the *Victoria,* Juan Sebastián Elcano.[2] They achieved the first continuous circumnavigation of the world, confirming Christopher Columbus's theory that the Orient could be reached by sailing west, a postulate thought to be ridiculous in Europe at the time. More importantly for this study, the Magellan expedition unexpectedly brought the first Basques to the Philippines.

Juan Sebastián Elcano was born in 1487 in Getaria, a fishing village in Gipuzkoa, at a time when Spain was emerging as one of the leading states in Europe. He was the eldest of nine children of Domingo Sebastián Elcano and Catalina del Puerto. Like most men in his village, the sea had a powerful influence on his life and destiny. He became a seafarer just like his two brothers and many other Basques of his time. As a novice crewman, he learned the ropes of navigation by ferrying contraband goods to French ports. Because of Spain's military engagements in Italy and northern Africa, Elcano, together with hundreds of other Basque sailors and soldiers, moved from the Atlantic to the Mediterranean Sea. He joined the military campaigns (mainly transporting regular and mercenary troops) organized by Cardinal Cisneros against the Moors in Algiers in 1509 and by the great Captain Gonzalo Fernandez de Córdoba in the Italian peninsula.

In his early life, Elcano had never shown much promise or signs of greatness. Instead, he led a prodigal and wayward life, piling up more debts than he could pay. Under pressure from his creditors, Elcano sold some of his ships to foreigners. Much later he found himself persecuted by the Spanish authorities for *estafa* (fraud). Out of desperation, Elcano offered his services to whoever was willing to recruit him. The Magellan expedition became his only option. By enlisting as a crewman, Elcano hoped to at least receive clemency for his previous offenses while clearing his name.[3]

Even then Elcano had to use his family connections. He was related to the Gaiza de Arzaus and the Ibarrola families, whose members occupied important positions in the Casa de Contratación in Seville. An Ibarrola was the former bookkeeper (more or less equivalent to the chief accountant in modern business parlance) of the Casa de Contratación. Undoubtedly his compatriots and relatives facilitated his recruitment. Perhaps his relatives thought that in the event he did not survive the expedition, his huge debts would be forgotten. It is an interesting irony that Elcano, who felt forced by personal and financial problems to join a daring expedition, would later succeed, redeem himself, and even receive the honor that Ferdinand Magellan wanted most.

Magellan was born to nobility in 1480 in Sarbosa, near Oporto, in Portugal. As a navigator, he first saw action as a member of an expedition to India (1505) led by Admiral Francisco de Almeida, later viceroy and governor of the Indies. He later served with distinction in the conquest of Malacca (1511), where he rose to become a captain. He would form part of the elite circle of Portuguese navigators whose stunning successes transformed Portugal from a tiny, backward kingdom into a first-class maritime power.

This transformation could have not been possible without the vision and wisdom of King Henry (1394–1460). Under his aegis, Portugal occupied the vanguard during the age of discovery. In 1419 Henry founded a nautical school in Sagres, the first of its kind in Europe, where he resided for forty years. Henry's nautical school attracted many talented cartographers, navigators, shipbuilders, carpenters, and other experts of different nationalities. Their goal was simple—to develop new navigational techniques that would ensure Portugal's success in maritime exploration. Because of his achievement, Henry earned the title "the Navigator," although he had never ventured upon the sea. In time, Portugal began reaping rewards from its investment. In 1449, the Portuguese sailed around Cape Bojeador and in 1457 discovered Cape Verde. Thirty years later, in 1487, Bartholomeu Dias sailed around the Cape of Good Hope. The following year, Vasco da Gama reached Calicut, India. His expedition was a huge success because it brought home a large shipment of exotic Oriental merchandise.

Henry's dream of sailing around the African continent to Asia thus became a reality. Portugal soon after succeeded in breaking the dominance of two Italian city-states—Genoa and Venice—in the lucrative trade with the Orient whose prized items were spices (pepper, cinnamon, clove, nutmeg, and mace), gold, silver, and slaves. Portugal, however, had a strong rival in Spain.

The rise of modern Spain began with the union of Castille and Aragon in 1475 and culminated in the conquest of the last Moorish kingdom of Granada in the same year. Spain, though a latecomer, would sponsor the outstanding maritime expedition of the epoch, resulting in the discovery of the New World on October 12, 1492, by an obscure Genoan navigator named Christopher Columbus. Earlier, Columbus, inspired by the Florentine cartographer Toscanelli, vigorously petitioned the Spanish Catholic monarchs, King Ferdinand of Aragon and Queen Isabel of Castille, to finance his daring expedition—to reach the Indies by sailing west. After seeing the success of neighboring Portugal in its maritime and commercial exploits, the Catholic kings granted the request of Columbus.

Although Columbus staunchly believed that what he discovered in 1492 was the "Indies," his successful voyage generated a bitter conflict of interest between the two Iberian states. King John of Portugal vehemently protested that the maritime expeditions of Columbus were incursions into the Portuguese sphere of influence. The intense rivalry between Spain and Portugal required the intervention of the pope, the ultimate arbiter of disputes among Catholic monarchs at the time.

On May 3, 1493, Pope Alexander VI issued the bull *Inter caetera,* which awarded the Catholic kings of Spain the full right to explore and claim the territories that were to be discovered on the western side of an imaginary line drawn a hundred leagues from the Azores. Conversely, everything found to the east of this line would belong to the Portuguese monarch. These concessions, however, were limited to the lands that were not yet occupied by any Christian ruler. On October 6, 1493, the pope extended said privileges to territories adjacent to the East Indies and authorized the Spaniards to settle there any lands discovered in the course of navigating toward the west.

The Portuguese king questioned the *Inter Caetera* under the suspicion that certain territories already under his dominion would be adversely affected by the demarcation line. As a result, representatives of the two Iberian monarchs met in Tordesillas to negotiate a treaty that would redraw the line of demarcation at 270 leagues to the west of the Azores. The Treaty of Tordesillas was ratified in 1494. The New World thereby passed largely to Spain, while India remained in the hands of Portugal. However, this treaty was never recognized by other European powers such as Holland, Britain, and France, who would later challenge the naval and imperial supremacy of Spain and Portugal. But, in the meantime, the two Iberian states would lord it over the seas and newly discovered territories. Soon Spanish colonizers and missionaries were all over the Americas, founding settlements, amassing wealth, and converting the natives to Christianity. But the possession of an extensive colony in the New World did not satisfy Spain's quest for the much-coveted Spice Islands.

Magellan vowed to finish the mission that Columbus failed to complete. He was convinced that Columbus's goal—of reaching the Indies by sailing west—was possible. However, his proposal to the king of Portugal was flatly rejected as absurd, aside from being too costly. Why bother to sail west to reach the east when Portugal already monopolized the route to the Indies under the Treaty of Tordesillas? Failing to get Portuguese sponsorship of his project, Magellan moved to Seville in 1517 and met with Diego Barbosa, a compatriot, who had good connections with the Spanish nobility. Through Barbosa, Magellan obtained an audience with Charles I and convinced him of the merit of his plan. He assured the Spanish king that the Spice Islands were not located within the Portuguese sphere of influence as fixed by the demarcation line. On signing the *capitulación* (royal contract) on March 22, 1518, and after receiving the prestigious title of Knight of Saint James, Magellan initiated preparations for his expedition.

Here we can return to Elcano and the Basque role in the Magellan expedition. The list of Basques involved in the preparation and manning of the expedition was notable. The resolute supporter of Magellan was the Bizkaian Matienzo, who would later become the abbot of Jamaica. He was then the treasurer of the Casa de Contratación. The contractor of the expedition was another Bizkaian, Domingo de Ochandino. Juan López de Recalde was the bookkeeper. Artieta, a native of Lekeitio, also had an important role in the organization of the voyage. He procured all the supplies and provisions from Bizkaia and Gipuzkoa. He also bought the flag ship *Trinidad* from Lequizamon, another Bizkaian. Others such as the Isasagas, Eguinos, Moniba-Alberros, Isastis, Urquizas, Onas, Irurruzas, Berospes, and Ibarrolas, also held pivotal posts.[4] Of the 275 men who made up the crew of the expedition, at least 35, or 12.7 percent, were Basques (see appendix 1).[5]

Interestingly, Magellan was joined by his slave, Enrique de Malaya, whom he had acquired while leading a Portuguese expedition to the Indonesian island of Ternate. Filipino scholars believe that Enrique was a native of the Philippines.[6] On September 20, 1519, the Magellan expedition left the port of San Lúcar de Barrameda in Seville. It was plagued by problems from the outset. First, the provisions were discovered to be inadequate. Second, members of the multinational crew, particularly the Spaniards, were hostile toward Magellan. Juan de Cartagena, appointed as co-leader of the expedition, started ignoring Magellan's orders the minute they left the Canary Islands after a brief layover.

Later, the Portuguese captain had to quell a mutiny led by Cartagena himself at the Bay of San Julian in southern America. The plot was discovered beforehand, and the culprits were promptly executed. One of those who died during the mutiny was Juan de Elorriaga, a trusted man of Magellan's and the Basque master of the *San*

Antonio. Others were pardoned in order to maintain the operation of the fleet. Among those spared was Elcano, who had played a minor role in the uprising. He had helped the mutineers take control of the *San Antonio.*

The expedition also lost two ships nearly halfway through the voyage. The *Santiago* was shipwrecked in the port of San Julian, and the *San Antonio,* with eleven Basques aboard, is believed to have perished as it headed back to Spain. In spite of the loss of these vessels and the threat of another mutiny by some restless crewmen, Magellan cruised through the strait that now bears his name. Later the expedition crossed a vast ocean whose unusual calmness led the expeditionaries to mistakenly call it the "Pacific." Death and starvation hovered over the expedition until a group of islands (the present-day Guam) was finally sighted on March 6, 1521. The Spaniards called it Islas de Ladrones (Islands of Thieves) because the inhabitants stole a boat from the flagship *Trinidad.*

After reprovisioning, Magellan and his crew hastily left the place, confident that the Moluccas were somewhere nearby. On the morning of March 16, 1521, they sighted the island of Leyte. It was the first glimpse by Europeans of the Philippine archipelago. Convinced that divine intervention had saved them from imminent death, Magellan christened the islands the Archipelago of Saint Lazarus because it was the feast day of the man Jesus Christ raised from the dead. Two Basques, Juan de Aroca and Martín de Barrena, would later die and be buried in Philippine soil.

On March 31, Easter Sunday, the first Catholic mass was celebrated in the Philippines. The natives, led by local chieftains Kolambu and Siagu, attended the celebration. Magellan erected a cross on top of a hill that faces the sea and took possession of the territories in the name of Spain. However, he would not live to harvest the fruits of his labor. On April 27, he was killed during a clash with the warriors of Lapu-Lapu, the chieftain of Mactan. In an attempt to impress Humabon, a chieftain of Cebu, with the might of Spain, Magellan led several soldiers to confront Lapu-Lapu. It was clearly a display of arrogance, overconfidence, and imprudence. Foolishly attacking a whole tribe with a handful of men in an unfamiliar territory, Magellan and his men were killed. Magellan's defeat also shattered the tenuous alliance that he had forged with Humabon, as the Cebuanos ambushed and killed other crewmen, including the Basques León de Espeleta and Rodrigo de Hurrira.

Only two ships, the *Trinidad* and *Victoria,* managed to escape, and both sailed to the Moluccas. However, King Manuel of Portugal, regarding the Magellan crew as pirates operating within Portugal's sphere of influence, had ordered their capture. As the Magellan expedition passed by Borneo, Domingo de Urrutia, a Basque mate of the *Trinidad,* was one of those taken prisoner by the Portuguese.

Gómez de Espinosa, who had taken over as leader of the expedition and captain of the *Trinidad,* ordered Elcano to proceed with the expedition, while Espinosa and fifty others remained in Tidore. When the *Trinidad* and its crew were eventually captured by the Portuguese, the prisoners included the Basque Antonio de Basozabal.

At this point Elcano finally assumed the command of the expedition and ordered the repair of the *Victoria* and procurement of provisions that would last for five months. On February 13, 1522, Elcano, together with a crew of forty-six Europeans and nineteen Malays, left the island of Timor to head back home. The crew faced two dangers, navigating the Indian and Atlantic Oceans and the possibility of being captured by the Portuguese fleet plying the route. Thus the challenge to Elcano and his men was to steer the *Victoria* to a nonstop crossing of the Indian Ocean, round the Cape of Good Hope, sail up all the coast of Africa without calling on any of the ports, and reach Spain.

While navigating the Indian Ocean, their provisions, consisting mostly of unsalted meat, begun to spoil and had to be thrown away to prevent pestilence. So the crew subsisted on only stale rice and water. Disease and death plagued the expedition. By May, some of the crew clamored Elcano to change route and, once near Mozambique, they thought of giving themselves up to the Portuguese rather than die of hunger. But Elcano remained firm about not surrendering the *Victoria* to their enemies. On reaching the African coast, they could not find water and provisions. At the Cape of Good Hope, a violent storm destroyed the main mast of the ship.[7] By the time the *Victoria* rounded the Cape of Good Hope, four Basques had died: Lorenzo de Iruña, Martín de Isaurraga, Juan de Santelices, and Lope de Tudela.[8]

On reaching Cape Verde, the crew consisted of thirty-one Europeans (including six Basques) and three Malays. Since Cape Verde was a Portuguese colony, the *Victoria* was in grave danger of being captured. Elcano took the risk of sending two men to buy provisions from the Portuguese stationed on the island. The two were careful not to identify themselves as survivors of the Magellan expedition. Out of camaraderie and without verifying the true condition of the damaged *Victoria*, the Portuguese welcomed them as guests and gave them water and food. The disguise, however, was later discovered when some of Elcano's men were caught exchanging spices for wine.[9] When a Portuguese contingent approached to seize the *Victoria*, Elcano gave the order to embark even with only eighteen men aboard. Two Basques, Pedro de Chindurza and Pedro de Tolosa, were among those left behind on Cape Verde as the *Victoria* escaped the pursuit of the Portuguese.

Finally, on September 6, 1522, the eighteen survivors of the expedition arrived triumphantly at the port of San Lúcar de Barrameda. Among them were four Basques: Elcano, thirty-five years old, captain; Juan de Acurio, thirty years old, warrant officer; Juan de Arratia, twenty years old, cabin boy; and Juan de Zubileta, no more than eighteen years old, page.[10] When Elcano requested provisions, Domingo de Ochandiano, then the treasurer of the Casa de Contratación, quickly sent a boat with a crew of fifteen, including the Basque Juan de Heguirar.

The success of the *Victoria* invalidated the prevailing nautical and scientific knowledge of the time. It forced European cartographers and navigators to revise their maps and calculations in order to explain a world much more extensive than previously thought. The feat of Elcano and his *Victoria* crew gave Spain the impetus to launch a series of maritime expeditions to uncharted regions of the globe. The fact that the expedition brought home samples of spices and exotic items from the Orient made the Spanish crown realized that the maritime expeditions, although costly and risky, were full of commercial opportunities. The cargo brought by Elcano from the Indies not only covered the entire cost of the expedition but even made a modest profit. More importantly, the Magellan expedition accidentally reached an archipelago that stretches along the southeastern fringe of the Asian continent. It was the prelude to the conquest of this chain of islands that would later be known as the Philippines.

Charles I of Spain (also known as Emperor Charles V of the Holy Roman Empire) honored Elcano with an annual pension of 500 ducats—which he actually never received. The Spanish monarch also awarded Elcano an elaborate seal on which a globe is depicted with the words *Primus Circundediste Me* (The First That Circumnavigated Me). Elcano, however, was not without detractors. Antonio Pigafetta, the Italian chronicler of the expedition, never mentioned Elcano in his memoir and thus did not recognize his achievement in steering the *Victoria* back to Spain.[11] He was apparently wary of the Basques, including Elcano, who plotted and mutinied against Magellan—and never forgave them. Stefan Zweig, a famous Swiss biographer of Magellan, in his book *Magallanes: El hombre y su gesta* (first published in German in 1957), even accused Elcano of secretly destroying Pigafetta's journal to hide any unflattering references from the Spanish king. He also attributed the mysterious loss of Pigafetta's original chronicles to those who wanted to obscure the Spanish crew's opposition to Magellan in order "to exalt the feat of the Basque Elcano."[12]

Elcano's achievement, though widely applauded, did not translate into personal greatness. He was given a place in the annals of navigation only belatedly. According to Mitchell Mairin, a British historian, the first statue raised in Elcano's memory was not in his native Getaria, or even in Spain. It was a wooden one found in Cavite, in the Philippines, although Mairin does not specify the date of its erection. The memorial was sent to Washington, D.C., after the surrender of Cavite to Commodore George Dewey in the Spanish-American War in 1898. Despite the epic achievement of the first circumnavigator, no statue was erected to him in his native land until 1800.[13]

Nonetheless, Elcano had not only redeemed himself but become a celebrity. The fame of this Basque navigator spread far and wide. More importantly, he was able to settle his financial accounts, and his previous mischiefs were largely forgotten. At thirty-five years old, he still had a long, promising career ahead of him. But it seems that he could not keep himself out of trouble. Moving to Valladolid, Elcano had a romantic escapade with a certain Maria de Vidaurreta, with whom he sired a daughter. When the relationship soured, Elcano avoided marriage. Vidaurreta and her kin threatened Elcano with death unless he faced up to his obligations. Elcano soon found himself fearing for his own life and begged the Spanish king for two special armed bodyguards to provide him protection. This was granted on May 20, 1524, mainly because Elcano's safety and services were vital to Spain. His knowledge of the Moluccas was badly needed by Charles I, who eventually appointed him as a special envoy to the important meetings held in Badajoz and Yelbes that tried to settle the disputes between Spain and Portugal on the status of the Spice Islands. Nothing came out of these talks, however, and the bitter rivalry between the two Iberian powers continued.

The new maritime route traced by Elcano further stimulated Spain's desire to control the lucrative spice trade and expand foreign commerce. Since there was a growing demand for spices and Oriental goods in northern Europe, the Spanish authorities decided to transfer the Casa de Contratación from Seville to the Galician port city of La Coruña in order to attract other European traders and financiers. The new location would also be closer to the northern markets. It was in La Coruña that the second expedition to the Moluccas was organized in 1524.

The Spanish monarch ordered a second expedition to establish the sovereignty of Spain in the territories reached by Magellan and initiate the colonization and exploitation of the islands, still thought to be the Moluccas. The leadership of the expedition was given to the Basque monk Fray Garcia Jofre de Loaysa of the Order of Saint John and the Knight of Barbales.[14] Little is known about his life and nautical knowledge. Nonetheless, Loaysa was ably assisted by Elcano, who served as assistant captain and chief navigator of the expedition. Besides, Elcano wanted to prove to his critics that his first feat was not a fluke.

Seven ships comprised the Loaysa expedition: the *Santa María de la Victoria, Sancti Espiritus, Anunciada, San Gabriel, Santa María de Parral, San Lermes,* and *Santiago.* Three of them, the *Santa María de la Victoria, Sancti Espiritus,* and *Santiago,* were commanded by Basques—Loaysa, Elcano, and Santiago de Guevara, a native of Arrasate.

Other Basques who participated in the expedition were Martín de Leriarte, first mate; Juan de Areizaga, priest from Gebara and brother-in-law of Elcano; and fifteen others, among them the Elcano brothers, Martín Péres Elcano, serving as first mate, and Antón Martín Elcano, assistant first mate.[15] Andrés de Urdaneta, a young sailor from Gipuzkoa, joined Elcano as a page on the *Sancti Espiritus.*

The Loaysa expedition was better prepared and equipped with provisions and arms than the Magellan expedition. It set sail on July 24, 1524, and anchored at Gomera in the Canary Islands. After resting for twelve days, the expedition continued its voyage. Like Magellan, Loaysa seemed doomed to fail. After four months at sea, the expedition lost the flagship *Santa María de la Victoria* and the *San Gabriel.* While traversing the Strait of Magellan, the *Sancti Espiritus* sank during a violent storm. Only four ships remained to navigate the Pacific Ocean. Their nightmare was aggravated when they discovered that there was nothing pacific about this vast ocean, contrary to the experience of the Magellan expedition.

On July 30, a year after the start of the expedition, Loaysa died, leaving the command in the hands of Elcano. But Elcano was in no condition to duplicate his previous achievement of circumnavigating the world. He also succumbed to scurvy and died barely a week after Loaysa. Elcano was succeeded by Alonso de Salazar, another Basque, whose leadership was likewise ephemeral. He died before reaching the Philippines. After the chain of deaths, the command of the expedition was passed on to another Basque, Martín Iñiguez de Carquizano, a native of Egoibar.

Under Iñiguez, the expedition arrived in Mindanao, the largest island in the southern Philippines. He and his men were received cordially by the natives. But the scarcity of provisions and the absence of spices forced them to abandon the island. They tried sailing northward, but the strong currents pushed them in the direction of the Moluccas. In Tidore, Iñiguez died mysteriously of poisoning, and the crew were later captured by the Portuguese. Only a handful survived the disastrous enterprise. Among them was Andrés de Urdaneta, whose valuable experience and nautical knowledge would serve him well in the Legazpi expedition forty years later.

Despite the dismal failure of the Loaysa expedition, Charles I ordered Hernando Cortés, the conqueror of Mexico, to organize an expedition to the Moluccas from Mexico. Cortés commissioned his cousin Alvaro de Saavedra to command a fleet. On the eve of All Saints' Day of 1527, the ships *Florida, Santiago,* and *Espíritu Santo* left the port of Zihuatenajo in Mexico. It was the first Spanish expedition launched from the American continent with the mission to reach the Indies. It had a small contingent of forty-five men, with an ample supply of gunpowder and medicine. Another objective of the expedition was to rescue the survivors of the previous expeditions to the Philippines.

But the voyage was worse than Loaysa's. While crossing the Pacific, two ships, the *Santiago* and *Espíritu Santo,* sank with a great loss of life. Only the *Florida* was left to continue the journey. With tremendous difficulty it arrived in Mindanao, but a storm impeded its sailing to Cebu. Saavedra desperately tried to find a return route to Mexico but failed. He died on the high seas on October 9, 1529. Much later, the rest of the expedition fell into the hands of the Portuguese. The degree of Basque participation in this undertaking is not known.

The repeated incursions of the Spaniards in the Moluccas became a source of bickering between Spain and Portugal. Their dispute was finally was settled in 1529. Armed with full powers, representatives of both kingdoms convened in Zaragoza in April and concluded a *pacto de retroventa,* an agreement whereby Spain would relinquish its rights over the Moluccas in exchange for Portugal's payment of the amount of 350,000 gold ducats. Spain's main reason for renouncing its claim to the Spice Islands was its financial woes and the need to make payment on maturing debts.

The disastrous expeditions of Loaysa and Saavedra and the 1529 pact did not, however, deter Spain from attempting to take possession of the rest of the Spice Islands. On November 1, 1542, an expedition led by Ruy López de Villalobos left the port of Navidad in Mexico. The fleet consisted of five ships: the *San Jorge, San Juan de Letrán, San Antonio, San Cristobal,* and *San Martín.* Three hundred sailors and eight missionaries joined the voyage.

After three months of sailing, the expedition reached Mindanao, which Villalobos called Cesareo Caroli in honor of Charles I. Like the Loaysa crew, they suffered starvation and were forced to leave the island. Some of the men headed north and reached the island of Tandaya, where they met friendly natives. Bernardo de la Torre, one of the members of the group, gave the name Felipenas to the chain of islands that presently form Samar and Leyte as a homage to the then prince of Asturias and later King Philip II. The name would later be extended to the whole archipelago.

Contrary winds blew the expedition toward the Moluccas, where its crew was captured by the Portuguese. According to legend, Villalobos later died in the arms of Saint Francis Xavier, the Navarrese Jesuit, hailed as the Apostle of the Indies. The Basque participation in this voyage included Guido Lavezares, a native of Bizkaia, who served as the bookkeeper of the expedition. Like Urdaneta, he would be an integral part of the Legazpi expedition. It is interesting to note that another Basque, Iñigo de Retes, captain of the *San Juan,* discovered Papua New Guinea, bestowing that name because the inhabitants resembled those of African Guinea.[16]

There was a hiatus of twenty-two years before Spain again attempted to conquer the Spice Islands. King Philip II's ascent to the throne gave a new impetus to the almost forgotten expedition to the Moluccas, which he steadfastly believed the papal bull of 1493 put within the Spanish sphere of influence. A new plan was conceived to establish Spanish sovereignty in that part of the world, and the Basques would play a vital role in its success.

Chapter Three

The Legazpi-Urdaneta Expedition

> It is clear that the Basques have contributed, in a large measure, to propagating Western culture and religion, and played an important role in the historical development of our people.
>
> E. B. Rodriguez, former director, Philippine National Library

Anyone strolling in Rizal Park at the corner of Roxas and Padre Burgos Boulevard in Manila will not fail to see a majestic monument of a proud conquistador hoisting a flag and a friar raising a cross with the open Scriptures at hand. Many Filipinos regard the monument as a symbol of Spanish hegemony over the Philippines. On the other hand, nationalists assert that it is a glaring emblem of the duplicity of Spanish colonial rule—the combined use of military might and religion to subdue the native population. In fact, the memorial was conceived by Basque residents in Manila in 1892 as a tribute to two outstanding Basques—Miguel López de Legazpi and Andrés de Urdaneta. Initially, they wanted to pay homage to just Legazpi as the founder of the city of Manila, but the plan was changed to include Fray Andrés de Urdaneta, the Augustinian monk who guided Legazpi during the voyage to the Philippines.[1]

Agustín Querol y Subirals, a famous Catalonian sculptor, was commissioned to design and cast the bronze statue.[2] But by the time it was finished and shipped from Barcelona to Manila, the Philippines was already a colony of the United States. The disassembled pieces of the monument languished for decades in the customhouse until they were finally erected during the time of American governor General Dwight F. Davis (1929–1931).[3] Amazingly, the memorial later survived unscathed during the fierce fighting between the American and Japanese forces that devastated Manila toward the end of World War II.

Legazpi and Urdaneta belong to an exclusive circle of great Basque navigators and conquerors of the sixteenth century, which includes, among others, Juan Sebastián Elcano, the first circumnavigator of the world; Juan de Garay, founder of Buenos Aires, the capital of Argentina; Bruno Mauricio de Zabala, founder of Montevideo, the capital of Uruguay; and Domingo Martínez de Irala, founder of Asunción, the capital of Paraguay.

Legazpi occupies a special place in Philippine history as founder of the first permanent Spanish settlement in Cebu, founder of Manila as the seat of Spanish power in the country, and first governor-general of the archipelago. He is the most famous Basque in the Philippines not only because of his achievements but because he died and was buried there. The inscription in the Capilla de Legazpi in San Agustin Church in Intramuros, Manila, where his remains are entombed, reads as follows: "Here lies a Basque captain and mariner, a Spaniard of whom destiny made a conquistador, although his calling was that of a man of peace. Spain pays homage to the memory of Legazpi and to the Order of Saint Augustine which in this historic temple has preserved through centuries the validity of the mission that brought Legazpi and Urdaneta to these Isles."

The epitaph largely ignores Legazpi's previous career, although the phrase "his calling was that of a man of peace" is suggestive. For his entire life prior to his naval expedition to the Philippines, he actually practiced a land-based civilian profession. To be exact, he was a bureaucrat turned businessman who spent most of his time in the relative comforts of an office, in contrast to the typical conquistadors of his generation who distinguished themselves by annexing territories through often bloody military campaigns. Interestingly, Legazpi is remembered as a captain and navigator. A closer look at his curriculum vitae shows that he was not even qualified for both positions.

Legazpi was born in the Gipuzkoan town of Zumarraga in 1503. He was the second son of Juan Martínez de Legazpi and Elvira de Gurruchategui. His father was a royal scribe in Areria, one of the three districts of Gipuzkoa. On his father's death in 1527, Legazpi inherited the position but held it only briefly.

The following year finds Legazpi in Mexico working as a secretary of the colonial administration—the Ayuntamiento. Many historians claim that he was greatly influenced by the famous Franciscan from Durango, and much later bishop of Mexico, Fray Juan de Zumárraga, who strongly encouraged Basque emigration to New Spain. With hard work and dedication, he prospered, becoming a town mayor, a high official of the Casa de la Moneda (Minting House), and a rich landowner. During the course of thirty-six years (1528–1564), Legazpi amassed great wealth and fortune. He married Isabel Garces and fathered nine children—five boys and four girls. This relatively peaceful and prosperous period of his life contrasts with what he would undertake in his twilight years—the conquest of the Philippines. This was an unusual task for someone who was never considered a colonizer. His election as commander of the expedition despite his advanced age (he was sixty-one when the expedition was launched) can only be explained through his close links with another man whose destiny was intimately intertwined with his and the future venture—Andrés de Urdaneta, a fellow Basque and a contemporary.

Urdaneta was born in the town of Ordizia in Gipuzkoa in 1498. His parents were Juan Ochoa de Urdaneta and Gracia de Ceraín. His father served as mayor of their village for a long time. As a boy, Urdaneta is said to have studied Latin and philosophy, since his parents wanted him to be a priest. But he became an orphan at an early age. And since he found military life more attractive, he enlisted as a soldier and joined in Spain's military campaigns in Italy and Flanders, where he rose to the rank of captain. It was during this period that his interest in navigation intensified, leading him to dedicate himself to the study of mathematics and astronomy. He was among the first to approach the study of navigation in a scientific and methodical manner rather than merely learning it by experience as most mariners did during his time. His combined knowledge of Latin, philosophy, cosmography, and military science qualified Urdaneta for various professions, since he was a "good soldier, good navigator, and good friar."[4]

As previously noted, he was recruited for the Loaysa expedition in 1525 and served as a page to Juan Sebastián Elcano, the circumnavigator, in the ship *Sancti Spiritus.* He was captured by the Portuguese in Moluccas when the rest of the ill-fated expedition accidentally sailed there. There, while a prisoner of the Portuguese in Ternate for seven years, he learned the Malay language, an asset that would serve him well upon his return to the Philippines.

Toward the end of February 1535, Urdaneta left the Spice Islands for India aboard the aptly named *Maluco.* From there he took another ship for Portugal. He finally landed in Lisbon on June 26, 1536. He was said to have confessed that he had fathered a daughter whom he abandoned in Lisbon to escape persecution by the Portuguese monarch, although there is no clear proof that he ever contracted marriage.

During the eleven years that he was away, he kept copious notes of the Loaysa voyage and his personal experience but unfortunately lost them. Nevertheless, when he was summoned by Charles I, he was able to submit a detailed and comprehensive account entitled *La relación de la armada de Loaysa* (*The History of the Armada of Loaysa*).[5]

In Spain, Urdaneta met Pedro de Alvarado, the conqueror of Guatemala, who recruited him to join the expedition he was preparing to go to the Moluccas and China. Urdaneta went with Alvarado to Guatemala, where Alvarado outfitted an expedition consisting of thirteen ships with the ultimate goal of conquering China. Alvarado also drafted another Basque captain, Martín de Islares, to the enterprise. In 1536, the Alvarado expedition left the port of Acajutla and arrived on the coast of Jalisco, Mexico, where the governor, a certain Cristobal de Oñate, a Basque, was facing an Indian revolt. Oñate requested Alvarado's assistance in suppressing the rebellion. Alvarado agreed but perished during the battle. Then viceroy of Mexico Mendoza, who had a stake in the expedition, proposed that Urdaneta be the new leader of the mission, but he refused the offer.[6]

Urdaneta eventually settled in Mexico in 1538 and got a job in the colonial government. In 1552 at the age of fifty-four, tired of his military and naval career, he finally fulfilled his parents' dream. He joined the Augustinian order and retired to a monastery in Mexico where he spent his first years as a teacher of the novices. He was committed to pious and religious work for the rest of his life when, in September 24, 1559, he received an order from King Philip II that forced him out of retirement. His mission entailed the preparation and direction of a maritime expedition to the Western Isles. In a letter dated May 28, 1560, Urdaneta expressed his willingness to follow Philip II's order and thanked him for the trust accorded him despite his age of "sixty-two winters and failing health." He also submitted a navigational chart and a description of the ports of Acapulco and Navidad. Philip II's ascent to the throne in 1555, after the abdication of Charles I, gave a new impetus to the almost forgotten expedition to the Moluccas. Philip relished the conquest of the much coveted Spice Islands and the opportunity to establish Spanish sovereignty in the archipelago that was to bear his name.

As a veteran army and naval officer with valuable experience in the waters of the Pacific Ocean during the Loaysa expedition, Urdaneta's services were crucial to the success of the mission. The four previous expeditions (by Magellan, Loaysa, Saavedra, and Villalobos) failed dismally in their attempts to establish a foothold in the archipelago. The Spanish crown could not afford another disappointment.

Philip II gave the order to colonize the Philippines to Don Luis de Velasco, Spanish viceroy of Mexico in 1559, but it took five more years before an expedition could be launched. The reason for the delay was that Velasco's mind was set on another goal. When news was brought by the expedition of Ponce de León of the existence of the so-called Fountain of Youth in Florida, Velasco shelved the Philippine mission and instead assembled and headed an expeditionary force consisting of two thousand men. The Florida expedition turned out to be a complete disaster, and Velasco subsequently died of illness and despair.

Nonetheless, Urdaneta continued preparing for the maritime venture. Being a friar, Urdaneta could not be made head of the expedition. So, he recommended Legazpi to the Spanish king. The Real Audiencia of Mexico, the colonial supreme court that took over the reigns of government after the death of Velasco, was shocked by the choice given that the aging but well-respected Legazpi had neither naval nor military experience. Indeed, taking into account the dangerous nature, high cost, and slim chance of success of an expedition to the Philippines at that time, the opposition to Legazpi's appointment was understandable. As a Basque writer correctly observed: "The designation of Legazpi as leader of the expedition was due to other circumstances and not to the aptitude that he had demonstrated in navigation, for neither did he have any experience in this field nor did he understand anything of ships since he could not even distinguish one from the other. His appointment could probably be attributed to Urdaneta, whose acceptance of the position of pilot was considered indispensable because he was the most qualified among the navigators who were residing in Mexico at that time."[7]

Urdaneta threatened not to board any ship unless Legazpi, his friend and compatriot, assumed command of the expedition. In the end, he prevailed. Moreover, to allay the fears of the Real Audiencia, Legazpi committed himself to spending his personal fortune to finance the expedition. Already a widower, Legazpi auctioned all his properties, with the exception of his house, to raise money for the project—with the assumption, of course, that he would be compensated for his labor and financial investments if the mission succeeded.[8]

The fleet consisted of 380 men with three ships and one *patarche* (a flat-bottomed boat): the *San Pedro, San Pablo, San Juan de Letrán,* and *San Lucas.* Legazpi and Urdaneta selected a number of fellow Basques to man the key positions of the expedition. Mateo de Saz, captain of the *San Pablo,* was at the same time master of camp (roughly equivalent to colonel) and second in command of the expedition. In the *San Pedro,* the 500-ton flagship, were Martin de Ibarra, a native of Bilbao, master; Francisco de Astigarribia, boatswain; Esteban Rodriguez, first mate; and Pierre Plin, a French Basque, second mate. In the *San Juan de Letrán* were Juan de la Isla, possibly a Bizkaian, and his brother Rodrigo, a mate; Andrés de Ibarra, a Mexican Basque, first lieutenant; Martín de Goiti, captain of artillery; Luís de la Haya, master sergeant; Andrés de Mirandola, nephew of Legazpi and auditor of the Royal Treasury; Felipe de Salcedo, grandson of Legazpi; Guido de Lavezares, treasurer of the expedition; and Andrés de Carchela, accountant. Martín de Rada and Pedro de Gamboa, both Navarrese, and Andrés de Aguirre and Diego de Herrera made up the contingent of Augustinian Basque missionaries.[9]

Other Basque crew members were Juan de Lazcano, secretary for Legazpi; Pedro de Guevarra, ironsmith; Amador de Arriaran, pilot; Juan de Aguirre, Pedro de Arana, and Alberto de Orozco, all soldiers; and Juan de Camuz, mariner.[10] Moreover, Ortuno de Ibarra, a Basque agent, was commissioned to procure the provisions and supplies for the expedition. Thus, on the whole, the Legazpi-Urdaneta expedition was mainly a Basque enterprise, with Basque leadership, Basque manpower, and substantial Basque capital.

Instructions from the Real Audiencia gave the enterprise two goals: to bring to the native inhabitants the knowledge of the Catholic faith and to discover the return route to Mexico.[11] The mission did not start well. Ten days after the ships left the port of Navidad, on November 21, 1564, the *San Lucas* deserted. Captain Alonso de Arellano and the ship's mulato navigator, Lope Martín, straggled behind, supposedly to go to Mindanao to fetch gold and spices and to head back to Mexico. Three months later, they anchored again in the port of Navidad and spread tall tales about their exploits in the Philippines and how Legazpi and his men perished.[12]

Actually, Legazpi and his crew navigated the Pacific without trouble and easily reached the island of Samar on February 15, 1565. Legazpi ordered Urdaneta, Mateo de Saz, and Martín de Goiti to search for a port or estuary and to initiate contacts with the natives. Their attempts to acquire provisions failed when the natives remained hostile despite the expeditionaries' show of goodwill. Andrés de Ibarra took possession of the island but to no avail. They left Samar on February 20, 1565, and landed on Leyte the following day. As on Samar, the natives met them with hostility. In March, they landed on the island of Bohol, where Legazpi first succeeded in making friends with the inhabitants.

Legazpi befriended the locals by entering into a blood compact with the local chief, Sikatuna. The blood compact (*sika sika* in Cebuano and *sandugo* in Tagalog, meaning "one blood") is a ritual performed by two men who draw blood from their arms, mix it with native wine or water, and drink the blood of the other to symbolize their newfound alliance or friendship. Legazpi's blood compact with Sikatuna was immortalized in a painting by Juan Luna, a famous nineteenth-century Filipino painter. It hangs to this day on the wall at the entrance to Malacañang, the presidential palace. It is a reminder to foreign guests and dignitaries that the Filipinos are open and friendly to those who respect their culture and tradition. It also highlights the pre-Hispanic Filipinos' form of diplomacy.

Since the island of Bohol could not serve as a permanent settlement because of lack of provisions, the expedition decided to transfer to Cebu on April 21. There it was met with hostility by Datu Tupas, the Cebuano leader, and his people, who immediately assumed that the Spaniards came back to exact revenge. As the Cebuanos learned from oral tradition, Datu Humabon and their forebears feted several members of the Magellan expedition (after Magellan fell), then hacked them to death. Legazpi sent emissaries to Datu Tupas, who tried to hold the Spaniards at bay while his people fled to the hinterland, taking with them everything of value. Legazpi ordered three rowboats under the command of the Basque trio of Mateo de Saz, Martín de Goiti, and Juan de Isla to attack, while the *San Pedro* and *San Juan de Letrán* bombarded the deserted settlement. The conflagration produced by the cannon shots destroyed most of the nipa (thatch) village. One of Legazpi's men, Juan Camuz, a Basque, discovered the image of the child Jesus in one of the abandoned huts. The Flanders-made icon is venerated in the Church of San Agustin in Cebu City to this day.

While the expeditionaries occupied Tupas's village, Legazpi strictly prohibited his men from venturing alone outside camp, for fear of enemies lying in ambush. Ignoring the command, the Basque Pedro de Arana strolled along the beach on his own with his harquebus. Before he could use his firearm to defend himself, his body was pierced by a spear and his head was cut off and carried away by his native assailants. Angered by the brutal killing, Legazpi ordered Mateo del Saz and some men to chase the perpetrators of the attack, who successfully eluded apprehension.[13] Through his recklessness and insubordination, Arana went down in history as the first Basque casualty of the expedition.

Despite his military superiority, Legazpi chose to negotiate peace with Tupas. He needed the natives to provide the expedition with food and as future allies. Fortunately, Sid Hamal, a Bornean settler in Cebu, approached Legazpi's camp to volunteer to act as an intermediary between the Spaniards and the Cebuanos. In the end,

Legazpi succeeded in persuading Tupas to stop resisting. The Cebuano chief agreed to recognize Spain's sovereignty and to pay tribute, while the Spaniards promised to conduct trade fairly. Legazpi also provided Tupas's wife with gifts and gave her special treatment, which the latter ostentatiously showed off to her subjects.[14]

Tupas himself tried to win the trust of Legazpi by offering him his widowed niece as wife and other women to serve him. The Basque commander instead introduced Tupas's niece to one of his men, who later married her. Legazpi initially gave the name San Miguel to their Cebu settlement and ordered the construction of a palisade fort and a bamboo chapel. In January 1571, shortly before he transferred his base to Panay and later Manila, he formally declared the place a permanent Spanish town, calling it Villa del Santísimo Nombre de Jesús, after the holy icon retrieved there.

Although lacking in nautical and military expertise, Legazpi was a gifted diplomat and administrator. His main assets were tact, patience, and a clear mind even under extreme pressure. As much as possible, he insisted on peaceful negotiations, always preferring them to outright armed conflict. Many of his men resented his pacifist style, but they respected him because of his firm leadership. His wise decisions were based on a realistic assessment of their situation. Besides, combat and disease had already caused expeditionary numbers to dwindle. Their provisions were running out, too. Legazpi knew very well that to avoid the dismal failure of previous Spanish expeditions, they had to hold out and await the arrival of reinforcements and supplies from Mexico. However, Legazpi's authority was defied and challenged several times by his men, some of them Basques. He had to quell one mutiny by the *gentilhommes* of the expedition, led by the Basque Pedro de Mena and a group of disgruntled non-Spanish crew that included Pierre Plin, the French Basque pilot.

A few days after the expedition landed in Cebu, Pedro de Mena challenged Legazpi's authority and bluntly told the Basque commander that he was fed up being a bodyguard for him, calling it "a job fit only for servants." As members of the upper class, the gentilhommes resented performing menial chores and guarding Legazpi while he slept (Legazpi also distrusted many of his crew). Mateo de Saz, the Basque aide-de-camp, relieved them of their positions. But unfazed and emboldened, Mena and his cohorts staged a revolt, signaling it by setting fire in one of the cabins of the flagship, which almost gutted some royal properties. The ringleaders, Mena and a certain Terrasan, were later captured and executed.[15]

Another incident involved a number of other Europeans, mainly Italian, Greek, and French, who grew restless after enduring hunger and deprivation during their time on Cebu. They were frustrated with Legazpi's inclination to build settlements and befriend the natives rather than seize and plunder wealth from them. They plotted to escape with the *San Juan*, bore holes in the other ships so that they could not be pursued, undertake piracy, and hopefully retire in France with their booty. Fortunately, Legazpi foiled the planned escape when one of the plotters confessed the matter to Mateo de Saz. The mutineers were all rounded up and many were punished with death, including the French Basque Pierre Plin and Jorge the Greek, both of whom were hanged.[16]

Legazpi's decision to settle in Cebu to wait for relief from Mexico and forge an alliance with the native population proved wise. The arrival of ships loaded with men, arms, and ammunition as well as news from New Spain augmented the dwindling ranks and effectively raised the morale of the troops. Then a powerful Portuguese fleet consisting of three big galleons and two small ones, two ketches, and twelve small boats appeared in Cebu on September 17, 1568. The squadron was led by Commander Gonzalo de Pereyra. The Portuguese resented the Spaniards for breaching the Treaty of Zaragoza. Fortunately, Legazpi and his men had already built a strong defense. Pereyra offered them assistance back to Mexico if the expedition would proceed to Ternate. Legazpi knew that if he agreed to the offer they would be as good as captives of the Portuguese. Pereyra occasionally ordered the cannons to be shot at the Spanish fortifications as a sort of target practice and to scare off the Spaniards. The Portuguese naval blockade of the port also deprived Legazpi of supplies from native traders of the neighboring islands. Again, Legazpi adroitly employed diplomacy in confronting the much better armed Portuguese. He dispatched Martín de Rada, the Navarrese Augustinian friar, to negotiate with Pereyra. The Portuguese commander took it as a sign of surrender, not knowing that the Basque leader had other plans. Legazpi insisted that he and Pereyra could not resolve the issue on their own and that the dispute must be submitted to the Spanish and Portuguese monarchs. This was actually a ploy to gain time. The talks dragged on until December, when the Portuguese finally realized they were exhausting most of their provisions. By that time Legazpi had already buttressed his defenses for any Portuguese assault and recruited more native troops to reinforce them. When conflict erupted, Legazpi's men successfully repelled the Portuguese attack. Thus Pereyra, seeing that his chances of victory were slim and not willing to risk losing more men in attacking Legazpi's fortress, retreated to the Moluccas in disgust.

Andrés de Urdaneta's involvement in the expedition was essentially confined to navigation. He barely conducted apostolic work in the Philippines since he had been ordered to accomplish what other navigators had never done—find a return route to Mexico. In June 1565, Urdaneta, accompanied by Felipe de Salcedo, Legazpi's grandson, Fray Andrés de Aguirre, and several men, embarked on the *San Pedro,* sailing north for the return voyage to Mexico. Salcedo was designated captain of the ship, although in reality Urdaneta was in command.[17]

Despite great odds, Urdaneta never lost hope and determination. By experience, he inferred that the prevailing wind in that part of the Pacific could take them back to Mexico. It was just a matter of traversing the correct latitude. For four months, the *San Pedro* navigated through rough and treacherous waters, drifting aimlessly in the northern Pacific until it reached the thirty-ninth parallel. There they found the westerly winds that carried them to the California coast. The ship made its way down to New Spain and finally reached the port of Acapulco on October 30, 1565. By the time of their arrival, scurvy had ravaged the crew, claiming sixteen victims, including a captain and two assistant pilots. The crew were so weak they could not even throw the anchor of the ship upon arrival in Acapulco. Four more men died of scurvy on reaching land. Urdaneta's *tornaviaje* was an impressive feat in the field of navigation, almost comparable to Elcano's first circumnavigation of the world.

More importantly in the short term, Urdaneta's success ensured the survival of Legazpi's forces in Cebu and Manila, since reinforcements were hastily dispatched from Mexico. Had he failed, the fragile Spanish settlements in Cebu and Manila could have been wiped out by hostile natives, the Portuguese, or the hordes of Chinese pirates that would later attack Manila. Mutinies and internal squabbles among the expeditionaries themselves also could have ruined their mission. The people in Mexico were overjoyed by the return of Urdaneta and his companions, whom they thought had perished based on the fabricated news disseminated by Captain Alonso de Arellano and Lope Martín of the *San Lucas.* When Urdaneta and Aguirre visited the court, they chanced upon the two deserters there, deceitfully claiming their rewards for having discovered the return route from the Philippines. They almost succeeded in getting it. Urdaneta's appearance exposed their wickedness, and the two were immediately arrested.[18] As punishment for their perfidy, they were to be sent with an expedition to the Philippines, where Legazpi himself would decide their fate.[19] It was said that Hernando Cortés, the famous conqueror of Mexico, thought of the idea.

In the Mexican capital, Urdaneta presented the viceroy and the Real Audiencia with a letter from Legazpi and a navigational map that must be followed by subsequent mariners on their way to the western Pacific and back to Mexico. After a brief rest, Urdaneta, accompanied by Fray Andrés de Aguirre and Melchor López de Legazpi, Legazpi's son, sailed to Spain to report their achievements to Philip II. Urdaneta neither solicited nor received compensation (unlike Melchor López de Legazpi who lobbied hard to get his father's rewards). Urdaneta was promised a reward for his feat, but in the end nothing materialized. He returned to the Augustinian cloister in Mexico. He thought of making another voyage to the Philippines, but his superiors opposed his plan because of his advanced age and failing health. He died on June 3, 1568, at the age of seventy. Arturo Campión, author of *El genio de Nabarra* (*The Genius of Navarre*), exalted him in almost mythical fashion: "The Basque is born with wings. No one of his race in that era adventured over so many fields as Urdaneta."[20]

Soon after the Portuguese squadron left Cebu in December 1568, Legazpi knew he would have to move his base from Cebu to another settlement to ensure a supply of provisions and if possible a defensible port. Again Legazpi entrusted the search to his Basque officers. He ordered Felipe de Salcedo, his grandson, and Captain Luis de la Haya to explore Panay; Captain Andrés de Ybarra reconnoitered Masbate, while Martín de Goiti remained in Cebu to prepare the patarche *San Lucas* for its voyage to New Spain. Legazpi also promoted Goiti to master of camp after Mateo de Saz died of malaria while exploring Mindanao looking for spices. On July 10, 1569, Felipe de Salcedo left for Mexico aboard the *San Lucas,* accompanied among others by Fray Diego de Herrera, the first Augustinian provincial of Cebu, to recruit more clergy for the Philippine mission.

In 1569, Martín de Goiti, together with a selected group of men, left for the island of Panay and founded a new colony at Iloilo. The place was originally called Irong Irong until the Spaniards, possibly Goiti himself, modified it to suit Spanish phonology. Iloilo would become a center of Basque business activity and immigration during the late nineteenth century. From Panay, Goiti's expeditionary forces sailed toward the island of Mindoro where they captured two Chinese junks. (Some versions of the story claim they aided the Chinese.) From their Chinese captives they learned of the existence of a bay settlement in the north that was said to be easily defensible and possessed a good port. The place was none other than Manila, the future capital of the Philippines. Manila's name was derived from the Tagalog phrase *may nilad* (there are nilad). *Nilad* is a mangrove that was abundant in the area at the time. Goiti must have interpreted the presence of Chinese traders in the archipelago as a clear sign of regular commercial relations between the northern islanders and the Chinese. He promptly reported his findings to Legazpi, who lost no time in outfitting an expedition.

In May 1570, Legazpi sent an expedition to Manila under the command of Martín de Goiti and his seventeen-year-old grandson, Juan de Salcedo (who had arrived with the expedition of his elder brother, Felipe de Salcedo, in 1569), 120 Spaniards, and hundreds of Cebuano and Ilonggo warriors. At first they were cordially received by Rajah Matanda, the elderly chief of Manila, and his nephew Rajah Sulayman. Rajah Sulayman must have learned about the Spaniards' presence in the Visayas and deeply suspected their aims. Soon, conflict broke out. Matanda's people fought valiantly against the foreign invaders and their Visayan allies, but they were soundly defeated.

On June 23, 1570, several ships from Mexico arrived in Cebu. The leader of the expedition was Juan de la Isla, one of the original members of the expedition that successfully returned to New Spain. Legazpi excitedly received the royal letters and orders instructing him to defend the Spanish settlement at all cost and awarding him the title of "Adelantado de las islas de los ladrones" (Ruler of the Islands of Thieves). The name "Philippines" apparently had not yet gained currency. He was also granted the position of governor-general for life of all the islands and territories that would be conquered for the Spanish crown. The expedition also included the

Basque Augustinian Diego de Herrera, with two Augustinian missionaries, Fray Diego de Ordoñez and Fray Diego de Espinar.

After spending five years on Cebu, Legazpi decided to leave for Manila. On the first day of 1571, he erected the Villa del Santísimo Nombre de Jesús and appointed Guido de Lavezares, the Basque royal treasurer, as *regidor* (councillor). Legazpi arrived in Manila in early June, and on June 24, 1571, the feast of St. John the Baptist, he established a permanent Spanish settlement in Manila and proclaimed it the "Distinguished, Most Noble, and Ever Loyal City," with its own coat of arms. He also renamed the island of Luzon as New Castille.[21]

Manila's geographical situation was indeed crucial to the maintenance of a permanent Spanish settlement. The city is situated on a beautiful bay of the same name, which at one end protrudes between the sea and the mouth of a river called the Pasig. With its fine harbor, it would be a magnificent location for conducting future relations with China, Japan, and Southeast Asia. It would also serve as a perfect outpost from which to establish regular communications with Mexico. Once the island of Corregidor was converted to a naval garrison guarding its bay, it was also easily defensible. Legazpi quickly began the construction of the city, laying out an extensive perimeter that would last for two centuries before being revised and extended.

Seeking to convert Manila into a trading entrepôt, Legazpi welcomed foreign merchants, whether Chinese, Moslems, or pagans of any nation, by providing fair dealing, security of persons and goods, and freedom from exactions by councillors and deputies. All of this was ensured in the first draft ordinances proposed to the Manila City Council on June 28, 1571, reiterating that special care should be taken to give good treatment to natives and foreigners alike.[22] The actual practice, as we shall see later, never followed Legazpi's original objectives.

In August 1571 further reinforcements arrived from Mexico in two ships, the *San Juan* and *Espíritu Santo,* under the command of another Basque, Juan López de Aguirre, a famous Bizkaian soldier. Aboard the ships were Diego de Legazpi, the founder's nephew, and other relatives, as well as the wife of Martín de Goiti.[23]

Once a permanent settlement in the archipelago was established, what remained was the military and spiritual conquest of the Philippines. Legazpi, however, did not live to see the realization of this project. In August 1572, he suffered a heart attack after reprimanding a subordinate. Ironically, Legazpi, the rich man who gambled his fortune to seek more fame and glory, died destitute, although he received royal honors and titles. His men found only 460 pesos among his personal possessions, an amount he actually borrowed days before his death. He never enjoyed the 2,000 ducat salary that Philip II granted him as governor-general for life. However, his son Melchor petitioned the Spanish king to transfer the land grants of his father in Luzon to Mexico. He also inherited Legazpi's title of Adelantado.[24]

Contemplating Legazpi's place in Spanish history, a Basque writer declared: "Perhaps it is worth reiterating the fact that the expedition to take possession of and to conquer the Islas Ponientes (Western Isles) of the Pacific Ocean was one of the most memorable events in Spanish history, and the primacy of this glory corresponds to a handful of distinguished Basques led by Legazpi."[25]

A contemporary Filipino scholar, on the other hand, sums up the greatness of Legazpi in the following way:

> Legazpi's enterprise cannot be looked on as simply the fifth of the various expeditions that reached the Philippines. It was of transcendental importance in the country's development. . . . Spanish historical writing has been, as expected, uniformly laudatory of Legazpi's work. American historians of the early twentieth century, from the perspective of a different culture, seem to have been in substantial agreement. The editors of the largest compilation of Philippine historical material, Emma Helen Blair and James Alexander Robertson, opined that his expedition "begins the real history of the Philippine Islands." Writing the historical introduction of this collection of documents, Edward Gaylord Bourne said: "The work of Legazpi during the next seven years entitles him to a place among the greatest colonial pioneers. In fact, he has no rival."
>
> Two generations later, less Eurocentric historians from the former colonies, the Philippines and Mexico, have weighed in with their own evaluations, which reinforce the high regard in which Legazpi has been held. The Filipino editors of a collection of source documents compiled on the occasion of the quadricentennial of the Christianization of the Philippines wrote: "There is no incontrovertible fact on which all historians agree than that the expedition, more than any other events, served as the turning point that changed the course of our history. The great enterprise . . . laid the foundation of our present-day political and social organization. . . ." In the introduction to his work, the Mexican diplomat, writer and scholar Rafael Bernal wrote: "It was an extraordinary moment in the history of the Philippines because, in those first ten years of Hispanic settlement here, the die was cast. . . . In those years the actual boundaries of the nation came into being. In those few years of history, the Philippines were molded in a cast that has solidified in time, never to be destroyed or thrown away . . . The documents in this volume reveal the action and thoughts, and the hopes of the men that made possible that conquest, with so little bloodshed, in comparison with the conquests done by other western nations.
>
> More recently, a Filipino historian has put it succinctly: "Before Legazpi there were no Philippines and no Filipinos. Some anthropologists have discerned a latent unity, based on shared cultural characteristics, among the numerous political units of the pre-Hispanic Philippines, but it was the positive act of Legazpi's expedition that gathered most of them together within a short span of time.[26]

The success of the Legazpi-Urdaneta expedition laid the foundation for Spanish hegemony in the Philippines.[27] The Basque contingent of the expedition clearly played a leading role in its accomplishment. The subsequent conquest of the archipelago can be considered the apex of the incredible expansion undertaken by Spain starting with the colonization of the Americas in 1492. Legazpi's belated aspiration to be a great colonizer came true, and Urdaneta's trust in his abilities to successfully lead the expedition was likewise vindicated.

Urdaneta's name is also immortalized in the annals of navigation because of his discovery of the return route to Mexico. This route would serve as the only line of communication between the Philippines and Mexico and would also be the basis of the Manila-Acapulco galleon trade that lasted for two and a half centuries. Equally remarkable is the fact that Urdaneta never really intended to sail to the Philippines. Under strict orders from the Real Audiencia, Legazpi did not open the sealed letter of instruction until they were crossing the Pacific. The instruction stipulated that the expedition was to split into three groups, bound for New Guinea, the Luzones (Philippines), and the Moluccas. Urdaneta's original choice was not the Philippines but New Guinea.[28]

Chapter Four

Conquerors

> The weapons that they [native Filipinos] use are three-wedged spears, in daily life, and during war a stack of lances, a bunch of sticks, blow guns, and some bows and arrows that they use with little accuracy and consistency. They have wars between them where they either kill or enslave each other. They showed great fear of our ships.
>
> Miguel López de Legazpi

Many scholars characterize Spain's conquest and pacification of the Philippine archipelago as relatively benign and amazingly swift. This sweeping assessment, however, must be viewed against the backdrop of Spanish expansion in the Americas and Spain's own national history. When the Legazpi-Urdaneta expedition arrived in the Philippines in 1565, the Spanish conquistadors had already subjugated the Aztec and Incan empires in Mexico and Peru. And decades before the Spaniards had conquered territories occupied by the Moors for centuries, a process culminating in the Spanish victory at Granada in 1492. Thus most Spanish conquistadors who came to the Philippines had plenty of combat experience (many were grizzled veterans of military campaigns in Europe and in the Americas) and were equipped with superior military armaments. How could the Philippines have not succumbed to one of the most powerful imperial nations of that epoch?

This does not imply that Filipinos put up merely token resistance. On the contrary, they fought fiercely to defend themselves against the encroachment of the Spaniards. Lapu-Lapu's victory over Magellan is a good example. But given the Filipinos' fragmented, poorly fortified communities (with the exception of the Sultanate of Sulu) and inferior weapons, the balance tilted heavily in favor of the Spanish invaders. In 1569, Legazpi himself made the following observation regarding the social organization and character of the native Filipinos, which, he believed, allowed easy conquest of the archipelago:

> Although there are large towns in some regions, the people do not act in concert or obey a ruling body; rather each man does whatever he pleases, and takes care only of himself and of his slaves.
>
> I think that these natives could be easily subdued with good treatment and

> the display of kindness; for they have no leaders, and are so divided among themselves and have so little dealing with one another—never assembling to gain strength, or rendering obedience to one another. If some of them refuse at first to make peace with us, afterwards, on seeing how well we treat those who have already accepted our friendship, they are induced to the same. But if we undertake to subdue them by force of arms and make war on them, they will perish and we shall lose both friends and foes; for they readily abandon their houses and towns for other places, or precipitately disperse among the mountains and highlands, and neglect to plant their fields. Consequently they die from hunger and other misfortunes. One can see a proof of this in the length of time which it takes them to settle down again in a town which has been plundered, even if not one of them has been killed or captured.[1]

Before the arrival of the Europeans, the native inhabitants of the Philippines lived in scattered communities called *barangay.* An organized settlement consisting of a hundred families, for instance, was normally governed by a chief called *datu.* Diversity characterizes Philippine society as well. Geographical fragmentation is a major cause of linguistic and regional differences among the Filipinos. More than eighty-five languages are spoken, with Tagalog (also called Filipino) and Cebuano as the dominant tongues. Although the Filipinos are predominantly of Malay stock, the traits of those living in the northern island of Luzon are different from those in the Visayan Islands. The southern islands of Mindanao and the Sulu archipelago are inhabited by a sizable number of Muslims.

Legazpi and company had surely learned from the four disastrous expeditions that preceded them. The ethnic diversity greatly facilitated the Spanish conquest of the Philippines. In addition, the Spaniards exploited the Filipinos' disunity and wisely employed the time-honored divide and conquer tactic, which they so effectively used throughout the conquest of the Americas. The traditional animosities among the Cebuanos, Tagalogs, and the Ilocanos, for instance, were further aggravated as the Spaniards played one ethnic group against the other.

The death of Legazpi marked the end of the first phase of Basque leadership in the colonization of the islands in the central Philippines and Manila. The Basques took the initiative again in the pacification of other parts of Luzon. After Legazpi's death, his men opened the sealed letter in his steel coffer from the Audiencia of Mexico, which named successors in the case of Legazpi's death. The next man in line was Mateo de Saz, the master of camp of the expedition, who had already died of malaria. The second name on the list was that of another Basque, Guido de Lavezares, the royal treasurer from Bizkaia, a veteran of the Villalobos expedition, and until then governor (*regidor*) of Cebu.[2] He was said to be "a man of much prudence, good intention, and advanced age."[3]

Lavezares's career is typical of that of many Basques of his generation. He possessed an adventurous spirit and was lured by the fame and riches offered by the Spanish exploration of and expansion to uncharted territories in New World. Like many aspiring Basque conquistadors, Lavezares moved to Seville, the gateway to the New World, before embarking for Mexico.[4] The scanty records of his life in Mexico reveal that he was granted a fief and that his first wife was murdered by Indians. But evidently Lavezares was not pleased with his initial achievements. On hearing of the expedition to the Moluccas being outfitted by Antonio de Mendoza, then viceroy of Mexico, Lavezares did not think twice about enlisting. He even sold part of his patrimony to finance a stake in the enterprise, a normal practice during the age of discovery. Thus in 1542 he joined the Villalobos expedition as a bookkeeper. He survived the disastrous mission, lived briefly in Mindanao, and was eventually taken prisoner by the Portuguese in the Moluccas. There he spent five years in captivity before returning to the Iberian Peninsula in 1549.

Lavezares sought the help of Fray Nicolás Witte to gain favors from the Spanish monarch. The friar wrote an emotional letter to Charles I on July 15, 1552, exulting Lavezares's merits and the valuable services he had rendered to the Villalobos expedition. The correspondence also recommended, among other things, the restoration of land Lavezares used to own that had been appropriated to the Indians. But nothing came of the petition.[5]

Frustrated by his life in Spain, Lavezares decided to return to Mexico to rebuild his fortune. He got a job selling books but kept an eye out for future expeditions. On September 5, 1558, Lavezares joined a reconnaissance mission to the newly discovered peninsula of Florida. He embarked on a ship that explored a bay along latitude 29°5' N that was called "the Philippines" and returned to Mexico in December of the same year. Lavezares wrote an impressive report of that voyage that subsequently guided another expedition in 1559, in which he participated. He spent three years in Florida, then came back again to Mexico in 1662. He was eventually designated as royal treasurer in the Legazpi expedition.[6]

The unexpected death of Legazpi made Lavezares the unlikely successor and governor-general of the archipelago. Lavezares with "much prudence, valor, and skill continued the conversion and pacification of the island."[7] Like Legazpi, Lavezares upheld the rights of the natives. During his term, he visited the provinces in the Visayas and initiated steps to check the abuses of Spanish *encomenderos* (landowners). Such steps had little effect and were totally ignored as soon as he returned to Manila. The envoy he sent to the sultan of Borneo failed, since the sultan never wanted any dealings with the Spaniards. He also granted *encomiendas* to Goiti, Salcedo, and other worthy soldiers.[8]

Lavezares also contemplated transferring the capital of the archipelago from Manila to the port of Cagayan, which was on the open sea and without the obstacles that ships coming from Mexico often faced when approaching Manila. He thought the area might also improve commercial traffic with neighboring countries. Among the inconveniences that beset the galleons was the monsoon in the straits of San Bernardino. Besides, news reached him that Cagayan had a big river.[9] More than this grand vision, it was Lavezares's successful defense of the incipient and feeble Spanish colony in Manila that earned him a place in Philippine history. Toward the end of 1574, the Spanish settlement came under threat of invasion from Chinese corsairs led by Li Tao Kiem, better known as "Limahong."

Limahong was born of a prominent family in the small Chinese port town of Tui-Chiu in the province of Cui Tam. At the age of nineteen, he offered his services to Tia-La Ong, then a famous corsair, who accepted him with great affection and admired his courage and ingenuity. Upon Tia-La Ong's death, Limahong was named his heir in charge of both the fleet and all the fortune of the dreaded pirate.[10]

The Chinese emperor tolerated Limahong's operations in exchange for his cooperation, though often without reciprocity. Eventually, Limahong's rapacity and relentless pillaging of coastal villages wore out the unusual tolerance shown by the Chinese emperor. He ordered the imperial forces to hunt down the Chinese corsair, dead or alive. With a prize on his head, Limahong looked for a safe haven. Upon seizing a Chinese junk in Pe-hung (off the eastern coast of Taiwan), he learned that it had just returned from Manila where it had made huge profits selling merchandise to the Spaniards. Limahong took control of the junk and interrogated the owners about the land they had come from. Their detailed story about the ideal port of Manila and the commercial activities there ignited Limahong's desire to abandon the Chinese coast, dislodge the Spaniards, and establish a base in Manila from which he could start building his own empire.

Limahong gathered all his vessels and subjects, which he considered the nucleus of a new state that he was contemplating founding. Using the captured crew as guides, Limahong steered his forces in the direction of the Philippines.[11]

On November 29, 1574, Limahong approached Corregidor island at the mouth of Manila Bay with a fleet of 72 junks and 3,500 women, 2,000 warriors and other sailors, quite a number of artillery, and many hand weapons and firearms.[12] The following day Limahong ordered Captain Sioco, his Japanese commander, to lead the attack on the Spanish colony. The first offensive was composed of 600 men and officers armed with swords and battle-axes. Sioco and his troops went ashore that night and disembarked in Parañaque, near Manila. The natives hastily informed master of camp Martín de Goiti, erroneously, about the arrival of enemies from Borneo. Goiti, convalescing from a sickness, dismissed the news. Soon Chinese pirates entered the gate of the Spanish fortress adjacent to Goiti's house and killed two guards and badly wounded one, Francisco de Astigarribia, a Bizkaian pilot, who managed to escape the massacre.[13] Lucia del Corral, the wife of Goiti, thinking that the commotion was caused by some rowdy natives, leaned out the window and shouted: "Go away dogs or you will all die today!" The Portuguese interpreter whom Captain Sioco brought with him caught the woman's insulting remark and translated it. The Chinese pirates went berserk. Captain Sioco furiously ordered the house to be set on fire. Goiti, who was then bedridden, charged out of bed, put on his robe, and got his sword. But he unwittingly jumped out of the window into the middle of the enemies. The Chinese corsairs chopped off Goiti's ears and nose with scimitars and presented them later to Limahong. They also killed the wife of a soldier who also was in the house at the time. Goiti's wife was also badly wounded but survived.[14]

Lavezares, who was living on the other side of the settlement, became aware of the enemy assault when he saw the blaze at Goiti's house and heard the shots of harquebuses. Although caught off guard, Lavezares recovered his composure and ordered the few men within his reach to move two artillery pieces into combat position. Captain Sioco, on the other hand, split up his troops into three units composed of at least two hundred men each. Sioco's forces executed a crescent-formation attack on Lavezares's post that quickly killed eight Spaniards. The Spanish defenders would have been hemmed in by the Chinese pirates if not for the timely arrival of Captain Alonso Velásques with twenty soldiers, including Amador de Arriarán, a Basque lieutenant, and Gaspar Ramírez, a lieutenant of Goiti's.[15] Despite the numerical advantage of the Chinese, the Spaniards bravely held on. Strangely, Sioco ordered a retreat instead of full-blown offense and sailed back to Limahong. Perhaps he thought his forces greatly outnumbered the Spaniards and that a second assault would yield them victory.

Sioco did not confess the botched mission to Limahong, who was excitedly waiting for good news. The Japanese commander explained that he had postponed the attack on the Spanish settlement because his forces had mistakenly landed too far from their target and his men were too exhausted by the long walk. Prior to reporting to Limahong, Sioco ordered his men to hide their dead and instructed the wounded to remain ashore. He profusely apologized for failing to accomplish his mission but promised to attack the following day.[16] Limahong, however, was so confident of an easy triumph that he rested his men for three days before giving the order to attack Manila again. It was a grave tactical mistake. Juan de Salcedo and his troops, composed of 45 Spanish regulars and about 200 natives, arrived in Manila just after the first Chinese assault.

Salcedo earlier volunteered to colonize the territory of Ilocos in northern Luzon. There he founded a Spanish settlement on Vigan that he called Villa Fernandina, in honor of Prince Ferdinand. Salcedo's men actually saw the Chinese pirates approaching Villa Fernandina. But the Chinese bypassed Ilocos and instead sailed in the direction of Manila. Alarmed by the numerical superiority of the Chinese fleet, Salcedo ordered his troops to immediately prepare to leave and raced back to Manila to help defend it.

The arrival of Juan de Salcedo and his troops boosted the Spanish morale and defense. In preparation for the second attack of Limahong's forces, Lavezares gathered all the Spanish soldiers and mariners, who numbered about 150 men along with a couple of hundred native troops. He distributed all the available arms in the arsenal and ordered the building of trenches and construction of makeshift platforms on which to mount the artillery. He also announced the appointment of Salcedo as the new master of camp to succeed the fallen Goiti.[17]

After resting for three days, Limahong signaled the siege of Manila by firing a cannon from the flagship. Captain Sioco vowed to take the Spanish settlement at all cost, knowing that failure would cost him his life. He disembarked with 1,200 men, double the number of the first assault, to ensure quick success. The gritty Salcedo gathered fifty men to impede the advance of Sioco's forces, but Lavezares argued against it, opting instead to ambush the Chinese when they entered in the city. Thus, Lavezares cleverly anticipated Sioco's battle plan. As he expected, Sioco passed through the same place, adjacent to where Goiti's house used to stand, and divided his troops into three squadrons to encircle the Spaniards—the first one toward the seaside, the second toward the fort, and the third near the Pasig River. Sioco led the first group. He commanded the second group to march to and stop by a plaza in the main street to await his orders. The minute the enemy forces converged there, however, the Spaniards suddenly opened fire with artillery and harquebuses that decimated them. Sioco's squadron fought back by charging at the Spanish trenches, hurling firebombs at them.[18]

The women and children who huddled together in the house of Lavezares started screaming and crying as Sioco's men approached. Salcedo, together with some infantrymen armed with pikes, came to the rescue. Little by little, the Chinese attack lost steam as they found the Spanish and Filipino resistance tougher than anticipated and as their casualties mounted. They also became disheartened when Sioco was killed during the encounter with Salcedo's contingent. Many begun fleeing from the fight. Limahong, in a desperate move, sent his 400-man reserve force, but they too were defeated.[19] It was indeed a decisive battle. Had Limahong won, Manila and its environs could have been turned overnight into a pirate's enclave.

Enraged by their stunning loss, Limahong's remaining forces sacked the village of Parañaque and razed it before finally retreating northward to the Gulf of Lingayen in Pangasinan. There the Chinese corsairs built a stupendous fort capable of holding 600 men on a small island near the mouth of a river. Limahong also ordered construction of special quarters for himself, adorned with much of his booty. Lavezares, on the other hand, frantically fortified Manila and raised all the money he could to purchase food and other provisions. He also sent messages to all Spanish settlers in Mindoro, Panay, and Cebu to congregate at and defend Manila.[20] The thought that their settlements could fall prey to the Chinese corsairs was enough for the Spanish residing outside Manila to rush for safety to the capital.

Salcedo was relentless in his pursuit of Limahong. With only a handful of Spanish and Basque soldiers, but aided by thousands of native troops, Salcedo laid siege to the fort of Limahong.[21] Repelled by the powerful Chinese artillery, he failed to penetrate its interior. During the assault, a Basque lieutenant, Pedro de Gamboa, was killed.[22] Salcedo decided instead to encircle the enemies and starve Limahong to surrender.

During this time, two Chinese junks led by Captain Aumon from the Chinese province of Fukien arrived in Pangasinan. His mission was one of the three dispatched by the Chinese emperor to search for Limahong and convince him to once again ally himself with the emperor. Salcedo kindly received Aumon and feted him in his tent. Aumon managed to convey the message of the Chinese emperor to Limahong, but the latter rejected the offer. Aumon decided to see Governor Lavezares, and one of Salcedo's officers served as guide as the Chinese emissary embarked for Manila.

Toward the end of 1575, two ships under Aumon arrived in Manila. There Lavezares gave a warm welcome to the Chinese delegation. Captain Aumon requested Lavezares turn over to him some of the captured Chinese rescued from Limahong, particularly some women who had been kidnapped by the Chinese pirates along the coast of China. Lavezares granted the petition and did not accept any payment from Aumon in exchange for their return. In fact, he himself paid their Spanish masters to release the Chinese women. Aumon was so impressed by the gesture that he offered to take Lavezares's emissaries to China. Lavezares was of course grateful, since it was his intention to open trade with China. As he wrote King Philip II in July 1574: "the Chinese continue to increase their commerce each year, and supply us with many articles, such as sugar, wheat and barley flour, nuts, raisins, pears and oranges, silks, choice porcelain and iron, and other small things which we lacked in this land before their arrival."[23]

Selected to join the diplomatic mission to China were two religious: Fray Martín de Rada, who was the head of the delegation, and Fray Gerónimo Marín, together with Miguel de Loarca and Pedro Sarmiento. They also brought a Chinese interpreter called Sinsay.[24] Lavezares's rapprochement with the Chinese was a pragmatic move. Although Chinese pirates like Limahong coveted the Philippines, the Spanish colony needed the goods the Chinese traders could bring to Manila. Years later in 1611, another Basque, Sebastián Vizcaino, was granted audiences by the Chinese emperor and the Japanese imperial prince.[25]

Trapped and with dwindling provisions, Limahong devised an ingenious plan to escape the Spanish encirclement. He ordered a canal dug toward the direction of a nearby river. It was covered by a fence in such a way that the Spaniards would not detect them. The Chinese also recovered pieces of their junks, mostly burned during the siege, and managed to assemble enough materials to build thirty-two boats. On August 3, 1575, after four months of being corralled, Limahong managed to slip away under cover of darkness while some of his men mounted a decoy attack against the Spanish camp.[26]

Notwithstanding his failure to capture Limahong, Salcedo's part in the successful defense of Manila made him a hero and firmly established this young master of camp as a military prodigy. He was often called the "Hernan Cortés of the Philippines." He was the wise counsel of Legazpi, and "for his astuteness, good character, and personal qualities, he earned the sympathy of the native Filipinos, subjugated his enemies, and brought them to peace and friendship with the Spaniards."[27]

Here, we'll back up to tell the story of Salcedo. Born in 1549, Salcedo was a first-generation Basque born in Mexico. His mother, Teresa López de Legazpi, was a daughter of Legazpi who married a certain Pedro de Salcedo.[28] He arrived in the Philippines on August 20, 1567, then barely a teenager, by joining the second voyage of his older brother, Felipe de Salcedo. Together with Martín de Goiti, he explored the Bay of Manila before its establishment as the capital of the archipelago. After the establishment of a Spanish settlement in Manila, Legazpi ordered Juan de Salcedo to subjugate the towns of Taytay and Cainta (in present-day Rizal Province), which he executed with dispatch. Salcedo then conquered the towns along Laguna de Bay, while Martín de Goiti subjugated the inhabitants of Pampanga. Salcedo later explored the gold mines in Paracale (Camarines Norte) in the Bicol peninsula.

In May 1572, Salcedo embarked on an exploration of northern Luzon with forty-five Spanish soldiers together with an unknown number of native troops. They arrived in the port of Bolinao and passed along the coast of Pangasinan, meeting with natives both friendly and hostile. Before leaving Pangasinan they also confronted three Japanese ships manned by either pirates or traders. The ships scuttled away when the Spanish squadron fired their cannons at them. Proceeding north, the Salcedo expedition reached the mouth of the Vigan River and found a village. The village chief resisted their intrusion and evacuated the people to the other village called Bantay across the river. Vigan was a beautiful settlement with about five thousand houses. Salcedo ordered the occupation of the village but told his men to spare the women and children.[29]

In Vigan, he heard about the existence of the territory of Cagayan, which was densely populated and had a navigable river. Cagayan River is in fact the largest and longest in Luzon. Salcedo's men, however, complained of exhaustion and argued that their ships, according to the natives, would not be capable of navigating the treacherous water near a cape in Ilocos Norter, later called Bojeador. Salcedo agreed to rest but proceeded with the exploration, this time by land.

On their arrival in Ilabay, Cagayan, the inhabitants were extremely hostile to the Spanish expeditionaries. A spear-brandishing warrior, perhaps a chief, even challenged Salcedo to a duel. Both leaders ordered their men not to interfere. The Ilabay warrior approached Salcedo and hurled his spear at him, but Salcedo adroitly deflected it with his shield. When it was the turn of Salcedo, the native scampered. Salcedo chased him, unmindful of an ambush. But on reaching a hill, he found himself surrounded by more than three hundred natives. Salcedo retreated toward a large boulder to guard his back side from attack and defended himself, bobbing, weaving, and shielding himself from the darts and spears that were showered at him and with his sword fending off those who frontally attacked him. He was at the point of exhaustion and his shield was being crushed when three of his soldiers came to his rescue. They were followed by seven more who fired harquebuses at the fleeing natives. This is just one of the many spectacular stories illustrating Salcedo's legendary courage. Later, Salcedo made peace with the Ilabay people. Despite the tough resistance he met in Cagayan, Salcedo was resolute in pacifying the province. He went back to Vigan and ordered the construction of a fort, with a view to establishing a settlement. He left there a captain and twenty soldiers.[30]

Salcedo left Vigan in three ships with the rest of the expedition of seventeen soldiers on July 4, 1572, and spent a night in an islet. The following day, after having navigated the feared Cape Bojeador, they reached Aparri, Cagayan. They entered the mouth of a large river and soon found a village called Tulay where the inhabitants were friendly. In order to earn the trust of the village chief, he left the Basque Luis de Guernica, gentilhomme of Legazpi, to guarantee that they came in peace. After exploring and reconnoitering both sides of the Cagayan River and crisscrossing the territory of Cagayan, Salcedo decided to return to Manila. He made the journey by land to accelerate their arrival in the capital, but it was fraught with difficulty. It is said that when Salcedo was crossing Laguna de Bay in an unwieldy boat, it capsized. The natives who were piloting it swam to the shore leaving Salcedo behind. Surprisingly, the intrepid and irrepressible Salcedo did not know how to swim! Thus, he stayed for hours in water clinging to the floating boat. Finally, almost drowned and unconscious, he was fished out by a canoe that happened to be passing in his direction. But before his arrival in Manila, Salcedo learned about the death of his grandfather, Legazpi.[31]

For unknown reasons, Lavezares was said to be initially cool toward Salcedo. The young captain reportedly did not render homage to Lavezares as new governor-general and was said to have left in a huff after paying his last respects to the remains of Legazpi.[32] Lavezares was evidently jealous of Salcedo's success and popularity and did not give him any orders for some time. Finally, Lavezares ordered him to conquer Camarines (Bicol), which he did with ease. Salcedo subsequently founded a Spanish settlement along the Bicol River that he called Santiago de Libon.[33]

Salcedo's report about his exploration of Cagayan and its great river was enthusiastically received by Lavezares, who thought of transferring the capital there. He dispatched Salcedo anew to northern Luzon, this time to occupy Ilocos and Cagayan. In Vigan, Salcedo founded a permanent settlement he called Villa Fernandina in honor of Fernando, son of Philip II, and his fourth wife, Queen Ana, daughter of Emperor Maximilian II. It was during this period that his men saw the junks of Limahong on their way to Manila.

The need to defend Manila finally forced Lavezares and Salcedo to reconcile their differences. Salcedo also contained the rebellion staged by Lacandula, the chieftain of Manila and Tondo, during the attack of Limahong. Lacandula would later help Salcedo during the siege of Limahong's fort in Pangasinan.

On the death of his father, Salcedo thought of returning to Mexico for two years to look after the situation of his mother and a younger sister. He had another sister who was a nun, and his elder brother, Felipe, was busy with his voyages to and from the Philippines. In March 1576, he went back to his encomienda in Ilocos to raise funds for the trip. There he fell ill of malaria. Ignoring his sickness, he continued visiting a mine. He apparently drank putrid water in a nearby brook, which violently purged him. He died three hours later at the young age of twenty-seven. Salcedo was regarded as an honorable and authentic gentleman. He is the only conquistador known to have bequeathed a great part of his possessions to the natives of his lands—his encomienda in Vigan.[34]

Lavezares, in a letter to King Philip II dated June 1573, detailed the expenses incurred by Salcedo in paying the debts of his grandfather, Legazpi. "What the governor left was so little and was not sufficient because he spent his wealth in helping the poor Spanish soldiers and in other things of service to the Spanish monarch."[35]

With the deaths of Legazpi, Goiti, and Salcedo, the first phase of Spanish conquest and the creation of permanent settlements in the Philippines concluded. The Spaniards now had four principal settlements, aside from the main one in Manila. They were in Cebu and Panay in the Visayas, Nueva Cáceres in Bicol, and Villa Fernandina in Vigan, Ilocos. More than half a million inhabitants had been brought under Spanish rule. Vast unconquered territories remained, especially in the mountainous areas of Luzon and the southern island of Mindanao and the Sulu archipelago, a stronghold of an Islamic sultanate. The initiative to colonize the southern islands would once again come from the Basques, though not until the nineteenth century. While military conquest made possible the pacification of the Philippines, the conquistadors' achievements were complemented by those of missionaries, many of whom were also Basques.

Chapter Five

Missionaries

For every friar in the Philippines, the king has a captain-general and an entire army.

Viceroy of Mexico

Pacification by force of arms alone could not bring about Spanish acquisition of the Philippines. The fact that the Philippines remains, to this day, the largest Christian country in that corner of the globe is proof of the important role played by the Spanish missionaries, since evangelization was intimately intertwined with military conquest. The conquistadors' hunger for land and wealth was matched by the friars' thirst for transplanting Christianity to Philippine soil. As an Augustinian friar asserted: "The sweetness of the gospel tempered the rigor of the sword; the cross and sword in perfect harmony, pursuing the same holy goal."[1] Thus the colonization of the Philippines is aptly described as a "temporal and spiritual" conquest. This peculiar relation between the sword and the cross dates back to the age of the Crusades and the so-called *patronato real* (royal patronage) granted by the pope to the Catholic monarchs of Spain and Portugal, charging them with the Church's apostolic mission in far-flung and newly explored territories.

Discussions of the outstanding Basque missionaries in the Philippines commonly start with reference to the apostolic work of Saint Francis Xavier, a Navarrese and a famous Jesuit missionary, on the island of Mindanao. Standard Philippine history books, however, do not contain any reference to Saint Francis Xavier's exploits, since the veracity of his travel and missionary work in Mindanao has yet to be confirmed.[2]

What is certain is that the first Spanish cleric, Fray Pedro de Valderrama, arrived in the islands during the Magellan expedition in March 1521. (There were supposed to be two clerics, but the other, a Frenchman, was left on the coast of Brazil.) His achievement was obviously limited. Although he celebrated the first Catholic mass and officiated the first baptisms, the seeds of Christianity never took root. The impact of the new religion on the natives probably dissipated right after the departure of the remnants of the Magellan expedition. The same thing happened with following Spanish expeditions.

It was only after the successful expedition of Legazpi and Urdaneta in 1565 that the Catholic Church was permanently established in the archipelago, starting in Cebu. As previously described, Urdaneta brought with him to the Philippines a contingent of fellow Augustinian missionaries, all of whom were Basques: Andrés de Aguirre, Pedro de Gamboa, Diego de Herrera, and Martín de Rada. Actually, Lorenzo Jiménez, a non-Basque, was also enlisted by Urdaneta, but he died in the port of Navidad before the expedition disembarked.[3] Thus the Basques became the real pioneers in preaching the gospel and teaching catechism in the archipelago.

Interestingly, when Legazpi landed on the shores of Cebu on April 29, 1565, one of his men, Juan Camuz, a Basque soldier from Bermeo, found the image of the child Jesus inside a large, abandoned house—the only one not burned by the fleeing natives. Thrilled by his discovery, Camuz reportedly yelled in Basque: "Swear to God, you have found the Son of God."[4] The Flanders-made icon, about two feet high, of tawny wood, dressed in cloth-of-gold embroidered with jewels and mounted on a gold pedestal studded with pearls, was actually a gift of Antonio de Pigafetta, the chronicler of the Magellan expedition, to Chief Humabon's wife. According to Pigafetta, after being baptized as Juana, "she asked us to give her the little child Jesus to keep in place of her idols."[5] Since then, the Cebuanos had developed a strong pagan devotion to it, which explains why the house where it was located was not put to torch. They implored its intercession in times of need. If they wanted rain, they would make a solemn feast and sop it into the water, and it is said they always got what they wished for.[6]

Legazpi wrote of the discovery of the icon: "A soldier went into the large and well-built house, where he found an image of the Child Jesus (whose most holy name I pray may be universally worshipped). This was kept in its cradle, all gilded, just as it was brought from Spain; and only the little cross which usually tops the globe in its hands, was lacking. The image was well-kept in that house, and many flowers were found before it, for what object or purpose no one knows."[7]

When the soldiers brought him the newfound image, Urdaneta said: "Let us build a church to house the Child." And when a small chapel was built, Legazpi proclaimed: "Cebu shall henceforth be called the Zion of the Philippine Islands, and the divine influence of Christianity shall go forth from Cebu to every part of this archipelago, and across the seas and distant shores."[8]

For the Basque missionaries, the discovery of the Santo Niño was an auspicious omen. They took the Santo Niño, later called by the natives "Diwata de los Castillas" (God of the Castilians), and placed it in the chapel, so that it could be worshipped by everyone in all its splendor. It was said that the Santo Niño granted favors to its faithful devotees, particularly to pregnant women praying for an easy childbirth. Hence it was popularly known as the "midwife."[9] The Santo Niño is strongly venerated in Cebu City to this day and is a patron saint of many towns all over the Philippines.

The image of the child Jesus is a fitting symbol of the start of Christianity in the

Philippines. The reverence accorded to it by the natives attests to the strong religious tradition of the pre-Hispanic Filipinos, who had their own *anitos* (ancestral gods) and *bathalas* (deities). The Basque missionaries were crucial in the establishment of the Catholic Church in the Philippines, especially during the first years. They supervised the building of churches and conversion of the natives. Their biggest challenge was to transmute the natives' religiosity by slowly introducing the Christian doctrine. They did not resort to mass conversion for fear of the instant apostasy that had occurred after Magellan's forces left. Besides, they were taking their cue from Legazpi, who without instruction from the Audiencia could not decide whether to embark on a full conquest and, as a consequence, evangelization.[10]

To start, the Basque missionaries used the time-honored approach of winning the minds and hearts of the youth as a long-term strategy. Children are generally receptive to new ideas. Besides, the adults, although respectful, were deeply suspicious of Christian teachings. The missionaries enticed Cebuano children to visit their convent and taught them reading and writing, Spanish customs and traditions, and, as soon as they were ready, Christian prayers and catechism. Accordingly, it took a reputed miracle before the skeptical Cebuanos understood what a Christian miracle was all about. On All Saints' Day of 1566, the Spanish camp caught fire, and more than thirty houses were incinerated. The convent was also burned, but to everyone's surprise, including the Basque friars themselves, the bamboo cross hanging on the door remained intact. The natives were awed by the event.

The first one to be baptized, however, was not a child but a young widow, the niece of Datu Tupas, who was later christened Isabel, in honor of Legazpi's late wife. The Basque missionaries made sure that the baptism ceremony would be followed by a lavish and ostentatious feasts to stress its importance. This amazed and impressed the natives, which was of course partly its purpose. When Isabel was married to Andrés, one of Legazpi's crewmen, an equally lavish wedding and feast were held. The same thing happened when their son was baptized. Sid Hamal, the Bornean Muslim settler in Cebu, together with his family, also asked to be baptized and converted. Since he was well known in the Visayas, the news of his conversation spread like wildfire among the natives. But the real breakthrough came when Datu Tupas himself and his son agreed to be converted in 1568. They were baptized as Carlos and Felipe (named after the Spanish monarchs), respectively. Legazpi and Felipe Salcedo stood as their sponsors. Soon after, many Cebuanos came to the Basque clerics to be converted to Christianity.

Urdaneta knew perfectly well that in order to carry out an effective evangelization, more missionaries had to be brought to the islands. So he took Fray Andrés de Aguirre with him on his return voyage to Mexico to recruit prospective clerics to reinforce their Augustinian brethren. Fray Aguirre managed to enlist three clerics for the Philippine mission. Their arrival in Cebu in 1567 was welcomed with great jubilation by the fledgling Spanish colony. As an Augustinian historian later wrote:

"their coming was very necessary to convert the people conquered by our captains to our religion and maintain their calm, which could not be achieved only by arms."[11]

Fray Aguirre was born of an aristocratic family in Bizkaia in 1523. He joined the Augustinian convent in Salamanca, and, in 1563, he was one of the missionaries sent to Mexico by Bishop Tomás de Villanueva, a future saint. Fray Aguirre was appointed as superior of the convent of Tolotapa, but he joined Urdaneta in the Legazpi expedition the following year.[12]

Upon their successful return voyage to Mexico in 1566, Fray Aguirre likewise accompanied Urdaneta for an audience with Philip II. After returning to New Spain, he stayed there. When Urdaneta died in 1568, however, Aguirre again decided to spend the remaining years of his life in the Philippines. He assembled eight missionaries for the Philippine mission. They arrived in Manila in 1575, and Fray Aguirre subsequently became the provincial of the Augustinians. He also attended the Manila Synod convened by the Basque bishop Domingo de Salazar, about whom more will be said later. Aguirre returned to Spain in 1582 and made a report to Philip II about the religious affairs in the Philippines. In 1593, despite reaching his twilight years, Fray Aguirre again decided to return to the Philippines to spend the rest of his life.[13]

In 1569, it was the turn of Fray Diego de Herrera to return to Mexico. He was accompanied by Fray Pedro de Gamboa, since Herrera had suffered from poor health ever since they arrived in Cebu. Before Fray Herrera's departure, he was elected as the first provincial of Cebu, although there were no more than six Augustinians there. Fray Martín de Rada became his successor.[14] A late-nineteenth-century Augustinian historian criticized Fray Herrera and his Augustinian colleagues for arbitrarily creating a province without consulting the head of the Augustinian order. Nobody, however, questioned Fray Herrera when he presented himself in Mexico as the Augustinian provincial from the Philippines.[15]

Fray Herrera returned to Cebu again in 1570 together with two missionaries. He left for Spain two years later and petitioned Philip II for more clerics. Thirty-six were selected, but only six eventually joined the Philippine mission. In 1573, while approaching Manila, the ship carrying Fray Herrera was wrecked because of pilot error. Many drowned, including Fray Herrera, and the ship's cargo was lost. The accident was a huge blow to the fledgling Spanish settlement in Manila since it was in dire need of people and supplies.

When Fray Aguirre returned to Mexico in 1566, Fray Martín de Rada became acting head of the Augustinian mission in the Philippines. Rada was born in Pamplona, capital of Navarre, on July 20, 1553, of illustrious parents, León de Rada and Margarita Cruzat. His father was a member of the Royal Council of Navarre, and his family was one of the twelve richest in the province. At the age of twelve, Rada was sent to Paris along with his brother to study. He excelled in mathematics, geography, and astronomy. He also studied Asian languages and showed great interest in nautical science and navigation.[16] He continued his studies in Salamanca, where he discovered his divine calling. He decided to become a missionary.

He joined the Augustinian order and resided in its convent of San Pedro. In 1556, he was recruited by Cardinal Juan de Tavera to carry out an apostolic mission in Mexico. There, he met Andrés de Urdaneta, whom he treated as "brother and friend in interests and ideals." He was proposed by Philip II to be the bishop of Jalisco in Mexico, but Aguirre decided instead to join Urdaneta as a missionary in the Legazpi expedition in 1565.

Rada taught catechism in Cebu and became provincial superior three years later. Upon the establishment of Manila as Spanish capital, Rada was elected as provincial and head of the Convent of Manila. It was a period of rapid ecclesiastical expansion, as parish priests were appointed in Cebu, Masbate, Otong, Mindoro, Tondo, Bay, and Pasig, and convents built in each. [17] Rada also officiated the funeral rites of Legazpi, whose remains were buried in the Church of Saint Augustine in the chancel.[18]

Rada authored various works, including *De recta hidrographiae ratione; Geometria práctica; Vocabulario y arte de la lengua cebuana; Diccionario y arte de la lengua china; Un breve tratado de las antigüedades, ritos y costumbres de los chinos,* of which we learn from Fray Jeronimo Román in his *Repúblicas del mundo;* and the *Relación* (*Account*) of their entry into China, which Rada coauthored with Fray Gerónimo Marín. This work was included in volumes eight and nine of the *Revista Agustina* and afterward in the religious journal *Ciudad de Dios* (*City of God*). Rada also left numerous astronomical tables, although a great part of his work has been lost. Only his *Relación* and some letters were published, since, at that time printing was nonexistent in the Philippines and there were no amanuenses to make copies of his works. In spite of his busy life, he found time to send voluminous letters to Fray Jerónimo Tomás and Fray Juan González de Menéndez, King Philip II, his brother Juan de Rada, and the *alcalde mayor* of Navarre, as well as to the provincial superior of the Augustinians in Mexico.[19]

Rada was an active defender of the natives against the abuses of the conquistadors. His humanism was evident in the letters (dated June 21, 1570, August 10, 1572, and June 10, 1573,) he sent to the viceroy of Mexico denouncing the abuses committed against the native Filipinos. In his letter after the death of Legazpi, he said: "With the passage of time, they (Spaniards) commit more atrocities, and there is less reprimand and punishment now than during the time of the Adelantado (Legazpi). The natives mourn for him, for in the past he treated them more like a father than do those of today."[20]

Described by his contemporaries as a Renaissance man—he was a math genius, geographer, astronomer, navigator, polyglot, scholar, etc.—Rada is best remembered in the annals of Philippine history as the head of the first diplomatic mission sent by Spain to China. Earlier, Legazpi used Rada's linguistic talent and diplomatic skills to conduct a protracted negotiation with Commander Pereyra while the Spaniards fortified their defenses against the superior Portuguese fleet.

As related in chapter 4, in 1575, after the siege of Manila by the Chinese pirates led by Limahong, Captain Aumon, the emissary of the viceroy of Fukien, sailed to Manila and requested Governor Lavezares to allow the return of some prisoners taken by the Spaniards from the Limahong fleet. When Lavezares not only arranged for their release but paid for it, Aumon, out of gratitude, offered to take a delegation appointed by Lavezares to China. Thus in June 1575, Lavezares quickly organized an embassy and appointed Fray Martín de Rada as chief of the mission. He was to be accompanied by Fray Gerónimo Marín, Miguel de Loarca, Pedro Sarmiento, and Sinsay, a Chinese interpreter.[21]

The mission did not come as a surprise to Fray Rada since he knew he would one day set foot on China. While in Cebu, he started learning the Chinese language from a native speaker who was living in the convent. Legazpi originally thought of sending a mission to the Chinese emperor, but death cut short his dream. Lavezares turned it into a reality.

Lavezares instructed the Rada mission to transmit his letters to the emperor of China and to the governors of the provinces of Canton and Fukien since the two provinces were nearest to the ports where the delegation would disembark. In those letters, Lavezares claimed that "the Philippines was occupied in the name of King Philip II and that when Chinese merchants come there, he (Philip II) would not allow them to be harmed or maltreated, as usually done by the inhabitants of these islands who capture them and rob of their goods, before our arrival; that at a cost the king had their captured goods rescued, set them free to the land of the Chinese and that the Chinese would be given full privileges and rights such as those enjoyed by the Spaniards without allowing any offense against them." He added an account of how they had repulsed the attacks of Limahong and his men. He also promised that once the dreaded pirate fell into his hands, he would be "carried in chains to the emperor's presence, let there be no doubt about this, and if already dead, his salted head would be served."[22]

Lavezares also gave the Rada mission two confidential instructions with two principal objectives: to obtain the rights to trade freely with China and to look into the ways of introducing Christianity in that extensive empire by allowing the free entry of missionaries. The instructions, imbued with strategic consideration, displayed the tact and sagacity of Lavezares: "The emissaries shall endeavor to learn the character of the people of the country and their mentality, customs, and conduct of relationships and contracts; if they are truthful and keep their word, and what merchandise could be obtained that would be of interest to both parties, and other things and secrets of the country that can be learned and obtained." The members of the Spanish delegation were prohibited from showing any overt admiration for the things the Chinese possessed or showed to them nor were they to mock their idols, such as those that the Chinese keep in their houses or in their temples. They were not to laugh at or scoff at their ceremonies, which the Chinese took seriously.[23]

Rada stayed for several months in China. By the time he returned to Manila, he had written on various aspects of Chinese civilization. In one of their journeys, the governor of Fukien boasted that only the Chinese knew the art of printing. Rada took out his breviary to burst that illusion. Rada's chronicles of his journey in the celestial empire became the basis of Fray Juan González Mendoza's *History of China*.

Upon the completion of the visit to China, Fray Rada reported that the mission was a complete success. The viceroy of Fukien reciprocated with precious gifts for Lavezares and in a reply to Lavezares's message said, among other things: "To you who has the image of heaven, although we are so different from one another, we are the sons of a father and mother, that is why we must love each other as friends and brothers. . . . From now on I wish to have great friendship with you and I will count my vassals as yours and yours as mine." Beyond the diplomatic courtesies, however, the viceroy of Fukien was most interested in the capture of the corsair Limahong, who must be "brought to him, if alive in chains, and if dead, his salted head," as promised by Lavezares. For this purpose, the viceroy sent three Chinese captains to sail to Manila as a reciprocal mission to Lavezares and to see the completion of his promise regarding Limahong. He also designated a port where the Spaniards could engage in friendly contacts and trade.

Rada's mission disembarked for Manila in early September 1575. On their way back, while on the island of Pehou, they were informed that Limahong had managed to escape from Pangasinan. The news caused a great consternation among them, particularly the Chinese. Though angered by the news, the Chinese envoys proceeded to Manila to deliver the message and gifts of the viceroy to Lavezares, arriving on October 28, 1575.

The three Chinese captains were received warmly in Manila. One of them stayed at the house of Lavezares, another one with Salcedo, while the last remained in his ship, most likely as a security precaution. The return of the Rada mission coincided with the arrival in Manila of Don Francisco Sande, the newly appointed governor-general. (Lavezares relinquished the post he assumed after Legazpi's death. As a sop to his pride, he was later appointed as master of camp.) Sande's assumption of duty as governor-general signaled a new era in the archipelago's colonial administration. As in the Americas, the conquistadors, who had successfully established a Spanish foothold in the Philippines, were now being eased out by powerful politicians and bureaucrats who unabashedly used influence to obtain high positions in the colonial bureaucracy. Not content with being a member of the Real Audiencia of Mexico, Sande coveted the position of governor-general of the Philippines as a stepping stone to higher office and also evidently to enrich himself. Totally ignorant of Asian culture, Sande's rude and tactless dealing with the Chinese envoys almost destroyed the friendly, commercial relations that Legazpi and Lavezares had painstakingly forged.

The Chinese emissaries presented exotic gifts to Lavezares even though he was no longer the governor, an act that irked Sande. They gave Salcedo luxurious porcelain and traditional Chinese weapons. They also regaled him with a white banner emblazoned with the name of the viceroy of Fukien. It was a token of their great admiration for the young master of camp for having inflicted great damage on Limahong. The remaining gifts were given to Governor Sande for distribution. The most important souvenir, however, was Fray Rada's account of their visit to China and of China's riches, which mesmerized the Spanish colonizers.

The Chinese delegation stayed for a while in Manila and waited for the monsoon rains to pass. The Chinese expected Governor Sande to reciprocate for the lavish gifts showered on the Rada mission in China, but the new governor never gave anything of value, only a letter described at the time as "exquisite writing."

Sande ignored the Chinese sensitivities and insisted on sending another mission to China. He appointed Fray Agustín de Alburquerque as head and relegated Fray Rada to the deputy position. There were also three native Filipinos and a Chinese interpreter. One of the Chinese captains, unable to control his anger, openly complained about the treatment. He even returned the jewel given to him, which the Spaniards claimed to be made of gold, saying it was not reciprocation for the gifts that they had brought to Manila. Still, they took the Alburquerque mission with them. But they decided to disembark on the island of Bolinao with the members of the mission. There they vented their anger over Limahong's escape and the shabby treatment they had received from Governor Sande and exacted revenge. First, they lashed the Chinese interpreter to death and beheaded the Filipino servants. Lastly, they stripped Alburquerque and Rada of their habits, tied them naked to a tree, and left the two priests there, thinking that the hostile natives would finish them off. After more than a day of exposure to the elements, the two missionaries were miraculously rescued by Juan de Moriones, a sergeant major, who was searching the area for mines.[24]

It took many years before relations between the Spaniards and the Chinese were normalized. Not until 1598 did another Basque, Juan de Zamudio, succeed in gaining entry into China to trade. Zamudio left for Canton and was received by the viceroy of the province when his ship arrived in the port of Pinal, twelve leagues from the provincial capital. The port was designated for commerce with the Spaniards.[25]

In 1576, Fray Rada again participated in an expedition, this time to Borneo. The Spanish colonial government had decided to help a friendly sultan defend himself against his enemies. The expedition proved to be a success, but, on their return, Fray Rada fell sick of beriberi and died on the high seas.

The religious missions in the Philippines from 1565 to 1576 were essentially an Augustinian monopoly. Fray Diego de Herrera and Fray Andrés de Aguirre in particular lobbied hard to get other religious orders to send missionaries, since the task ahead was monumental. Fray Herrera's call for apostolic reinforcement was heeded by the Franciscans, who arrived in the Philippines in 1577. They were later followed by the Jesuits (1581), the Dominicans (1581), and the Augustinian Recollects (1606).

In 1580, the pope elevated Manila to a diocese. The new status, however, necessitated the appointment of a bishop. To the disappointment of the Augustinians, Philip II chose a Dominican for the position. But as it turned out, the new bishop, Domingo de Salazar, was also a Basque.

Salazar was a native of Araba. He joined the Dominican order and studied in the famous Convent of San Esteban in Salamanca. His contemporaries included some of the illustrious Dominican theologians of the epoch, such as Fray Domingo Ibañez and Fray Bartolome de Medina. Salazar was himself a brilliant student and could have been counted among the great theological scholars had he pursued an academic career. Instead he decided to serve God by becoming a missionary in the Americas. Inspired and challenged by the obstacles facing the Dominicans in establishing their mission in Mexico, he volunteered to go to New Spain to convert many Indians into Christians.[26]

In Mexico, Salazar carried out intense apostolic work, conversion, and catechism. He was a factotum, performing various ministries, baptizing and preaching to the natives, surprising others with how he could do so many tasks alone. He had taught many students, mostly Creoles, some of whom eventually acquired superior education and virtues under his patient guidance. He later earned the title of Master of Theology, the highest award that could be bestowed in the Dominican order for outstanding attainment and virtue. Fray Salazar was also a prior of the province of Mexico and provincial vicar, to the great satisfaction of the religious. He was also the first consultor that the Holy Inquisition had after the tribunal was set up in that city.

All in all, Salazar stayed in Mexico for forty years, and during those four long decades, it is said, he never violated in any manner the sacred constitution of his order. Thus his entire religious life was exemplary, a kind of *non plus ultra,* that which cannot be surpassed. It was said to be so supernatural and divine that the holy pontiff remarked that "Salazar can easily be canonized for having faithfully guarded the canons of our religion."[27]

Being a man of action, however, Salazar sought other challenges and adventures rather than being content to stay in the Mexican capital. He volunteered to go to Vaxac, then a newly conquered territory, to preach the gospel to the natives. He also accompanied Fray Domingo de la Anunciación in a failed expedition to Florida. During their journey, the scarcity of food was such that they resorted to eating the leather straps of helmets, sword belts, roots of weeds, and barks of wild trees.

Salazar's zeal in proselytizing was matched by his fervor in defending the rights of the Indians against the abuses of Spanish colonizers. This led to clashes with the authorities in Florida. The turning point came when he publicly denounced the abuses being committed by the Spaniards against the natives of the Islands of Guadalupe (Barbados). Salazar even sought an audience with Philip II and pleaded against the cruel treatment of the Indians. Atrocities committed against the native Americans had long been the crusade of Bishop Bartolomé de las Casas (1474–1566), another famous Dominican, with devastating effect on the moral authority of the Spanish monarchy. De las Casas condemned the brutality of Spanish colonization, which led to the banning of all expeditions in the New World for more than a decade (1549–1560). Seeing another de las Casas in the making, Philip II decided to silence Salazar by appointing him as head of the newly created bishopric of Manila. The elevation of Manila into a diocese was decreed by Pope Gregory XIII in the bull *Illius fulti presidio,* dated February 6, 1579. Understandably, Salazar was at first reluctant to accept the position since it was tantamount to banishment. In the end, his Dominican superiors persuaded him to consent, as it was an opportunity for him to continue his missionary work with the native Filipinos, not to mention having the honor of being the first Dominican bishop of Manila, a position much coveted by the other religious orders, particularly the Augustinians.

Salazar requested that Philip II send other Dominicans with him, but majority of his companions died or got sick during the crossing of the Atlantic when an epidemic ravaged their ship. Those who survived the ordeal refused to join Salazar in the Philippine mission. He had to make do with a lone companion, Fray Cristobal de Salvatierra, a young Basque from Araba, who would later faithfully serve Salazar. Together they erected the cathedral of Manila, a great financial burden since they did not have ecclesiastical earnings. Salvatierra also served as supervisor of the diocese of Manila and acting bishop during Salazar's absence.[28]

Bishop Salazar arrived in the Philippines in March 1581 together with the first Jesuits. A number of Augustinians and Franciscans also disembarked with them. Upon assuming his position, he dedicated himself to introducing reforms in the colony and to remedying the abuses being committed by the Spanish colonizers against the natives. Salazar bemoaned the situation he found in Manila on his arrival, comparing the new diocese to a flock without a master. He was appalled by the corrupt and venal practices pervading in the capital. He would not tolerate louche morals, profanities, and blasphemies. Because of his zeal in carrying out his mission, he drew down the wrath of the Spanish residents, including then governor Diego Ronquillo. A number of them did not conceal their opposition to the Basque bishop. Some Spanish soldiers brazenly warned Salazar that he should go easy on them because they would not hesitate to aim their harquebuses at him. But Salazar never lost heart and became even more determined to address the important issues that would improve the management of the church and religious missions in the Philippines.

To push ecclesiastical reforms, Salazar convened a council, later known as the First Synod of Manila (1582–1586), which made several important decisions regarding the evangelization of the native Filipinos. One was the teaching of Christian doctrine in the native languages rather than Spanish. Another was to gather together the dispersed clan villages, as far as was possible, into larger communities to facilitate their methodical instruction in Christian life and worship. It is to this decision that many Philippine towns owe their origin, as well as their characteristic arrangement around a central plaza or square dominated by the town church and its bell tower.[29]

The synod was not an exclusive gathering of theologians and jurists but also included leading military officials and encomenderos. The initial meeting was tension filled and eventually turned into a fiasco when the religious condemned the encomenderos for their abuses of the natives and for their failure to live up to the tenets of Christianity. During a heated argument, an irate encomendero even punched an Augustinian friar in the face. The Basque bishop and the governor likewise clashed, defending one side against the other. Only through the intervention of cooler heads did the disputants calm down.[30]

Bitter infighting persisted, however, even among the religious orders. The regulars, especially the Augustinians, being the pioneers, resented Salazar's proposals to divest the religious orders of their ownership of properties and jurisdiction in parochial administration. They staunchly defended their privileges, but Salazar, supported by the newly arrived Jesuits and secular clerics, held tenaciously to his position.

The Basque bishop threatened the Augustinians with censure and excommunication if they did not obey the decision of the synod. He petitioned Governor Ronquillo, in his capacity as vice patron, to relieve the Augustinians of their ministries and to allow them to live in their convent in Manila according to their religious norms and to sustain themselves through royal subsidy. The Augustinians took this as an affront and a total disregard of their role as pioneers in the evangelization of the archipelago.

Governor Ronquillo, contemptuous of Salazar's criticism of his lackluster Christian practice, tried to use his royal assistance (*real auxilio*) to derail the initiatives of the bishop. He admonished Salazar to desist from his zealous reforms, but only succeeded in fanning the flames of discord. Fray Andrés de Aguirre, then the Augustinian provincial, having taken offense at the various allegations of Bishop Salazar against his order, decided to appeal to the ecclesiastical court (Corte de Procuradores) and to beseech the Spanish king to take appropriate measures to decide the fate of the religious orders in the Philippines. Taking matters into his own hands, he selected Fray Juan Pimentel as companion and took the first ship for Mexico. On reaching the Mexican capital, Aguirre wrote two scathing letters to the bishop of Mexico and other authorities complaining about Salazar's heavy-handed treatment of the Augustinians and his alleged excesses.[31]

Meanwhile, many Spanish residents in Manila supported the embattled bishop.

They admired the Basque bishop for his lucid doctrine, preachings, and sermons, he being a learned theologian and excellent orator. But his strength lay in the example he set. Although his detractors described him as priggish and at times truculent, he practiced what he preached. He was a simple and ascetic man. He was parsimonious, wearing the same old habit, a woolen tunic, that he used in Mexico. He slept on a wooden bed; his meals consisted mostly of eggs and fish; and his house was bare of frills and adornment. He did most household chores by himself, although he had domestic helpers.

Deeply concerned about the state of literacy in Manila, he ordered the religious to give instructions in their convents to those people who wished to be taught, and he petitioned the king for a regular subsidy for those religious who doubled as teachers. It was granted by the king in a royal decree from Barcelona in 1583. He was also a principal proponent of the construction of a hospital for the Chinese settlers. He made prison and hospital visits on Fridays without fail. He consoled the prisoners and sick with kind words and dispensed alms according to their needs. He collected all the tithes and meticulously counted them, taking care not to lose a single cent. He allocated a certain amount for the poor and sternly warned his helpers not to put their hands on the church funds. He bought idle lands and converted them into productive farms. He also sold his pectoral cross and other valuables and gave all the proceeds to the poor.

His detractors, nevertheless, were not convinced. They circulated malicious rumors questioning the Basque bishop's vow of chastity, alleging that he may have fallen into temptation and become tainted while providing shelter to prostitutes, many of whom he gathered from the streets. Even some religious tended to agree, since Salazar "received and defended those women of loose morals with great care."[32]

One of Salazar's lasting legacies was the urban construction of Manila. Before his arrival, the Spanish settlement in the capital was made of flammable materials such as wood, bamboo, and grass. The settlement was at grave risk, and in fact had burned down on several occasions. In February 1583, a great fire consumed the city, including the cathedral, the Augustinian convent, the royal hospital, and the citadel with all its arms and ammunition. Besides, the city was vulnerable to attack by Chinese corsairs.

Bishop Salazar petitioned Governor Ronquillo and the city council to reconstruct the city out of stone and durable materials. His suggestion was well received in principle but ultimately opposed by the colonial government because of the scarcity of stone and the cost of construction materials. With the great zeal and energy that marked his apostolic mission, Bishop Salazar took a Chinese barge up the Pasig River in search of quarries. He later found adobe in Makati and ordered its extraction. To enable a quantity of large stones to be cut, he ordered that the necessary tools be fashioned. Since they were the first such tools ever made in the Philippines, and there were no ironsmiths familiar with their manufacture, they cost him a great deal.[33]

With great expense and effort, he was able to build his convent, the first concrete structure in the city. The other Spanish settlers followed his example, and little by little the facade of the city changed. The profits derived from the fledgling galleon trade provided the financial resources for such construction. There soon followed a stone fort, a hospital, a cathedral, and religious quarters, all of them inside the walled city called Intramuros.

The Basque chronicler Antonio de Morga was very impressed when he saw Manila for the first time toward the end of the sixteenth century. He wrote: "The streets of the city were lined with houses, the majority of which were of stone, and some with wood, many roofs were of tiles, and others with straw; balconies and iron railings adorn them, and every day more were being constructed and perfected."[34] In sum, while Miguel López de Legazpi was the Basque founder of Manila, another Basque, Domingo de Salazar, was its first urban builder.

Salazar's achievements, however, were almost overshadowed by his bitter conflict with the Holy Office of the Inquisition in Mexico. In his single-minded pursuit of cleansing the colony of heretics and blasphemers, he was accused and, later on, found guilty of illegally usurping the powers of the Holy Office.

Before the formal establishment of the Holy Office in the Americas, the bishops exercised inquisitorial powers. They prosecuted, condemned, and even burned at the stake those found guilty of heresy. But these episcopal powers were lost when the Holy Office was formally created. On January 25, 1569, Philip II signed a royal decree establishing the Holy Office of Inquisition in Lima and Mexico. Lima was given jurisdiction over all of South America, while Mexican jurisdiction included Guatemala, Honduras, Costa Rica, the Antilles, and the Philippines.[35]

Although the Holy Office of Inquisition in Mexico appointed commissioners in all the cities within its jurisdiction, none was designated to take charge of the Philippines. Many years passed, and the inquisitors never thought of appointing a commissioner in the archipelago. Even when the newly designated Bishop Salazar passed through Mexico in 1581, the Holy Office never discussed this point with him because "the Philippines was a new territory and hardly inhabited by Spaniards." But they soon realized the omission when Bishop Salazar shortly upon his arrival in the Philippines exercised inquisitorial powers without prior approval from the Holy Office in Mexico.

The Basque bishop had closely witnessed the prestige, power, and the fear inspired by the Holy Office and decided on arriving in his diocese to bestow on himself and his episcopal dignity the attributes of the Holy Office. When news and complaints reached the authorities of the Holy Office in Mexico, they hastily dispatched Fray Francisco Manrique, an Augustinian commissioner, to Manila to investigate Salazar.[36]

Bishop Salazar, in his letter to the Holy Office in Mexico dated September 8, 1583, defended his action by claiming that the Mexican inquisitors had never discussed the matter with him and he therefore thought that his diocese was not under their jurisdiction. Bishop Salazar's auto-de-fé (religious prosecution) also gained the strong support of the Franciscans and the Jesuits. But their warning to other Spanish residents that recognizing the Augustinian commissioner was commensurate with committing a mortal sin aggravated the conflict. It had begun to look like a turf dispute between the Augustinians, the pioneers, and the newcomers, Franciscans, Jesuits, and Dominicans. Recall that Fray Andrés de Aguirre earlier complained to the Mexican ecclesiastical authorities, then Philip II and the Roman Curia, and denounced Salazar based on the report of Fray Manrique, whom he appointed as vicar while he was outside the Philippines.

The fact-finding mission also started off on the wrong footing. Fray Manrique antagonized Salazar and his religious supporters when he demanded the appointment of a panel to be composed of canon and legal experts, claiming that "the theologians (referring to the Franciscans, Jesuits, and Dominicans) know little about law and nothing will come from them." Other Manila residents such as Juan Convergel Maldonado and Benito de Mendiola backed Fray Manrique and later criticized Salazar's approach as heavy-handed. Both Maldonado and Mendiola later testified that, because they sided with Manrique, they were forcibly arrested and imprisoned in the inquisitorial cell under the orders of the Basque bishop. Governor Ronquillo had to intervene to secure their release. Fray Manrique, exasperated by the hostility he faced from the other religious orders and feeling increasingly impotent in carrying out his work, desperately appealed to Philip II to issue the necessary directive before he proceeded with his mission.[37]

On September 24, 1583, Governor Ronquillo threw his support to Fray Manrique, and reported to the Holy Office in Mexico that Bishop Salazar indeed was obstructing the work of Fray Manrique, "putting anyone who would follow the orders of the commissioner of the Holy Office under the pain of ex-communication" and that he (Ronquillo) had offered to Fray Manrique all the favors and assistance he had been deprived of because of Salazar's irritation with the whole affair. Thus the Holy Office of Mexico petitioned the Spanish king to order the bishop of Manila to cease and desist in his usurpation of inquisitorial powers. The petition was granted. In a letter to Bishop Salazar dated May 26, 1585, Philip II rebuked the Basque bishop and ordered him not to encroach on affairs under the jurisdiction of the Holy Office in Mexico and deauthorized the officials Salazar had appointed to constitute the hierarchy of the Manila inquisition. The king also ordered Salazar to turn over to the Holy Office in Mexico all the cases and proceedings that he had already undertaken so that they could be reviewed and decided upon.[38]

What happened to Salazar in the Philippines had also occurred, more or less, in the Americas, where several bishops defended their inquisitorial powers from the ministers of the Holy Office. But the latter, supported by the Spanish king, demanded exclusive exercise of their jurisdiction in matters of faith. Not surprisingly, the bishops always ended up losing their case. With the rebuff, Bishop Salazar had no choice but to shut up and respect the authority of the Holy Office in Mexico. He divested himself of all his inquisitorial functions and turned over all the proceedings he had initiated. Seeing his compliance with the king's directive, the Holy Office, in a rare exception, treated him kindly and spared him from the scandal by not publicly announcing the deauthorization of his inquisitorial powers.[39]

In a report to the Holy Office in Mexico dated April 28, 1587, Salazar enumerated the six pending cases of inquisition before him. Interestingly, two of them dealt with a Basque and a Basque descendant. One of them involved Francisco de Zuñiga, a twenty-year-old Basque bachelor. When admonished for indulging in lascivious acts, he, according to some witnesses, haughtily responded: "What do I care? Fornication is not a sin!" According to others, although he confessed and begged for forgiveness, he later denounced the Basque bishop, who retaliated by ordering his arrest and the seizure of his properties. Zuñiga underwent public trial barefooted. Holding a candle and gagged, he recanted. Finally he was sentenced to ten years of banishment in the Americas and, in case of refusal, two hundred lashes.[40]

Another case dealt with Martín de Goiti, the fourteen-year-old son of the former master of camp of the same name and a native Filipina, for committing sacrilege against the image of Our Lady and inciting the native girls to fornicate with him. Some witnesses testified that Martín even showed the girls the image of Our Lady and told them that she was not a virgin because he had already corrupted her. Martín denied the accusation, saying that while reading in Spanish some words got mixed up with the local language, resulting in a misunderstanding by the witnesses. In short, he merely committed linguistic errors. Goiti's case was still pending when Salazar submitted his report.

When Salazar returned to Spain to defend himself against his enemies, many assumed that Philip II would not receive the Basque bishop. But the Spanish king granted him an audience and ended up enjoying their meeting. Salazar made an impressive report about Philippine ecclesiastical affairs and the reforms he had initiated. As a result, he obtained a huge amount from the king and other nobles to augment the meager stipend of the prebendary. Salazar also succeeded in increasing the number of prebendary so that the Manila diocese would be better served. Since the bishop could not attend to the confirmation and other bisphoric acts in all the islands, he proposed the division of his diocese into four: an archbishop and three bishops and indicated the term for each one. Rome eventually approved Salazar's proposal and named him archbishop of Manila.

But before the papal bull could be promulgated elevating Manila into an archdiocese, Salazar was afflicted with a grave illness and died in 1594. It was said that Salazar died poor, with only six reales in his possession, much like the poor people that he served. He never gave a single real to his poor sister because he was attending more to the most needy. Salazar's penury came to the attention of Philip II, who hastily paid the cost of his burial. A solemn funeral ceremony was held in the honor of the first bishop of Manila in the convent of Saint Thomas of Madrid, where all the members of the Royal Council attended. The funeral, however, coincided with that of the archbishop of Toledo, Gaspar de Quiroga, also cardinal of Rome. Toledo was then the richest archdiocese in all Christendom. Archbishop Quiroga died a day before Salazar and was scheduled to be interred in Madrigal. Since the royal court could not attend both funerals, they consulted the king, who ordered them to attend the burial of Salazar, the poor bishop. Thus the epitaph in his tomb says: "Here lies Don Fray Domingo de Salazar of the Order of the Preachers, Bishop of the Philippine Islands, lucid in his doctrine, faithful follower of religious life, intimate pastor of his sheep, father of the poor, he himself being truly poor. He died on December 4, 1594."[41]

The ships that arrived in Manila in 1596 from New Spain brought the sad news of Salazar's death. The Spanish residents, particularly the poor and the religious, deeply mourned his loss; even his foes belatedly recognized his achievements. But few could equal the suffering felt by Fray Cristobal de Salvatierra, his ever loyal companion and provisor. Great men often had great collaborators. Salazar was no exception. In Salvatierra, he had an invaluable vicar. Salvatierra was described as a "pillar, immovable and firm, resisting all temptation and never letting the bishop down, always staying by his side."[42]

Salvatierra was an outstanding graduate of the prestigious Dominican convent of San Esteban in Salamanca. In his desire to be one of the first founders of their congregation in the Philippines, he joined Salazar with thirty others. Many of them perished during the crossing of the Atlantic, and after arriving in Mexico many more became sick. The voyage from Spain to the Philippines was torturous, with the crossing of the Atlantic just the first step. Upon disembarking in the port of Veracruz, Spanish passengers and merchandise destined for Manila had to traverse inland to reach the port of Acapulco, and from there navigate the Pacific Ocean. The whole voyage took not just months but a year or so to complete.

Therefore many Dominicans were terrified to continue their journey to the Philippines after their initial harrowing experience. Despite the pleadings of Salazar, many of them stayed in Mexico; only Fray Salvatierra heeded the Basque bishop. Salazar appointed Salvatierra as administrator of the new diocese of Manila, a task he performed with great competence and devotion. He also served as a senior inquisitor. He took care of the ministry in the province of Bataan, traveling there mainly by foot. Indefatigable, he still joined expeditions to Nueva Segovia (Ilocos) and the Moluccas, serving as chaplain of the soldiers.

Salvatierra was both loved and feared. He defended the rights of the natives and pursued sinners with extraordinary zeal and courage, sometimes to an embarrassing degree. He would break into the houses of adulterers and catch them "in flagrante delicto." He also ordered the arrest of prostitutes and their clients and would personally drag an erring cleric to prison. One of his controversial actions was the prohibition of Chinese plays. After learning Chinese language, calligraphy, and customs, Salvatierra found the theatrical plays to be full of superstition and idolatry and therefore offensive to God. The Spaniards enjoyed the plays because of their fast actions and vivid costumes, despite not understanding a word of the dialogue. The fact that they were held in the evening added to their popularity. Salvatierra claimed that many of those who patronized the Chinese plays, "Spanish men and women as well as their chaperons and maids, indulged, under the cover of darkness, in activities that were not worthy of doing in Christian lands."[43]

Since the Chinese were great aficionados of this entertainment, they resented Salvatierra and sought the assistance of Governor Ronquillo, claiming that there was nothing wrong with the plays. Salvatierra ordered the excommunication of those who went to see them. But since the governor had a different position, nobody dared published the excommunication order. The provisor himself had to post it on the doors of the churches, accompanied by some friars, since no civilian was willing to join his crusade. Salvatierra stood his ground despite strong opposition to his order. He only allowed the staging of Chinese plays that he had previously expurgated of superstitious and idolatrous elements.

His relentless ministry in Bataan, then a day's travel by sea from Manila, took its toll on him. He attended to his pastoral work with great care and love, covering an area so extensive that he had to trek muddy trails, always barefoot, along the base of the mountains, rugged seacoast, and mosquito-infested swampy lands. It later took four missionaries to do what Salvatierra did during his prime. In addition, he was afflicted with asthma, which later caused his death. He died in the Dominican-run Chinese hospital he helped establish in Tondo.

Other outstanding Basque missionaries followed the examples of Aguirre, Herrera, Rada, Salazar, and Salvatierra. There was Pedro Arce (1560–1645) who served as bishop in Cebu and Nueva Cáceres (present-day Camarines) and as interim archbishop of Manila. Another was Melchor Oyanguren (1688–1717), who was regarded as a great preacher in Tagalog and author of a trilingual dictionary in Tagalog, Spanish, and Basque.[44]

A number of Basque missionaries were martyred in the course of their religious activities in the Philippines, Japan, and the Pacific islands. Domingo Ibañez de Erquicia and Miguel de Aozaraza, both Dominicans from Gipuzkoa, were martyred in Nagasaki, Japan, in 1633. Ibañez de Erquicia was a superb preacher and professor of philosophy in Manila. The two of them were beatified on February 18, 1981, by Pope John Paul II during his first visit to Manila. It is also worth mentioning that the first Filipino saint, Lorenzo Ruíz de Manila, was a lay missionary who joined the Ibañez mission in Japan. Fray Francisco Ezquerra was tortured in Guam; Fray Francisco Mendoza in Mindanao; a Basque Jesuit, José de Esandi, was killed in an undetermined place, while a fellow Jesuit, Juan Bautista de Larrauri, was martyred in Leyte.[45]

Truly the Basque missionaries played an active rule in the foundation of the Catholic Church in the Philippines. In general, all the missionaries served not just as guardians of the religious life of the people but also as police of the social order. They performed multifarious roles, as teachers, administrators, farmers, judges, and, at times, entrepreneurs. They were the chief agents of Hispanization.[46] Their influence grew ubiquitous and pervasive. Even the British, after their retreat from Manila in 1764, acknowledged the impact of the missionaries on the islands and recognized their mistake in maltreating them. In a pamphlet they published after their departure, they admitted: "had we known better, we would have corrected the violence committed against the religious fathers, to whose persuasion and fidelity were owed the maintenance of this country. . . . It is certain that Dr. Salazar [referring to Simón de Anda y Salazar, the Basque resistance leader against the British invaders discussed in greater detail in chapter 7] has acted like a gentleman; we praise his magnanimity and love for his King, but it was only due to the protection of the religious fathers that he overcame the major difficulties and sustained the loyalty of the natives."[47]

Even during the first half of the nineteenth century when there was a grave need to reinforce the colonial forces in the Philippines to preserve Spanish hegemony, the role of the missionaries was still very much valued. As Marcelo Oráa, a Basque governor-general of the Philippines (1841–1843), told Ferdinand VII, the king of Spain: "Send me a company of friars; they would serve me more than forty battalions."[48]

Chapter Six

Galleon Traders and Merchants

> How not to live and prosper in the Philippines when its people more than in any other nation wonderfully adjust to adaptation in the new lands of the planet?
>
> Pedro Feced, "Are There Basques in the Philippines?" 1892

Even before the arrival of the first Europeans in the Philippines in 1521, Manila was an incipient commercial entrepôt frequented by Chinese, Indian, and Muslim traders. The Basque chronicler Antonio de Morga noted in his accounts that "merchant ships from China, Japan, Moluccas, Borneo, Siam, Malacca, and India sail to the bay and river of Manila."[1] The early Filipinos in particular maintained commercial contacts with Chinese merchants, who regularly came to the archipelago to barter for tropical products and shells much sought after in China. Once the Spanish hegemony was established in Manila in 1571, the Spaniards effectively exploited the city's geographic location as a transshipping hub.

The galleon trade actually began in June 1565 with the return voyage of the *San Pedro*. Under the command of Legazpi's grandson, Felipe de Salcedo, and piloted by Andrés de Urdaneta, it left Cebu for Mexico. The discovery of the *tornavieje* (return route) four months later established the maritime link between the Philippines and Mexico through the ports of Manila and Acapulco. Although the main objective of the Salcedo-Urdaneta expedition was to discover a return route to Mexico, Legazpi also sent a small quantity of cloves from Mindanao.[2] The cloves had been purchased using royal funds by a group of men led by the Basque master of camp Mateo de Saz in northern Mindanao during a reconnaissance mission.[3]

In 1572, Legazpi sent the first shipment of Chinese goods consisting of silk and porcelain to Mexico. It was the start of a lucrative commercial venture that would guarantee the survival of the Spanish colonists in Manila for over two centuries. Trade with China was officially encouraged, with Mexican silver as the key medium of exchange. Soon Manila, with its fine harbor, was converted into a trade emporium that encouraged other Spaniards to settle in the Philippines. During the first years of the galleon trade, there was a great euphoria among those participating in the commercial traffic, for clearly large profits could be had and wealth amassed in a short time.

In order to protect its commercial interests and encourage settlement, the Spanish crown granted a monopoly of the galleon trade to Manila residents, with the conviction that the "only source of wealth for the islands as well as attraction for Spanish emigration was trade with China."[4] But the monopoly also created a motivation for the Manila residents to suppress the number of potential settlers. In 1593, they requested that Philip II exclude merchants based in Mexico, Peru, and other Spanish colonies in the Americas from participating in the trade between the Philippines and the Americas. In the long run, only a minority of the most powerful merchants in Manila benefited from the galleon trade. The reliance on the galleon trade had other negative consequences. Living complacently on this trade, Spanish settlers did not worry until much later about the economic development of the islands.[5]

Thus life in Manila was centered on the arrival and departure of ships and galleons. The Manilans served as intermediaries for the galleons that arrived from Asia and those that left for Acapulco in Mexico. No hard labor was expended on establishing plantations or on developing agriculture and livestock or industries.[6]

It is not difficult to understand why trade and commerce became the only occupation. The variety of goods the Chinese brought to trade in the port of Manila was overwhelming for most Spaniards. Dazzled by what he saw, the Basque chronicler Morga wrote the following:

> The goods that they [Chinese] usually bring and sell to the Spaniards are raw silk in bundles of the thickness of only two strands, and other silk of inferior quality, soft untwisted silk, white and of other colors in small skeins, much smooth velvet, and velvet embroidered in all sorts of colors and patterns; and others with the background of gold and embroidered by hand with the same materials; brocades of gold and silver upon silk of various colors and designs, many other brocades, and silver twist in skeins, upon thread and upon silk, but all the spangles of gold and silver were false and upon paper; damask, satins, taffetans, and gorvarans; glossy silks; and other stuff of all colors, some finer and better than others; quantity of linen made of grass, which they call handkerchief stuff, and white cotton tablecloths of different kinds and sorts, for all sorts of uses; musk, benzoin, ivory, many ornaments of beds, hangings, coverlets, and curtains embroidered on velvet, damask and gorvaran of many shades of colors, table covers, cushions, carpets, caparisons of horses of the same stuff, and with bugles or seed pearl; some pearls and rubies, sapphires, stones of large assortments, nails of all sorts, sheet iron, tin, lead saltpeter and powder, and other fruits from China, hams of pig, and other salted meats, live fowls of good breed, and very fine capons, much fresh fruit, oranges of all kinds, very good chestnuts, walnuts, peas, *chicueys* fresh and dried, which is a very delicate fruit; much fine thread of all kinds, needles, knick-knacks, little boxes, and writing boxes; beds, tables, chairs, gilt seats painted with all sorts of figures and design,

> tame buffaloes, geese like swans, horses, some mules and donkeys and even caged birds, some of which talk and others sing, and they make them play a thousand tricks; and a thousand other gewgaws and ornaments of little cost and price, which were valued among the Spaniards; besides much fine crockery of beads of all kinds, and carnelians on strings, and other beads and stones of all colors; pepper and other spice; and curiosities, to recount all which would never come to an end, nor would much paper be sufficient for it.[7]

At first there were no prohibitions on the trans-Pacific trade. But then the textile producers of Andalucía protested that the availability of cheap Chinese textiles was ruining their business. Furthermore, the trade caused an alarming drain of silver from the New World to China. Therefore, in 1593 the Spanish crown imposed strict rules on conduct of the trade. However, given the vast distance and peculiar situation of the Philippines, many of the rules were not obeyed. In general, the Philippine trade with Mexico was confined to Acapulco, and goods were disposed of to Spanish American buyers during an annual fair. The Spanish state owned the galleons, while the Royal Treasury shouldered the costs of their construction and operation.

Only two vessels were allowed to carry Asian merchandise and ply the trans-Pacific route each year. In addition, the value of the shipment from Manila was limited to 250,000 pesos per year and the value of the whole sale in Acapulco was pegged at 500,000 pesos. These restrictions, however, were not observed for the simple reason that they were impractical. Although the Spanish government put a limit on the volume and value of trade, this did not necessarily reduce its profitability. A single trip could provide a windfall of profits or, of course, tremendous loss in the case of shipwreck due to violent storms in the Pacific. Then, too, British and Dutch pirates frequently pounced on the galleons.

In carrying out the restrictive system, it became necessary to measure cargo space on the galleons and allot rights to it among the shippers. A committee measured the ship's hold and divided the space into equal parts corresponding to a bale, or *fardo,* of definite and uniform size. Each bale was subdivided into four packages, or *piezas,* and the right to ship on the galleon was represented by a *boleta,* or ticket, corresponding to one pieza. Dividing 4,000 boletas (representing piezas) into the return quota of 500,000 pesos gave a value of 125 pesos for each boleta in Manila. This provided a convenient criterion for assessing duties and compiling statistics, although in practice the boleta's value could be much higher.[8]

In the early years of the galleon trade, distribution of the boletas was the prerogative of the governor-general. But in 1604, a *junta de repartimiento,* or board of allocation, was created, consisting of the governor, the senior *oidor* (judge), the attorney general, representatives of the municipality, and representatives of the merchants. Detailed norms were drawn up to ensure that the entire Spanish community had a share in the trade according to merit and need. Boletas were normally awarded to widows of Spaniards, orphans, and government pensioners as a form of social security. Even if such persons did not have the money to ship anything, they could always sell their boletas to the highest bidder.[9]

Shippers who lacked capital borrowed extensively from the *obras pías.* These were accumulations of pious legacies for religious, charitable, and educational purposes administered by institutions such as the Confraternity of Mercy and the Third Order of St. Francis. Since these institutions also insured the goods shipped on the galleon, they acted, in effect, as the colony's commercial banks. Because of the risks of the voyage, their premiums and interest rates were high; yet shippers paid them with little hesitation because of the even greater profits.[10]

One of the principal aims of the galleon trade was to provide the means to maintain the colonial administration of the islands. The traditional view was that the Philippines was a financial burden to Spain. The colony did not possess the spices much sought after in the European markets, and had only small quantities of precious metals such as gold and silver. In order to survive, the colonial government depended to a great extent on the viceroyalty of Mexico, which provided the *situado,* or a quantity of silver with which to pay the salaries of royal functionaries, of the religious, the expenses for fortification and defense of the islands, and other maintenance costs.[11]

In fact, frustrated Spaniards, civilian and military, proposed the abandonment of the islands for economic reasons. The religious, however, objected to the plan. The missionaries insisted on maintaining the Philippines for the sake of its Christianity. The Basque bishop Salazar led the other religious orders in petitioning Philip II to retain the Philippines and to improve its administration. Bishop Salazar, in fact, even offered to present the case to the Spanish king in person but was prevailed on to remain in his diocese in Manila. In the end, a Jesuit priest, Fray Alonso Sánchez, was sent to Spain on behalf of the residents of Manila.

Recent studies by Dennis Flynn and Arturo Giráldez, however, contradict the traditional view that the Philippines was a burden to the Spanish treasury and that it was kept only for religious reasons. As they convincingly argue,

> Textbooks tell us that the Philippine Islands were a profitless archipelago for mother country Spain. If this were true, why did Spain remain in the Philippines for centuries in the face of continuing losses? We are told that religious motivations dominated. This colony was a financial loser, in other words, but saving souls was worth the financial punishment. The Philippines were in fact a major profit center that helped finance the Spanish Empire, generating something like 200,000 pesos per year in net profits during the seventeenth century. Half of the *situado* sent to Manila from Mexico each year was financed by taxes collected on the galleon trade itself. Moreover, most of the *situado* financed the war against the Dutch for control of the Moluccas and simply passed through the Philippines. Financially, global reasoning requires that we include in Crown

> revenues profits gained from the actual mining of the 50 plus tons of silver passed annually through the Pacific. A global, rather than local, view of the Manila galleon trade makes clear that (1) this trade was huge, (2) it did not shrivel as claimed by Pierre Chaunu [a noted French scholar on the Manila-Acapulco galleon trade], and (3) the galleons provided major financial support for the Spanish Empire.[12]

In the end the Spanish crown decided to keep the Philippines as an outpost of the Spanish Empire. Spain could not just renounce its authority over the Philippines without losing prestige. Besides, the Philippines could serve other purposes. Religious missions to China and Japan were launched from Manila. The islands would also become an important military and naval base in the Far East to deter the advances of the Dutch in the seventeenth century and the British and French in the eighteenth.

Who really profited from the galleon trade? Very few persons, a well-to-do minority, invested their money. In 1743, for example, the cargoes of the galleons *Nuestra Señora del Rosario* and *Los Santos Reyes,* whose shipments reached the limit of 4,000 piezas (shares), were distributed among only forty-eight individuals. Among the forty-eight persons that participated in the shipment, fourteen were of Basque origin. The following are their names and piezas (shares of cargo space):[13]

Felipe de Exquisia	320 piezas
Captain Luís de Arechaga	248 piezas
Captain Martín de Arauzana	211 piezas
Sergeant Major Tomás Justo de Endaya	192 piezas
Captain Francisco Ustáriz	108 piezas
Andrés de Yrabien	108 piezas
Captain Tomás de Pardinaur	71 piezas
Captain José Sarrate	37 piezas
Captain José Rodríguez de Ortigosa	28 piezas
Simón Carranza	28 piezas
Captain Miguel de Iturriaga	21 piezas
Admiral Juan Bautista de Carranza	20 piezas
Sergeant Major Diego de Aristizábal	19 piezas
Captain Francisco de Estrarona	13 piezas

Taken together, the Basque participation amounted to 1,391 piezas, or 38 percent of the total. It is also evident that most of them held military and naval posts. Indeed, a substantial, even disproportionate, percentage was given to the few Basque residents in Manila at the time. Although one cannot generalize from this one instance it does give an idea of the weight and significance of Basque commercial interest in the trans-Pacific trade.

In sum, the galleon trade became the lifeblood of the Spanish settlers, including Basques, in the Philippines. As noted earlier, however, the profits to be made in the shipments killed the initiative of the settlers to cultivate the land and exploit the mineral resources, as was the case in other Spanish colonies in the New World. Why bother to develop plantations or excavate gold mines in the hinterlands when trading with the Chinese would provide high margins with less effort? As a consequence, the vast majority of the Spaniards settled only in a few large settlements like Manila and Cebu. Notwithstanding the encomiendas given to them, they relied too heavily on the galleon trade. Except for shipbuilding, the Spaniards did not bother to harness the native talents of the Filipinos to produce goods. The vast distances, the danger of crossing the Pacific, and the royal restriction on the number of voyages (only two a year) did little to encourage development of the colonial economy in the Philippines during the first two hundred years of Spanish rule.

No wonder there was little incentive for Spaniards to emigrate to a colonial outpost like the Philippines. In 1768, the Basque Simón de Anda y Salazar, a former judge of the Manila Audiencia and later governor-general, out of exasperation wrote the Spanish king: "settlers are badly needed, because in 200 years since the conquest, all Spaniards are confined in reduced numbers in Manila, and there is not a single one in the provinces."[14]

There were several advocates of reforms to improve the economic situation of the Philippines, but their efforts usually came to naught. One exception was Francisco Leandro de Viana (1730–1804), a Basque from Araba, whose audacious views and ideas provided the bases for a new economic policy for the Philippines.

Francisco Leandro de Viana

Francisco Leandro Viana was born in Villaverde, Araba, in March 1730. He came from an elite family whose members held important positions in the military establishment and government service. He was a brilliant law student at the University of Irache, where he graduated in 1748. He then studied advanced law (*licenciatura*) in Salamanca, where he obtained the distinction *nemine discrepante* in 1755.[15] In February 1756, Viana was appointed as attorney general of the Audiencia of Manila. He traveled to Mexico and from Acapulco set sail to the Philippines in a frigate that he described as "small, uncomfortable, and exposed in its bad state to many dangers during the long trip." He finally assumed office in September 1758.

Young, idealistic, and energetic, Viana immediately dedicated himself to his position. He took great interest in the study of the economic problems of the Philippines and proposed a number of plans to remedy them. His zeal in upholding the interest of the Spanish state and protecting the rights of the native Filipinos quickly earned him powerful enemies, including the Basque governor-general Pedro Manuel de

Arandía and Arandía cohorts such as Francisco Zapata and Santiago de Orendain, a son of a Mexican Basque. His economic ideas, particularly his proposal to open a direct trade route between Spain and the Philippines via the Cape of Good Hope, clashed with the views of prominent members of the Consulado—the board of merchants created in 1769 to supervise the Acapulco galleon trade and adjudicate disputes among the members of the business community—such as the Basque Pedro Lamberto de Asteguieta, Pedro Iriarte, Felipe Erquizia, and Pedro Echenique.

In May 1760, he wrote his first report about abuses in the collection of the *almojarifazgo,* or sales tax on goods sold in Mexico, and advocated a prudent and wise conduct of the galleon trade. This was followed six days later by another bold report that exposed the fraud in the galleon trade from Acapulco; the extraction of silver without authorization; the connivance of the governors and other officials of the islands in this trade; and at the same time proposed solutions to these problems.

The young attorney general observed that since the discovery of the Philippines, the Royal Treasury had benefited little because of the "bad conduct of the governors who only thought of their own interests." Viana lamented the deplorable state of Manila: "all the walls and the fort of Santiago were in ruins; the major part of the artillery was almost unusable; the hospital was falling down; the Colegio of San Felipe (a boys' school) little by little is becoming uninhabitable, and that of San Potenciana (girls' school) is in danger of collapsing at the first light tremor."[16]

Viana deplored the sorry state of the port of Cavite, "where the sea was already flooding all parts."[17] He also blamed the previous administrations of Francisco José de Ovando (1750–1754) and the Basque Pedro Manuel de Arandía (1754–1759) for not constructing a single ship. He warned that the money minted in Spanish territories was being siphoned out to the other kingdoms of Europe while enticing them to come to China.

After the British occupation of Manila (1762–1764), Viana wrote another report on "the misery and deplorable state of the Philippines" (*Demonstración del mísero, deplorable estado de las Islas Filipinas*) in 1765. In this work, he outlined the creation of a trading company with exclusive Spanish capital that would initiate direct trade between Spain and the Philippines via the Cape of Good Hope. The central idea was to achieve fiscal balance in the colony, converting the Philippines from a financial burden to a source of wealth.

The first part of his report described the state of the Philippine economy and emphasized the importance of its retention. He argued that if the Spanish crown abandoned the islands, the British would readily occupy them, "since they had become fond of and coveted the uses that the islands could offer." In the second part, Viana defended the use of the route of the Cape of Good Hope by stating that no papal bull or treaty prevented the Spaniards from taking this trajectory.

Viana also outlined a trading plan. Ships would leave Spain with cotton, wine, hats, silk stockings, mirrors, tableware, and other articles made of glass, paper, and various textile fibers; then unload part of their cargo in Manila and take on such goods as edible birds' nests, mother-of-pearl, seashells, cochineal, indigo, and other dyes from Pampanga, sea slugs, dried deer meat, deer sinews, leather, sapan wood, ebony, and other woods; and proceed to Canton to exchange these products and the remainder of the European cargo for the Chinese goods hitherto taken to Europe by foreigners. On their return voyage, they should again call at Manila to take on Philippine products salable in Spain, such as woven mats, palm leaf hats, raw cotton, tortoiseshell, sapan, and various kinds of other woods. Cinnamon could also become an article of commerce if its cultivation were pursued.[18]

To conduct this trade, an East India Company should be organized, with the king holding a portion of the shares. The company's shipyards would be located in the Philippines to take advantage of its excellent timber reserves. Once organized, the company could embark on large-scale enterprises. After giving pride of place to cinnamon, pepper, and other spices, Viana mentions sugar, cocoa, coffee, rice, wheat, tobacco, indigo, the mulberry tree, and cotton. Weaving existed in Ilocos, Cagayan, Bicol, and Panay, especially Iloilo, but was underdeveloped; master weavers could be imported to train the native operators in achieving domestic self-sufficiency, obviating the need to import textiles from the Chinese, Dutch, and English. Minerals such as iron, gold, sulfur, and rock crystal awaited exploitation.[19]

Viana's plan was endorsed by the Basque Simón de Anda y Salazar, who became governor-general in 1769. In view of the country's damaged condition following the British occupation (see next chapter), he suggested making no immediate changes to the commercial system but advocated revisiting the matter after a few years. He enumerated the country's commercial products, such as spices, gold, indigo, rattan, high-grade cotton, beeswax, and hardwoods. He also advocated resumption of iron mining.[20] Actually, the Spanish crown took a keen interest in Viana's economic proposals for the Philippines. In fact, Philip V issued a royal decree on March 29, 1773, creating a company with the name "Philippines." But the project never materialized.[21]

In July 1776, Viana wrote yet another critical report, this time focusing on ways to generate local revenues to maintain the colony without depending on the subsidy from Mexico. He questioned the wisdom of exempting the Spanish crown from paying the expenses of the missions and the annual costs of "wine for masses and oil for lamps as well as the professorial chair that is maintained in the university in Manila." He suggested ways to increase taxes and to expand the *corregimientos* (territories still to be pacified). He advocated felling of timber and prevention of its theft; reorganization of the arsenal of Cavite; and an improvement in accounting at the royal warehouse. He also defended the creation of merchant guilds.

Even after the end of his tour of duty in Manila, Viana continued his crusade. In a report submitted to the Council of the Indies, on which he sat as the count of Tepa, he denounced the boleta system as the root of all evil in the galleon trade. He favored assigning boletas only to bona fide merchants and deplored the despotism and greed of the governors; the intrusions of the clergy, the military, and the bureaucracy; and the provisions for widows and the poor among the *boleteros* (boleta holders). He observed sarcastically about this unique scheme of social security that "there did not remain anyone in the Philippines who did not share in the *repartimiento*." He proposed that the churches, pious foundations, widows, orphans, soldiers, and city councillors not be deprived of the distribution quota "with which it has been customary to help them"; but instead they would be given the same amount they would have received from the sale of their boletas. This would be underwritten by the merchants, which could then assign all boletas to qualified individuals. The aid would last until the beneficiaries could amass a sufficient endowment, but in no case would it exceed ten years, after which time the merchants could ship in their own vessels or buy boletas directly from the royal government. His proposal was also refreshing in trying to link the allocation system with investment and economic growth; boletas should be given to registered merchants with various qualifications "and principally to those who may distinguish themselves in developing with their capital agriculture, manufactures, and industry . . . that they may be rewarded with boletas according to the greater or less capital invested in the said fields.[22]

Much later, Viana was appointed as *alcalde de crimen* (criminal judge) and oidor in Mexico. He also became an active member of the Royal Economic Society of the Friends of the Country. He died in Madrid in August 1804.[23] Viana failed to implement his liberal economic ideas during his stint in the Philippines. But many Basques imbibed his ideas during the latter part of the eighteenth century. They would take the initiative of developing the economic potential of the archipelago by founding the Royal Economic Society of the Philippines and the Royal Philippine Company.

The Royal Economic Society

Upon his arrival in Manila in 1778, governor-general José Basco y Vargas, an Andalusian of Basque descent, engaged the participation of the elite of Manila in the creation of an economic development society. He believed that this body would serve as a vehicle to promote social and economic development similar to most successful royal societies in Europe. Thus, in 1781, the Sociedad Económica de los Amigos del País (Economic Society of the Friends of the Country) was formally organized, with Basco as president. The basic goal of the Economic Society was to achieve self-reliance through the cultivation of cash crops.

Basco hoped to realize his goals through exhortations and decrees. Cash awards and distinctions were offered to those who would open up and run plantations of cotton, mulberry trees, and spices such as cinnamon, pepper, nutmeg; to those who established factories for the manufacture and processing of silk, hemp, cotton, linens, and porcelain; to practical inventors; and to those who excelled in the sciences, liberal arts, and engineering. Basco also issued instructions on the cultivation of plants such as cinnamon, cotton, sugar, and pepper. The instructions for pepper (issued January and March 1781), for example, stipulated that there be at least one *caván* (sack) in each hacienda; the government was to buy up the entire crop of the natives during the first five years; and incentives such as exemption from the tribute were offered to the five natives who sold the most pepper.[24]

Even before the formal establishment of the Economic Society in 1781, the Royal Basque Society in Manila was already receiving the protection and encouragement of governor-general Simón de Anda during his second term (1769–1772) in carrying out agricultural and mineral production in the archipelago, in promoting industry and specific studies on the cultivation of rice, and the planting of indigo, the raising of honey bees, and so forth.[25] In fact, before the end of his tour of duty in 1776, Anda, in his desire to establish commerce with the kingdom of Nabob Myder Alican (Hyder Ali of Mysore, in English) on the coast of Malabar (West India), sent two representatives: Ramón Ysasi, a Basque, and the engineer Miguel Antonio Gómez. Both left aboard the frigate *Deseada,* arriving at Malacca in May 1777, then continuing to the port of Mangalore, their port of destination. Unfortunately, Ysasi died there, leaving Gómez to discharge their mission. Anda had died by the time the mission returned to Manila. The Manila-Mangalore trade project, however, would receive the full support of Governor José Basco y Vargas.[26]

British admiration of Simón de Anda extended beyond his political and military leadership. An English businessman traveling to the Philippines in 1848 had only praise for Anda's economic management of the country: "Simón de Anda was about the first person who showed any desire to augment the trade of the islands; and his election to the highest office of the colony, after its restoration by the English, was a most fortunate event for Manila. Although, unluckily, many of the steps he took with the best intentions, notwithstanding being infinitely in advance of those of his predecessors in office, were not always in the right directions, and consequently unattended by the highest degree of success that he aimed at, partial results were obtained by them, and a beneficial change began to regulate affairs."[27]

But it was Governor Basco y Vargas who implemented most of the economic proposals of Anda and the other Basque businessmen. A closer look at Basco's initiative, however, shows that the economic society he founded was patterned after a Basque economic society and later evolved as an affiliated local chapter. The Royal Basque Society of the Friends of the Country (Real Sociedad Bascongada de los Amigos del País) was established in 1765 by young, idealistic Basques who aspired to create an association that would promote economic and social development while enhancing the unity of the Basque Country. The Royal Basque Society traced its origin to the efforts of Manuel Ignacio de Altuna, who in 1745 became the mayor of Azkoitia in

Gipuzkoa. Altuna was a contemporary and friend of Jean Jacques Rousseau, the great French philosopher.

Together with his two friends Joaquín de Eguía and Francisco Munibe e Idiaquez, the count of Peñaflorida, Altuna sponsored academic seminars in 1746 that dealt with science, history, current events, and music. Although short-lived, the efforts laid the intellectual foundations for the establishment of an economic society. In 1763, the count of Peñaflorida and fifteen other young men presented a plan to the Juntas Generales, or legislature, of Gipuzkoa to set up an economic society to be called the Academy of Agriculture, Science, and Useful Arts and Commerce Adapted to the Particular Circumstances and Economy of Gipuzkoa. The idea appeared to be modeled on several similar French societies. In 1764 the project was approved, and late that winter the society began to function. By this time the concept had been broadened to include the three Basque provinces of Araba, Gipuzkoa, and Bizkaia. The new organization was called the Royal Basque Society of the Friends of the Country.[28] The members of the society were divided into four commissions: agriculture, science, and practical arts; industry; commerce; and humanities (*bellas artes*). The society held an annual meeting where each of the commissioners made a report. The reports were collected and published under the name of the *Extractos*.

Later, the society's membership expanded, with many members residing in the most important and sensitive nerve centers of the Spanish Empire. Of the 1,181 members listed in 1793, the largest contingent, or 496 persons, resided in the New World, while 378 members lived in parts of Spain other than the Basque Provinces. In contrast, only 211 members, or slightly more than one-sixth of the total, resided in the Basque Country. Forty-four members were listed with their regiments (post unknown); 28 resided in parts of Europe other than Spain; 1 lived in Africa, 1 was traveling, and 23 resided in the Philippines, of which 21 lived in Manila.[29]

It is also interesting to note that the number of members of the Royal Basque Society in the Philippines, with the exception of Vitoria (24), exceeded those of other Basque cities such as Bilbao (20), Donostia (15), and Iruñea (13), "which justifies stating that it seems that the love of the Basques [for their country] increases in relation to their distance to it."[30] Equally impressive were the occupations of the members in the catalog of membership in 1793, which included some of the most prestigious posts within the Spanish Empire. In Manila, one was a justice, one was the regent of the Royal Treasury (regente de la Real Hacienda), and there were two directors and the treasurer of the Royal Philippine Company.[31]

Governor Basco spearheaded the monopoly of palm wine, areca nuts, gunpowder manufacture, and tobacco. The tobacco monopoly, in fact, became Basco's greatest economic legacy. It lasted until 1880.[32] In 1781 Madrid approved Basco's proposal that the cultivation, manufacture, and sale of tobacco be made a state monopoly. Certain regions—principally the Cagayan Valley and what is now Nueva Ecija—were designated as tobacco regions. The cultivation of tobacco outside them was forbidden. In these regions only tobacco could be produced. Cultivators were obliged to deliver their entire crop to government collectors, who graded the leaf, paid for it at a set price, and destroyed what they did not buy. The leaf tobacco was then taken to government factories where it was manufactured into cigars and cigarettes for export and for local sale in government shops or *estanquillas*. This system was fully enforced in Luzon. In the Visayas and northern Mindanao, because of the difficulty of enforcement, tobacco cultivation was permitted, but only for exclusive sale to the government. In one important respect the tobacco monopoly was a startling success. It balanced the colony's budget. Not only that, it actually reversed the flow of revenue. After a few years of operation, it was the Philippines that was sending subsidies to Spain, in cash or credits or in the form of easily salable cigars and tobacco leaf.[33]

Mining also received Basco's attention. The Basques in particular played a key role in the development and exploitation of the mines. María Isabel de Careaga got a lease from the Basco administration to operate the Santa Inés mines. Another Basque resident in Manila, Lorenzo Buicoechea, operated the Angat iron mines.[34]

After the departure of governor-general Basco from the Philippines in 1787, the Royal Economic Society he founded gradually lost steam. In the midst of Spain's political vicissitudes at the time, such as the war against England in 1796, the Napoleonic invasion in 1808, and the loss of the Spanish colonies in the Americas, not to mention the lack of interest from succeeding governors, the Economic Society became moribund.

The Royal Economic Society was revived in 1819. But it really became active only three years later. This time the society's membership included a larger spectrum of Philippine society, consisting not only of merchants and government bureaucrats but also lawyers, judges, planters, and clerics. In 1823, the society established a chair for agriculture and gave special prizes to outstanding agricultural projects.

In the same year, the Royal Economic Society started the publication of the *Diario Mercantil* (*Trade Journal*), with 250 copies per issue. It lasted for ten years, the longest Philippine publication of the epoch. Two of its three writers, José Nicolás Irastorza and José de Azcárraga, were Basques. In 1826, Azcárraga resigned and was replaced by another Basque, Tiburcio Gorostiza. Although it was a lofty project, the trade publication never made money to cover the cost of printing. Nonetheless, the society supported it until it ran out of funds.[35]

The Royal Economic Society made important contributions to Philippine agriculture by promoting projects in diverse areas, such as stockbreeding of horses, cows, and carabaos; Manila hemp and textile (silk and cotton) production; as well as scientific cultivation of sugarcane, coffee, and indigo. It advocated the establishment of a savings bank, the Monte Piedad, which opened its first branch in 1855. In 1831, the society also supported the establishment of the Casa de Moneda (Mint House) in the Philippines.[36] During that time only Mexican, Bolivian, Peruvian, and Chilean coins circulated in the Philippines. It would take another thirty years, in 1862, before the

Casa de Moneda would mint the first Philippine coins, which were popularly known as *isabelinas* and *alfonsinos.*[37] In 1852, the society lobbied for the opening of the posts of Iloilo and Cebu to foreign traders. The petition was granted in 1855.

The Royal Economic Society also involved itself in cultural affairs. It donated 1,547 pesos to the museum of the University of Santo Tomas in 1850 and assisted the Spanish colonial government in sending Philippine exhibits abroad. Thus the Philippines as a separate entity participated in the Great Exposition in London in 1851 and the Philadelphia Centennial Exposition in 1876. The Philippines won awards in both expositions. The society likewise set aside one-fifth of its funds as interest-free loans to the colonial government for the improvement of public buildings and housing for the poor.[38]

To conclude, the Basques played a significant role in the Royal Economic Society, which contributed to the economic development of the Philippines. But it was during Governor Basco's term of office that another Basque-initiated project—the creation of the Royal Philippine Company—brought about profound changes in the Philippine economy.

The Royal Philippine Company

The idea of creating the Royal Philippine Company came from the economist Francisco Cabarrús, who proposed an alternative he called "commercial union of America with Asia." He justified his plan on the grounds that the distant islands of the Philippines needed the support of a trading company of this type for its economic takeoff.[39] Cabarrús, a French Basque, was also then director of the National Bank of San Carlos. He was supported by other prominent Basques in Madrid, such as Bernardo Iriarte, member of the Supreme Court of the State; Francisco Leandro de Viana, former attorney general in Manila and later member of the Council of Indies; Diego de Gardoqui, Spanish consul in Boston; and others, including Governor-General José Basco y Vargas. The establishment of a trading company with a monopolistic character under the patronage of the Spanish crown was seen as way for Spain to compete commercially with other European nations. At the same time the new venture hoped to promote the development of the Philippines, whose economy was stunted by the galleon trade.

Direct trade between the Philippines and Spain was not an entirely new concept, although it is rather remarkable that the Basques were among the first to attempt to carry it out. In April 1732, four Basque merchants based in Cádiz (Manuel de Arriola, Francisco de Arteaga, Juan Martinez de Albinagorta, and Juan de Leaequi) obtained a royal permit to set up a company to traffic with Manila for ten years. They planned to load their ships in Cádiz with wine, spirits, olive oil, and European textiles destined for sale in Manila. On the ships' return, they would carry "copper, silk, tea, porcelain, lacquerware, cotton cloth, pepper, clove, nutmeg, *raíz de China,* rhubarb, galanga, cocoa, guta, rubber, atincar, musk, menjui, and other genres as well as herbal medicines." To ensure its viability, Philip V granted the Basque trading company an exemption from customs duties and extended it other privileges. But even before the enterprise was launched, the Spanish king revoked its license and instead opted to support ventures that a greater number of merchants could join.[40]

Since the beginning of the eighteenth century, as a natural consequence of the proliferation of economic theories, Spanish intellectuals started conceiving the creation of a powerful trading company whose models and immediate precedents were the politico-mercantile societies created a century before by Holland, France, and England for commercial traffic with the Orient.[41] By this time Spain was lagging far behind Holland and England, who were already operating profitable trading ventures such as the Dutch East India Company and the British East India Company.

The Basques pioneered the creation of a trading company patterned after the Dutch and English models. In 1728, they founded the Royal Gipuzkoan Company of Caracas (Real Compañía Guipuzcoana de Caracas), the first private trading company in Spain. It received a royal concession for a monopoly on trade with the province of Caracas (Venezuela), particularly cocoa. This was intended to counter the Dutch, who had been selling cocoa in the European markets, even to their archenemy Spain. Despite its rather checkered history (a rebellion erupted in Venezuela against its commercial monopoly), the Caracas Company operated profitably, with average annual dividends of 20 percent during the 1730s and 5 percent from 1751 to its closure in 1785.

In October 1778, a new regulation (Reglamento para el libre comercio) on free trade was enforced in selected ports in Spanish America. Although Caracas kept its monopoly status, it was nevertheless opened to free trade in February 1781, thereby erasing the crucial commercial advantage of the Caracas Company. Earlier the company's operation was severely affected by the war against England in 1779. As the Caracas Company started losing money, the shareholders decided to liquidate it. It was at this point that Francisco Cabarrús proposed the creation of the Royal Philippine Company. As previously mentioned, Philip V created a "Philippine Company" in 1773, but it never got off the ground. Thus, in March 1785, with the closing of the Royal Gipuzkoan Company of Caracas, it was succeeded by the Royal Philippine Company (Real Compañía de Filipinas) when Charles III signed a royal charter.

In reality, the Royal Philippine Company was only a reincarnation of the Royal Gipuzkoan Company of Caracas. The transformation of the Caracas Company to the Philippine Company did not substantially change the Basque presence in and ownership of the new company. The former management team remained, as did many of the old shareholders, such as the province of Gipuzkoa, the *consulado* (board of merchants) of San Sebastián, the city government (*ayuntamiento*) of Donostia (San Sebastián),[42] the University of Oñate, as well as individual investors such as Zuaznabar, Lopeola, Arbaiza, and Goicoa.[43]

The new list of shareholders also included the Spanish crown and the five major guilds in Madrid. Other assets and properties of the Caracas Company, such as its shipyard in Bizkaia and its weapons factory in Placencia, were passed on to the Philippine Company. Even the *factores* (financial inspectors) were retained on the payroll of the new company. Its initial capital was valued at 8 million pesos.[44]

The royal charter given to the Philippine Company granted it exclusive rights to sell merchandise from China and India and to transport it directly to Spain via the Cape of Good Hope (instead of the route to Mexico). It also enjoyed incentives such as an exemption from customs' duties in Cádiz and Manila. In return the Philippine Company was obliged to invest 4 percent of its earnings in the promotion of economic development in the Philippines. Moreover, the Royal Treasury could also borrow from its coffers for the needs of the Spanish state, borrowing that grew as Spain became involved in international conflicts (most of the loans were never repaid).

Although created on March 10, 1785, the Philippine Company did not operate until the first of July. Its first ship was dispatched from Cádiz to Manila via Lima and was followed by two ships in January 1786 via the Cape of Good Hope. In 1787, the Philippine Company received its first shipments from Asia, amounting to 17,115,347 reales maravedis, which was a huge amount at the time. Since profits exceeded all expectations, the board of directors of the Philippine Company boasted that that no corporate body had delivered more spectacular results to the Spanish state than the Philippine Company during its first phase of operation from 1785 to 1790.[45] During this period, the company paid a 27 percent dividend to its shareholders, even higher than the Caracas Company, which also yielded an impressive 20 percent dividend from 1730 to 1735.[46]

The Philippine Company employed a total of 2,822 crew members. However, its business was not confined to the Philippines. Of the forty-two expeditions during this period, of which two were private ships, only twelve went to the Philippines, while the rest traded in various points in the Americas.[47] In fact, in 1786, for example, the company even explored the possibility of trading for sea otter skins in California.[48]

The company deployed agents in Manila and appointed as manager the Basque Juan Francisco Urroz, who also acted as a farmer, manufacturer, and trader at the same time. They all buckled down to work, establishing branches in the provinces of Ilocos, Bataan, Cavite, and Camarines. They purchased land, distributed farm tools, and put up textile factories. They even paid native farmers in advance for future production.[49] Indeed, the Philippine Company had an immense impact on the development of the colonial economy. Together with the members of the Royal Economic Society, it supported the cultivation of cash crops such as indigo, sugar, rice, cotton, and pepper.

Meanwhile, the Philippine Company faced fierce opposition from Manila traders, who were mainly dependent on the galleon trade. But the trans-Pacific trade was slowly being displaced by the Philippine Company since it already had a lock on the European markets, the final destination of large shipments to Acapulco. However, the company suffered large losses because of the inexperience of its personnel and lack of capital. Totally ignorant of Asian markets, its agents in the Philippines paid more than the prevailing market price. For instance, they had purchased pepper for 13.5 pesos per pecul (one pecul is equivalent to 117 pounds), when the same quantity could have been bought in Sumatra for only 3 or 4 pesos. Overconfidence also cost the company dearly. Its principal agent in Manila boasted to the headquarters in Madrid that production of pepper would reach 9,600 peculs, enough to supply Spain and a great part of Europe. The results were far below projections, as production yielded no more than 64,000 pounds (547 peculs).[50]

In addition, many products that the Philippine Company bought from China and India were either unknown or old fashioned. The government regulation that required ships to call on Manila also increased transportation costs. The company also had to work solely with Spanish and Basque capital, inasmuch as foreigners were banned from owning shares in the enterprise. This restriction on foreign investors and capital was lifted in 1803 by Charles III, provided that the investors' sovereigns were not at war with Spain.

Despite its losses, the Philippine Company acquired a better knowledge of markets and business practices in Asia and, as a result, substantially expanded Spanish trade with the continent. More importantly, the regular supply of textiles, mainly from India, lessened Spain's dependence on France and Germany. The company also gave impetus to the Spanish maritime industry, which provided jobs to a great number of seamen.[51] Many of them, as we will see later, were Basques.

The greatest threat to the success of the Philippine Company came from the Spanish government itself, as it dipped into the company's capital. The company was constantly under pressure to allocate part of its funds to government projects that were totally unrelated to its operations. When the Spanish state needed loans, the company lent it 43 million reales. And if its tax payment, amounting to 64 million, is added, at least a third of the company's funds went to benefit the Spanish government.[52]

Spain's international conflict was also a setback for the Philippine Company. In 1796, another war against England gravely affected the activities of the company, and its operations almost collapsed. After the conflict ended in 1802, however, the company tried to get back on its feet. Charles III renewed the company's licence in 1803, extending its operation to 1825. This time it got a better deal from the Spanish crown. Its privileges included the opening of the company to foreign investors, building of factories in other parts of Asia, shipment of goods from China and India directly to Spain, and shipment of goods (limited to half a million pesos annually) from the Philippines and other parts of Asia to Lima and Buenos Aires as well as other ports of South America. The company and its agents, however, were restricted from engaging in the trans-Pacific galleon trade (except in the indigo trade) and were barred from conducting business in the domestic market as well as in other ports in Asia where Filipino traders were present.[53]

But the tides of history were simply against the Philippine Company. Napoleon's invasion and occupation of Spain in 1808 wiped out any incentive to continue the commercial traffic with the Philippines. The company had to wait for better times. In 1809, Juan Manuel de Gandasegui, director of the Philippine Company, was forced to go to England, where he obtained the license to send merchant ships from English ports under English flags to Lima, Veracruz, and Buenos Aires. But because of an insurrection in Buenos Aires, only the voyage to Lima materialized.[54]

The restoration of Ferdinand VII to the Spanish throne after the Napoleonic Wars did not improve the Philippine Company's balance sheet. Rather, the crown resorted to company funds to finance its losing battle against the independence movements in the Americas. The opening of the Philippines to international trade in 1815, the last year of the Acapulco galleon trade, gave a new impetus to the Royal Philippine Company. Again, in 1820, the Spanish Constitutional Court ordered the abolition of its trade privileges, but these were restored three years later. The company's license was revoked in October 1834, thus ending its almost fifty years of existence.[55]

Legazpi-Urdaneta monument in Manila. The Basques Miguel López de Legazpi and Fray Andrés Urdaneta laid the foundation for Spanish hegemony in the Philippines in 1565. The monument was built through the initiative of Manila Basque residents in the 1890s. Courtesy of Filipinas Heritage Library, Philippines

Legazpi tomb. Miguel López de Legazpi founded Manila, the capital of the Philippines, in June 1571, but the Basque governor-general died of a heart attack the following year. His remains lie in San Agustin Church, Manila. Courtesy of Antonio M. de Ynchausti

Simón de Anda Monument. The Basque Simón de Anda was a young judge (oidor) *during the British invasion of Manila in 1762. He refused to surrender to the British forces and waged a protracted guerrilla warfare against them until a peace treaty was signed between England and Spain in 1764. He was governor-general of the Philippines from 1769 to 1772. Courtesy of Filipinas Heritage Library, Makati, Philippines*

Banco Español-Filipino. The Basque governor-general Antonio de Urbiztondo established the Banco Español-Filipino de Isabel II, the first bank in the Philippines, in 1851. Its name was changed to Bank of the Philippine Islands in 1912. The bank came under the control of Ayala Corporation (successor to the Basque firm Ayala y Compañía) in 1969, which still owns the majority of its shares. Courtesy of Filipinas Heritage Library, Makati, Philippines

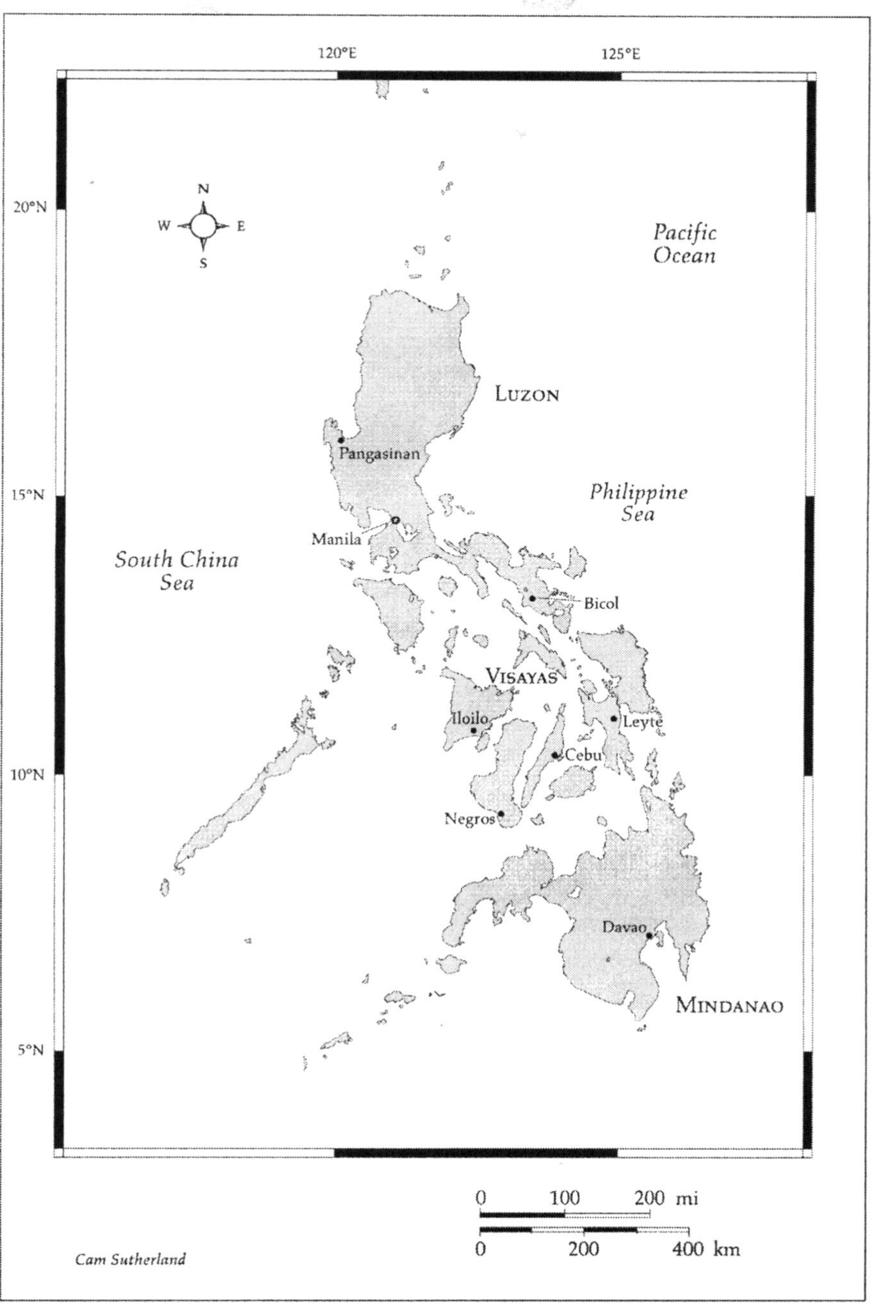

Major areas of Basque immigration and settlement in the Philippines during the nineteenth century.

Puente Colgante. The Puente Colgante was the first suspension bridge built over the Pasig River in Manila. The bridge was 110 meters long and 7 meters wide. Its construction was directed by a Basque engineer, Matías Mechacatorre, from 1849 to 1853. Ynchausti & Company financed its construction. It was replaced by a new structure in the 1930s. Courtesy of Antonio M. de Ynchausti

The rope factory of Ynchausti & Company was located at the Muelle de la Industria in Manila along the Pasig River. This first high-quality-industrial product from the Philippines, known as Manila Hemp, *was exported worldwide. Courtesy of Antonio M. de Ynchausti*

Port of Iloilo. When the port of Iloilo was opened to international trade in 1855, it quickly became a center of Basque commercial activities and immigration. Photo engraving of the wharf in 1898. Courtesy of Ayala Museum, Makati, Philippines

Marcelo de Azcárraga. Marcelo Azcárraga (1834–1915), a Philippine-born Basque, became a general in the Spanish army at the age of thirty-six. He also became Spain's minister of war in the 1890s and served briefly as president of a transition government in 1905. Courtesy of Filipinas Heritage Library, Makati, Philippines

José Rizal. José Rizal (1861–1896), the Philippine national hero, used Basque characters in his immortal novels Noli Me Tangere *(1887) and* El Filibusterismo *(1891)—two literary works that inspired the Philippine revolution against Spain in 1896 and 1898. It was the first time that Basques figured prominently in Philippine literature. Courtesy of Filipinas Heritage Library, Makati, Philippines*

Puente de Ayala. The original Puente de Ayala in 1902. The construction of the bridge was funded by Ayala y Compañía and was named after the Basque Antonio de Ayala, the patriarch of the Ayala clan of the Philippines. Courtesy of Filipinas Heritage Library, Makati, Philippines

Family of Paulino Aboitiz, 1901. Paulino Aboitiz, a native of Lekeitio (Bizkaia) and the patriach of the Aboitiz clan in Cebu, came to the Philippines in the 1870s and worked as a merchant mariner in Leyte Island. He later married Emilia Yrastorza, a Philippine-born Basque. They had ten children. His eldest son, Ramón (standing at the center of the picture), founded Aboitiz y Compañía Incorporada in 1920, the forerunner of Aboitiz & Company, one of the biggest conglomerates in the Philippines today. Courtesy of Andoni F. Aboitiz

Jai alai fronton. The war-torn jai alai fronton in February 1945. Basque pelota was formally introduced in the Philippines in 1899, and the Manila fronton was contructed in 1939. It was then considered a sport of the elite. Jai alai was a popular betting game during the 1970s and early 1980s until it was banned in 1986. The Manila fronton briefly reopened in 1998 only to be padlocked a year and half later. The building was finally ordered demolished by the Manila city government in September 2000. Courtesy of Filipinas Heritage Library, Makati, Philippines

[above] *Makati, 1969. The Ayala family is synonymous with the development of Makati as the Philippines' financial and commercial district. The main avenue traversing the district carries the family name. Some of the exclusive residential and commercial enclaves were named after Basque pioneers such as Legazpi, Urdaneta, and Salcedo. Courtesy of Filipinas Heritage Library, Makati, Philippines*

[bottom, facing page] *Manuel María de Ynchausti. Manuel María de Ynchausti (1900–1961), a third-generation Philippine Basque, was heir to Ynchausti & Company (YCO), the biggest firm in the Philippines during the second half of the nineteenth century. In 1933, he sold the company and voluntarily divested the Ynchausti family's properties and distributed them to the Filipino poor. He and his family later settled in the Basque Country. He played an active role in the Basque movement. He cofounded the International League of the Friends of the Basque in 1938 and helped refugee Basque children of the Spanish Civil War. Courtesy of Antonio M. de Ynchausti*

Chapter Seven

In Defense of Spanish Sovereignty

> If the king of Spain abandons the Philippine Islands, it would be like leaving the Spanish possessions in the Americas wide open and highly vulnerable from the southern flank.
>
> Simón de Anda y Salazar, governor-general of the Philippines (1762–1764, 1770–1776)

Maintaining the Philippines as a Spanish colony required the construction of fortifications and recruitment of troops to defend the Spaniards from local uprisings and external threats. When Legazpi established the first Spanish settlement in Cebu on May 8, 1565, Mateo de Saz, the Basque master of camp, built the first Spanish fortification—a bamboo palisade. Saz was considered the "prince of amateur military engineers who worked in the Philippines."[1] Saz's crude but sturdy fortification helped the Spanish expeditionaries withstand the Portuguese attempt to dislodge them from Cebu in September 1568.

Legazpi replicated the Cebu experience in Manila when he proclaimed it the Spanish capital in June 1571. A fort called Santiago and a walled city—the Intramuros—were constructed at the mouth of the Pasig River, strategically chosen because the river serves as a natural moat, while another side can be attacked only from the sea. Finally, the swampy terrain on the two sides facing the interior would slow down any enemy offensive from inland.

The bamboo and wooden palisade was replaced by a concrete fortification in the 1580s when Bishop Domingo de Salazar arrived in Manila. The Basque bishop was a major exponent of urbanization of the city, although his idea was to prevent conflagration, a much more real and frequent threat, rather than to improve the defense of its citizens. At the beginning of the seventeenth century, Manila was in full expansion. Intramuros had been eclipsed by the extension of the city into the contiguous areas. The increase of the Chinese population became a security problem for the feeble Spanish colony in Manila. As already recounted, during the initial years of the founding of Manila, the Spaniards faced a fierce attack by the Chinese corsairs led by Limahong. If not for the heroism of Juan de Salcedo, Guido de Lavezares, and the other Basques, the Spanish settlement might have been obliterated. Despite, or perhaps because of, the defeat of Limahong, the Chinese presence in Manila actually expanded considerably. The flourishing trade between the Spaniards and the Chinese encouraged permanent settlement in Manila. Eventually the Spaniards realized that the Chinese greatly outnumbered them. Given the dangers, it was a miracle that the Spaniards managed to hold onto the Philippines.

Manila in 1572 had only eighty Spanish citizens, excepting the clergy in churches, hospitals, and monasteries, some of them located outside the city walls. Fifty of the men had Spanish wives; some of the others were married to native women. In addition to clergy and citizens, there were usually 200 Spanish soldiers in the area, because Manila was also a fort. The soldiers were generally a low-class sort, poor and living on alms; some were quartered in the houses of the Spanish citizenry, others in nearby native ones.[2]

Understandably, the Philippines was the last choice for Spanish colonists. They preferred to settle in the Americas, which was nearer to home, richer, and possessed well-developed settlements. The journey to the Philippines was long and dangerous. Hardships and uncertainty also awaited the new Spanish settlers. As the writer Wenceslao Retana y Gamboa, a *madrileño* of Basque extraction, lucidly explained: "Life in the Philippines, especially during the old times, meant deprivation, sacrifice, and continuous exposure, not only to the diseases typical of torrid zones, but also to enemy attacks, be they Dutch, Chinese, Malay Moslems, Malay gentiles, even the Christian ones, revolting in great frequency, more than history can promptly record: those who risked going to a colony of such conditions would have to be, as many of them were, outlaws, desperate men, and, of course, adventurous types."[3]

The Spanish military establishment was convinced that the best way to defend the islands against foreign intrusion was to increase the number of Spanish soldiers. However, the task of recruiting new troops to serve in the Philippines was almost as daunting as the search for settlers. The quality of recruits from Mexico left much to be desired. Nobody wanted to go the Philippines, and it was necessary to resort to less than noble means to recruit the number of soldiers required each year.[4]

The soldiers resorted to selling uniforms and ammunition. There were drunkards, gamblers, and men of many vices, indeed to such a degree that the penalty and punishment established by military ordinances could not be enforced. Abandonment and desertion were rampant.[5]

As explained in the previous chapter, the galleon trade between Manila and Acapulco became the lifeblood of the colony and the principal attraction that lured nonclerical Spaniards, including the Basques, to the Philippines. The goal was to get rich quickly and return to Spain or settle in Mexico. The key was to capitalize on the trade with the Chinese. But as the trade flourished, Chinese emigration to Manila also increased. Many also settled permanently. They were not only merchants, but craftsmen, skilled laborers, and domestic servants. They supplied all sorts of Asian products to the Spaniards, who thereby became too dependent on the Chinese middlemen. In order to control the Chinese population, the Spaniards subjected them to close surveillance.

The Spaniards' fear of the Chinese was understandable. In 1570, there were only 40 married Chinese in the Manila. In 1589, there were already 4,000, and by 1600 the number had increased to 15,000. During the Chinese insurrection of 1603, around 24,000 Chinese were killed, leaving only 500 to work in the galleys. In 1605, when the Chinese were instructed to rebuild the destroyed walls of Manila, only 1,500 were around to comply with the order. But eighteen years later, in 1623, there were as many as 20,000. After the Chinese revolt in 1610, the vanquished Chinese were forbidden from living in *Intramuros.* They were concentrated in a district called *parian,* some meters away from the walls and within easy reach of the Spanish cannons. The Spaniards estimated that around 23,000 Chinese were killed during the second Chinese insurrection in 1639. After the uprising, the population of the *parian* rapidly swelled until it reached 15,000 in 1649.[6]

The fear of the Chinese was counterbalanced by those who looked on them as indispensable agents in the development of Manila as a prosperous colony. Others like Bishop Salazar looked favorably on the Chinese because many had embraced the Catholic faith. He was also impressed by their skills and knack for learning new trades. In a letter to Philip II, he wrote:

> There are in this *parian* tradesmen of all the trades and crafts that flourish in a commonwealth, and all in great numbers; their handiwork is much more skilled than that of Spain, and some of it they sell so cheaply that one is ashamed to admit it. . . .
>
> In this parian are to be found physicians and apothecaries, with signs in their language over their shops specifying what is sold therein; many chophouses also, where the *sangleys* [Chinese] and natives go to eat, and Spaniards too, or so they tell me. The Spaniards have given up being tradesmen altogether, for everyone orders his clothes and shoes from the sangleys who make everything very properly, Spanish style, and at very moderate prices. The silversmiths cannot do silver-plating because this art is unknown in China, but otherwise they do marvelous work in both gold and silver, and they are so skilled and cunning that having seen an article made by a Spanish craftsman they are able to produce one just like it. . . .
>
> We have been vastly entertained here by what befell a bookbinder from Mexico who came to this country with materials of his trade and set up a bookbinding shop. A sangley attached himself to him saying that he wished to be his servant, but covertly without his master's knowledge observed how he went about binding books; and in less than [blank in ms.] he left his house saying that he wished to be a servant no longer. He then set up his own bookbinding

> shop, and I assure Your Majesty that he turned out to be such a superlative craftsman that he forced his erstwhile master out of business, for everyone now takes his custom to the sangley, who does such excellent work that no one misses the Spanish tradesman. Even as I write I have my hands on a Latin Navarro bound by this man which in my opinion could not have been turned out in Seville.[7]

While the Chinese settlers in Manila remained a security concern, the real danger to Spanish hegemony in the Philippines in the early part of the seventeenth century came from the Dutch. Toward the end of the sixteenth century, Spain's naval supremacy was already being challenged by Holland, England, and France, whose colonial and commercial interests coincided with those of Spain. These great powers also did not adhere to the Treaty of Tordesillas between Catholic Spain and Portugal. It was therefore inevitable that an armed conflict would threaten Spanish interests in the Philippines.

The conflict between Spain and Holland was both political and commercial. The Netherlands, which Philip II inherited from his father, Charles I, revolted against Spain in 1581 to gain independence (although fighting continued until the signing of an armistice in 1607). Spain retaliated by barring the Dutch from trading in the port of Lisbon. This was a huge blow since Dutch traders were dependent on Portuguese middlemen for the lucrative spice trade. Their only recourse was to get the spices from the source itself.

After gaining independence from Spain, Holland embarked on an aggressive naval buildup that rivaled its former colonial master. In 1602, Holland also established the Dutch East India Company. The company later developed into a powerful trading concern and spearheaded the expansion of Dutch commercial interests in the Far East. When Portugal was annexed by Spain from 1580 to 1640, the Portuguese colonies and trading stations in what is now Indonesia became the target of Dutch expansion.

In 1598 the Dutch sent five expeditions consisting of twenty-two ships to the East Indies. A squadron commanded by Oliver van Noort blockaded the port of Manila. Luckily, the Spanish authorities got wind of the impending Dutch attack. Governor Francisco Tello de Guzmán relied mostly on Basque officers to defend the colony. He summoned Antonio de Morga, then a member of the Audiencia, to lead the defense preparation. Morga hastily assembled a motley battalion in Cavite and armed it with harquebuses and muskets. Governor Tello also commissioned Basque captains Juan de Alcega and Agustín de Urdiales to command the Spanish fleet.

Morga was appointed as lieutenant governor of the Philippines in 1593, although he did not arrive there until June 1595. He spent eight years in the archipelago, which he described as "the best of my life." He served in various capacities: as vice governor (*teniente de governador*), interim governor general, and judge (*oidor*) after the reestablishment of the Real Audiencia of Manila in 1598.[8] After his stint in the Philippines, in 1603 Morga was appointed as *alcalde de crimen* (criminal judge) of the Real Audiencia of Mexico. His account of the Philippines, *Los sucesos de las Islas Filipinas,* published in 1609, became a classic reference during the epoch. Morga's multiple posts and successful tour of duty in the Philippines had earned the admiration of Filipinos. In his annotation of the *Sucesos,* José Rizal, the Philippine national hero, likened Morga to a politician in ancient Rome—man of letters, warrior, legislator, and historian.[9]

In his prologue to the 1890 reprint of the *Sucesos,* Ferdinand Blumentritt, the famous Austrian Philippine expert, wrote: "The work of Morga always enjoyed the fame of being the best chronicle of the conquest of the Philippines. Spaniards and foreigners alike agreed with this verdict and assessment. No historian of the Philippines can underestimate with impunity the wealth of information that the work of the renowned judge offers, but neither can they satisfy their desire because the *Sucesos* of Morga is a rare book, so very rare indeed that very few libraries possess it and they guard it with the same care as if it were an Incan treasure."[10]

During the Dutch naval attack on Manila, the Spanish defenders, led by the Basque admiral Juan de Alcega, engaged the Dutch in what would become the first of many Spanish-Dutch naval battles in the Philippines. The Dutch were forced to retreat, although they sank the Spanish flagship. But the Spaniards suffered heavy losses as well. The casualties included the Basques Juan Zamudio, Agustín Urdiales, and Domingo Arrieta. Antonio de Morga almost drowned swimming back to shore.

Dutch raids continued. Naval campaigns against the Spaniards were carried out in 1602, 1616, 1617, and 1626. When Portugal broke away from Spain in 1640, King Juan, the former duke of Braganza, proclaimed that all former Portuguese colonies would do the same. In the same year, the Dutch seized Malacca from the Portuguese and also took over the Portuguese garrison in Formosa (Taiwan) in 1642. The Dutch prowled Philippine waters unmolested and attempted to blockade Manila on several occasions to intercept Chinese junks, though with limited success. The Spaniards in the Philippines again braced for a possible Dutch invasion, but it was not forthcoming.

The Dutch also indirectly aided Muslim rebellion against Spanish rule. In 1644, the newly arrived Governor Diego Fajardo made the mistake of reducing Spanish military deployment in Zamboanga and Jolo. Seeing the weakened Spanish defenses, Salicala, the crown prince of Jolo, went to Batavia and requested Dutch help in dislodging the Spaniards from his island. He succeeded in acquiring two ships to attack the Spanish garrison. The Spaniards tenaciously defended their position, thanks to the bravery of the Bizkaian captain Estevan Ugalde, who forced Salicala's troops to give up the siege. Salicala and his troops retreated to Batavia, although they vowed to return the following year.[11]

Those who came back in 1645 were the Dutch forces, but this time they would carry out an assault on Manila. Twelve warships approached Manila and circled around the bay with impunity. Eleven ships anchored off the coast of Bataan, while the flagship reconnoitered the coast of Cavite. Seeing that Cavite was defenseless, the Dutch commander postponed the assault to the third day, which gave the Spaniards enough time to reinforce themselves. During the fighting, the Basque provincial governor, Andrés Azaldegui, with his skillful handling of the cannons, wreaked havoc on the Dutch invaders, forcing them to flee to Pampanga. Despite their attempts to blockade Manila, the Dutch suffered great losses and had to retreat to Batavia.[12]

Again, in 1646, the Dutch attempted to seal off Manila not only from China, but also from the Americas. A squadron of five ships was stationed off the Ilocos coast to intercept Chinese junks, while another squadron of seven ships cruised near the entrance to San Bernardo Strait to waylay the incoming Acapulco galleons. Governor-General Diego de Fajardo dispatched veteran Basque naval commander Lorenzo de Ugalde and his men to confront the Dutch squadrons. Ugalde had previously been commissioned to bring the annual subsidy from Mexico to Manila. All that Manila could send out against the Dutch were two aging ships, the *Encarnación* and the *Rosario,* which had just sailed from Acapulco.

Astonishingly, Ugalde was victorious and was hailed a hero. A deeply religious man, Ugalde attributed his victory to "the intercession of the most holy Mary, Queen of Angels, under the invocation of the rosary."[13] The event became known as La Naval de Manila, a feast that is still celebrated today to commemorate Spanish victory.

Until the signing of the Treaty of Westphalia in 1648, the Spanish colony in Manila lived in a nearly perpetual state of siege from the Dutch. In the final assessment, the Dutch failed to dislodge the Spaniards from the Philippines because of the skills of the Basque naval officers, the loyalty of the Christian Filipinos (who made up most of the crew in the Spanish vessels), and the sturdy construction of the galleons, which were made from Philippine hardwoods.[14]

The Dutch ceased their offensive against the Spaniards in the Philippines when Spain finally relinquished its claims to the East Indies (Indonesia). Soon both sides slowly set aside their differences and entered into a new form of commercial partnership. Some Basques, like Captain Juan de Ergueza, were quick to take advantage of the Spanish-Dutch rapprochement. He made a profitable trading voyage to Batavia, returning to Manila with oil, wine, cheese, and other merchandise. In turn he exported currency, gold, and deerskins. He also brought to Manila several slaves he purchased from the Dutch.[15]

Meanwhile, the succession of the Bourbons to the Spanish throne in 1700 and their policy of "Family Alliance" (Pacto de Familia) with their French cousins implied that Spain would be dragged into conflict in the event of war between France and England. Thus there was a great need to double the security precautions and defenses in all the Spanish colonies. The Philippines, being close to the British bases in India, had to be always on guard.[16]

In the waters of the Pacific, the increasing presence of English pirates, who pounced on the galleons heading to Acapulco in the first half of the eighteenth century, alarmed the military officials in the Philippines. The capture of the ship *Covadonga* by the British admiral Anson in 1743, during the full-scale war between Spain and England, caused the suspension of the galleon trade for many years.

As a consequence of the Seven Years' War (1756–1763) between Great Britain and France, Great Britain declared war on the Spanish monarch because of the Bourbon alliance. In August 1762, a potent British expeditionary force, under the command of Rear Admiral Samuel Cornish and Brigadier General William Draper, and consisting of eight warships, three frigates, two supply ships, and two Indian vessels with about 1,000 British soldiers, 300 British sailors, 600 *sepoys* (Indian infantry men), and 40 mercenaries from different countries sailed from India to attack the Spaniards in Manila.

Manila residents were caught by surprise. Compounding their problem was the fact that the Basque governor, Pedro Manuel de Arandía, had died in 1754 and had not yet been replaced. The archbishop of Manila, Antonio Rojo, was serving as interim governor, and the city's defenses were vulnerable. There were only 556 Spanish regulars and a number of native troops from the neighboring provinces.

As expected, the British thrashed the token resistance and occupied the city. Archbishop Rojo, seeing the futility of further resistance, surrendered the city to the British. Cornish and Draper demanded the payment of 4 million pesos and the immediate capitulation of all the Spanish military establishments in the archipelago. Meanwhile the British and Indian troops and foreign mercenaries plundered and looted the residences. Women of course did not escape the rampage. A recorded case was that of a Basque widow Feliciana de Arriola, who was raped, stripped of all her belongings, and even left with nothing to wear.[17]

Although the British became the masters of Manila, the Spaniards organized a tough resistance movement led by the Basque Simón de Anda y Salazar, a member of the Audiencia. Anda was born in Subilana, Araba, in 1709. He was a highly educated man, having finished a doctorate in canon law at the Universidad de Henares, and then held various academic positions. In 1735 he married María Cruz Días Montoya from Mixankas, Araba. They had two children: Tomás and Joaquina. Two years later he joined the Academia de Santa María de la Regla, where he specialized in the new Laws of the Indies. In 1755 he was designated as oidor of the Audiencia of Manila, but did not assume the position until July 1761, six months before the arrival of the British forces.[18]

When the British took full control of Manila and its environs, Simón de Anda became their fierce adversary. Anda gathered Spain's loyal followers in Bulacan and, in October 1762, he issued a circular proclaiming himself as governor-general and president of the Royal Audiencia. Many Filipinos assisted the resistance movement by secretly sending gunpowder, lead, and war materiél to Anda's camp. Other Basques, like Francisco de Viana, at the time another member of the Audiencia, also joined Anda.

After General Draper landed in Manila and assumed command of the city, Manila residents were obliged to swear allegiance to King George III within fifteen days. Draper also demanded the payment of a million pesos as part of the capitulation agreement. Only 700,000 pesos were collected. The British started arresting functionaries and distinguished residents. Archbishop Rojo was forced to order the captain of the galleon *Trinidad* to deliver the amount of 1.3 million pesos in addition to the 2 million drawn from the Royal Treasury to cover the demanded payment. However, Anda made sure that the earnings from the galleon would not reach Draper.

Draper forced Archbishop Rojo to order Anda to collaborate with the British, but the Basque rejected the offer, saying that since the archbishop was a prisoner of war, he himself would execute the powers of governor-general of the island. He added that he would not in any way surrender the sovereignty of the Philippines to the British. In November 1762, the British organized a force composed of 200 regulars, 500 sepoys, and a considerable number of Chinese to attack the rebel's stronghold in Bulacan. In December, about 900 Chinese immigrants in the Pampanga revolted against the Spaniards and allied themselves with the British.[19]

Meanwhile, Anda received reinforcements from José Pedro Busto, an Asturian, who managed to escape the city during the siege. Anda made Busto his assistant. As the British navigated the Pasig River, they met stiff resistance from the native inhabitants who had remained loyal to the Spaniards. In Marikina, the British were repelled three times before they overpowered the local defenders and captured their chief, Ali Mudin, who was also the sultan of Jolo.

In March 1763, Ali Mudin signed a defense pact with the British brokered by Santiago de Orendain, a lawyer and a son of a Mexican Basque. Ali Mudin also ceded the coast of Borneo to the British. Orendain was a controversial personality at that time. Earlier he had ingratiated himself with the Basque governor-general Pedro de Arandía, who made him a personal adviser. He made many enemies, particularly among the friars, who blamed him for Arandía's anticlerical stance. In 1759, the interim governor-general, the Basque archbishop Miguel Lino de Espeleta, tried to prosecute Orendain. But the latter astutely evaded charges. In his memoirs, Francisco de Viana described Orendain as "sly, wicked, and perverse." Orendain earned more notoriety when he defected to the British and offered his house as a repository for the books and documents the British confiscated from the Convent of San Agustin, many of which he later sold. After the peace settlement, Orendain and his daughter, whom he married to a British soldier, fled from the country. When they reached the port of Tonkin, however, they were murdered by natives there.

Simón de Anda assembled his troops in Bulacan and Pampanga to attack Manila. In December 1762, Anda's forces blockaded the capital at the points of Malinta and Maysilo. They were almost defeated, saved only by timely reinforcement under the command of José Bustos. The British recovered lost terrain when they ransacked Bulacan in early 1763, killing at least 1,500 Filipino soldiers and 70 Spaniards. Again

Anda's troops, composed of 3,000 Pampangos, wrestled the province away from the British. The last major battle between the British and Anda's forces took place in Malinta and Maysilo in June 1763. The British forces included about 600 Chinese. Nevertheless, Anda and his men were victorious.

In July 1763, the British received an order from the English king to cease hostilities. But protracted conflict continued until negotiations between the two sides took place in Cavite in March 1764. It was only then that the news arrived of a peace settlement, signed by Spain and England on February 10, 1764, which included, among other provisions, the abandonment of Manila by the British. When the British forces finally left Manila, they took with them every vessel in the harbor that could float.[20]

A new governor-general, Francisco de la Torre, arrived in the Philippines in the same month and relieved Anda of his command. Anda returned to Spain as a hero in 1767 and received an appointment from Charles III as a minister of the Council of Castille. Two years later, in April 1769, Anda was appointed formally as governor-general of the Philippines and assumed his duties in July of the same year. He prosecuted and imprisoned a number of functionaries and top officials, including some members of the Audiencia, such as Basaraz and Enrique de Villacorta, who had collaborated with the British invaders, and those who impeded the expulsion of the Jesuits in 1768. However, Anda's orders were revoked by Madrid, and he was fined 12,000 pesos for abuse of authority. He instituted various reforms in the Philippines, among them the secularization of the parishes to promote the development of the native clergy and the rationalization of taxation of the natives.[21] His zeal in performing his duties was met with fierce opposition by the religious orders and other colonial officials who saw the Basque governor-general's policies as inimical to their own. Anda also issued an edict expelling all the Chinese from the Philippines, but the order was revoked by Governor-General José Basco y Vargas. Anda was also a member of the Royal Basque Society from 1769 to 1773 and became a knight of the Order of Charles III in 1772. He died of dysentery in October 1776 in Cavite. Because of Anda's heroism and achievements, a monument was constructed in his honor that still stands in Intramuros, Manila.

The Basques certainly played a pivotal and, in many instances, a leading role in the defense of Spanish sovereignty in the Philippines. By any standard, the heroism and valor they displayed was extraordinary. Without the Basque defenders, the archipelago could have easily fallen into the hands of Chinese pirates and Dutch invaders. Had the Basque Simón de Anda given up the resistance against the British forces, the historical outcome would of course have been different. In fact, the Philippines continued to be a colony of Spain until the end of the nineteenth century. This is crucial, because it was during the last century of Spanish occupation that a greater number of Basques settled in the Philippines.

Chapter Eight

Nineteenth-Century Settlers and Entrepreneurs

> Basques in the Philippines! In all ranks, all categories, all activities, and in every corner of that constellation of islands.
>
> Quioquiap

The Philippines in the beginning of the 1800s was still largely underdeveloped, notwithstanding the belated efforts of Spain to improve its situation. Spain itself was in an irreversible decline, ruined by years of foreign wars and internal strife. Two centuries of overdependence on the Manila-Acapulco galleon trade killed the incentive to exploit the economic potential of the Philippines and, as a consequence, limited the number of potential settlers from the Iberian Peninsula, including Basques.

Even so, the Philippines in the nineteenth century presented better opportunities for economic progress than in the previous two centuries. Technological advances in navigation and transport had made the trans-Pacific journey relatively safer, shorter, and cheaper. A regular direct trade had begun between Spain and the Philippines via the Cape of Good Hope, initiated by the Royal Philippine Company. Excepting the Muslims in western Mindanao and the Sulu archipelago, most Filipinos had been converted to the Catholic faith by the incessant labor of Basque and Spanish missionaries.

At the same time, some significant events favored Spanish migration to the Philippines. In 1808 Spain was invaded by Napoleon Bonaparte, who installed his brother Joseph on the Spanish throne. Then the Spanish colonies in the Americas took advantage of Spain's weakness and started agitating for political independence. The invasion naturally disrupted communications and trade between the Philippines and Spain. The Basque-controlled Philippine Company, which was just recovering from the heavy losses it had sustained during Spain's war with England in 1796, braced for another debacle.

In the early years of the nineteenth century, independence movements swept through Spain's New World colonies. By 1825 all of the continental and mainland former colonies had achieved their autonomy, reducing Spain's influence in the Americas to a foothold in the Antilles. The loss interrupted Spanish emigration to the New World. The previous opportunities for Iberian-born persons in the colonial, civil, military, and ecclesiastical structures were gone. Of equal significance for the Basques, who were heavily involved in merchant marine activities, commerce between Spain and the New World was reduced to a trickle.[1]

Predictably, xenophobia, and particularly anti-Spanish sentiment, characterized the early years of Latin American independence. Spanish nationals were faced with either leaving the new Latin American nations or renouncing their Old World citizenship.[2] It was, in fact, a Basque descendant, Simón Bolívar, who led the war of independence against Spain. In the end, only Cuba, Puerto Rico, and the Philippines remained as Spanish colonies. Given the limited options, the Philippines became a beacon to prospective Basque emigrants seeking fortune, properties, and jobs in the colonial government.

Another important event that contributed to Basque emigration to the Philippines was the Carlist wars, the first from 1833 to 1839 and the second from 1872 to 1876. In 1833, a civil war, known as the First Carlist War, erupted in Spain. This was caused by the refusal of Carlos, brother of Ferdinand IV, to recognize the ascension to the throne of his young niece, Isabel II. More than a succession issue, the conflict became a clash between the conservatives and the liberals.

In response to the policies of the liberal government in Madrid, which was both centralist and anticlerical in its philosophy, the deeply Catholic and regionalist Basque Provinces supported the claim of the pretender (Carlos) to the throne. The struggle broke out with all the virulence that characterizes civil conflicts. To finance the war, most of the rural areas of the Basque Country were subjected to heavy taxation and military conscription by the Carlist forces. Many of the battles were fought in the Basque Provinces. The defeat of the Carlists in 1839 saddled the Basques with the payment of heavy war retribution. Under the Treaty of Vergara, the Basque fueros were to be respected, but only insofar as they did not conflict with the Spanish national interest.[3]

By 1872 the Carlist forces in Spain were once again powerful enough to trigger a civil conflict. The Second Carlist War was a repetition of the first. Initial successes of the Carlist forces, financed through heavy taxation and military conscription in rural Basque areas, were reversed. The victorious government forces stationed an army of occupation in the Basque Country and exacted heavy retribution. This time the fueros were all but abolished by the central government.[4]

It is not surprising that many Basque liberals and Carlist supporters decided to leave their home to emigrate to the Philippines to escape political persecution and to start a new life. This was the choice of Basques such as José de Azcárraga, José Oyanguren, and Eusebio Ruíz de Luzurriaga.

Fear of military conscription and the fact that battles were fought in Basque territories contributed greatly to the Basque diaspora. Basque males of military age opposed to the war had to flee their homeland. Records show that some boys as young as thirteen or fourteen were encouraged by their relatives to emigrate to save them from the horrors of war and give them the opportunity to build their fortunes in the remaining Spanish colonies.

Although Basque emigration was spurred primarily by economic and political motives, there were other factors like the lure of adventure and the flight from criminal penalties. Lastly, the Basque Country during the nineteenth century remained entrenched in its traditional land tenure and inheritance practices. The principle of single-heir inheritance, meaning that one person in each generation inherited the family patrimony, was a strong socioeconomic inducement to other members of the family to seek their fortunes in other places.

The success of Basque commercial houses like Ynchausti and Company and Ayala and Company, among others, became an inspiration to new Basque emigrants to settle in the Philippines. Having toiled in developing uncharted territories and acquiring properties, Basques found their desire to return to the Iberian Peninsula, specifically to the Basque Country, counterbalanced by their success and newly acquired economic status in the Philippines.

As previously explained, independence movements in Latin America, in particular in Mexico, spelled the demise of the Manila-Acapulco trade and later the Philippine Company. The last galleon, aptly called the *Magallanes,* sailed from Manila in 1811. However, by that time (circa 1820) Basques were not only firmly established in Asia, they had business relations with other Basques in Latin America, notably in Acapulco and Peru. These included men like Azaola, Arrinda, Azcárraga, Arrechea, Salaberría, and Ayala.[5]

The Spanish colonial government in the Philippines therefore had no choice but to gradually open the country to international trade. Besides, tariffs and customs duties provided new sources of revenue to maintain the colonial administration. Soon, English, German, French, American, and other foreign trading companies opened branches in Manila, Cebu, and Iloilo. Although Asian, mainly Chinese, products were still important trade commodities, efforts gravitated toward agricultural production. The cultivation of cash crops such as sugar, tobacco, indigo, coffee, and abaca (Manila hemp) for export became the trend. Philippine-born Basque Manuel de Azcárraga, who became an outstanding lawyer and politician in Spain, hailed this as "the beginning of the true prosperity in the Philippines."[6]

It was also the beginning of an influx of European emigrants to the Philippines. As a Spanish observer wrote: "By 1837, the white population, both national and foreign, has considerably increased since 1820. We are seeing new faces everyday."[7] With the opening of Manila to international trade in 1834 came the opening of foreign consulates in Manila. In 1842, there were already five: Belgium, Denmark, France, Sweden, and the United States. There were also thirty-nine foreign commercial houses, including eighteen British, two American, one French, and one Danish.[8]

Indeed, better economic prospects in the Philippines attracted a growing number of Basque settlers. Basques from the four Spanish Basque provinces were present in the archipelago. Most numerous were the Bizkaians, because the opening of Philippine ports to international trade attracted seamen (captains, pilots, and shipbuilders). The second most important group was the Navarrese, who were involved in trade and in the planting of abaca, coconuts, and, later, sugar. The third group was the Gipuzkoans, involved in exploration, such as José Oyanguren and his friend Joaquín Urquiola (from Gaviria) on the island of Mindanao, or in trading, such as José Joaquín de Ynchausti from Zumarraga, the founder of Ynchausti and Company. (His later partners were Navarrese: Elizalde, Teus, Yrrisari, and others.) The Arabans were less numerous, being mostly involved in government administration and later in their own business—for example, the Ayala family. The very few French Basques were established in Manila.[9]

Basque settlers were predominantly male, young, single (or in some cases widowers), and semiliterate. They often married the daughters of earlier Basque immigrants, who, in most cases, were their employers or sponsors. Failing this, some would marry into prominent peninsular or mestizo families. How many Basques came to the Philippines? Based on the study conducted by the late Jon Bilbao of the University of Nevada, using sources from the Philippine National Archives, an estimated 1,500 Basques resided in the Philippines between 1830 to 1910.[10] Although this is certainly not a definitive figure, we could surmise that about 2,000 to 2,500 Basques resided in the Philippines during the nineteenth century.

The first batch of Basque settlers concentrated in Manila. For instance, Basque trading companies such as Otadui, Marcaida, Matía y Menchacatorre, and Orbeta specialized in importing European goods and agricultural machinery.[11] However, succeeding Basque immigrants who arrived during the second quarter of the nineteenth century did not establish themselves in Manila. Instead, the provinces with underdeveloped lands and economic potential provided an excellent opportunity for Basques with a strong agrarian background. Besides, they were latecomers and most of the Spaniards were already entrenched in the urban areas.

Not all Basque immigrants were welcomed with open arms. Some, because of their rude behavior and their stubbornness, ran afoul of the Spanish authorities and the natives alike. One recorded case was that of Darío de Ansotegui from Vitoria, Araba, who arrived in Manila in 1842 and settled on Romblon Island. He married Ana de Rojas and had a child. The Spanish provincial commander of Romblon, Joaquín Vidal, complained to the governor-general in October 1855 that "Ansotegui's behavior is not the appropriate one for the natives because of his domineering character, violent temper, and the way he interprets things for his own benefit." The commander requested Ansotegui's transfer to another place. The governor-general, however, ordered Commander Vidal to grant Ansotegui his residence on condition that he restrain his behavior and respect the Spanish authorities. "Otherwise he will be sent back to Spain." The governor-general also ordered the commander to read his note to Ansotegui in the presence of the local priest.[12] Fortunately incidents like this were isolated and did not in general harm the image of the Basques. Owing to their pioneering spirit, propensity for hard work, and special business acumen, many Basques became successful entrepreneurs. This collective success, however, elicited resentment.

Soon, the Basques became actively involved in the four main exports of the Philippines at that time—sugar, abaca, tobacco, and coffee. The lucrative sugar trade was a strong magnet for Basque settlement in the Philippines. At the start of 1850, the Philippines joined Cuba in becoming a major exporter of sugar to the world market. British demand for Philippine sugar increased after the emancipation of African slaves in the West Indies and the subsequent decline in sugar production there. The extensive plains of the periphery of Manila and Pampanga and on the islands of Panay and Negros made possible the cultivation of large-scale sugar plantations. As a consequence, the Basques, using native labor, pioneered the construction of roads, bridges, railways, seaports, warehouses, sugar mills, and factories. Most importantly, they also introduced new farming and production techniques.

Aside from agriculture, the Basques were also active players in the development of domestic industries such as cordage, distilleries, paints, and dyes. Ynchausti and Company, for example, produced and commercialized ropes made from abaca fibers grown in the company's haciendas in Bicol to meet the great demand for use in ships—particularly in Europe and America—because of their strength, durability, and resistance to the effects of saltwater.

When the port of Iloilo on the island of Panay was opened to foreign traders in 1855, it quickly became a leading commercial center in the Visayas. The fact that the British government established a vice-consulate in the port city attested to the growing its economic importance. It should be recalled that the first Basques who settled in Iloilo were led by Martín de Goiti, Legazpi's aide-de-camp. It could have been the Basques who changed the name of the place from Irong-Irong to Iloilo, finding the native name hard to pronounce. The same thing probably happened when Legazpi and his men renamed Maynilad as Manila. Naturally, Iloilo attracted a Basque contingent, and the place ultimately emerged as the second most important focus of Basque settlement in the Philippines after Manila.

Important Basque companies of Manila, like Ynchausti and Company, which controlled half a dozen large sugar plantations and a fleet of more than twenty vessels in the inter-island trade, opened branches in Iloilo. Iloilo had Basque-owned businesses of all kinds, and a number of hotels and boarding houses.[13] Some Basques also became involved in the cultivation of coffee in Tayabas (present-day Quezon Province), such as Iñigo González Azaola, who in 1846 won two prizes from the Royal Economic Society for his coffee plantation. Tayabas then was a leading coffee producer.[14]

The settlement and development of hitherto unexplored lands, particularly in Bicol, Negros, Panay, and the hinterlands of eastern Mindanao, gave a new impetus to the colonization and development of the areas with an eye toward commercial ventures. Some Basques would practically hack their way into the thicket of lush forest and grasslands to establish settlements and plantations. This was the case with José Oyanguren.

Oyanguren was born in Bergara, Gipuzkoa, at the end of the eighteenth century and gained fame as a lawyer. In 1825, however, after becoming a target of political persecution because of his liberal views, he took refuge in the Philippines, where he dedicated himself to business. Active, robust, and enterprising, Oyanguren decided in 1830 to explore the coast of western Mindanao, reaching the Gulf of Davao, and the other remote islands. Initially he did well in his legal profession. He registered as a lawyer in Manila in 1837, and, in 1840, he became a judge in the district of Tondo (Manila), a position he held until 1846 when judges were appointed from Madrid.[15]

An agreement between the Sultan of Sulu and the Spanish authorities in Manila had ceded the region of Davao to Spain. Oyanguren conceived the idea of colonizing the area. Before Oyanguren's pioneering effort, Mindanao was a vast unexplored island for the Spaniards. It remained a frontier territory throughout the Spanish colonial period. Spain had only a token presence, in Dapitan on the northwestern tip of the island. After reconnoitering the Davao area for the second time, Oyanguren petitioned then governor-general Narciso Clavería y Zaldúa for permission to undertake a mini-*conquista* on terms not much different from those granted by the Spanish kings to conquistadors during the sixteenth and early seventeenth centuries.

Governor-General Clavería was receptive to the idea. Although he was born in Gerona (Catalonia), he had spent his childhood in Bizkaia, and his familiarity with the Basques could have influenced his favorable decision.[16] By a decree of February 27, 1847, Governor Clavería bestowed on Oyanguren jurisdiction for a ten-year period, and exclusive trading rights for the first six years, within the limits of the territory he might conquer in the Gulf of Davao. He also let him have some artillery, muskets and munitions, and authority to organize a company of territorial troops. Oyanguren sailed for Davao with a small squadron of vessels he had fitted out at his own expense, or more precisely at the expense of a joint stock company he had organized.[17] On the other hand, he promised to subject to the Spanish authorities the territory comprising the Cape of San Agustín to Sarangani point; to expel the Muslims, or at least reduce the number residing there; to establish Christian settlements, in order to facilitate the cultivation of fields; to raise livestock of all types; and to establish friendly relations with the natives in the interior and attract them to civilized life under Spanish tutelage.

In just a little over a year the lawyer-turned-conquistador achieved the almost impossible mission of colonizing a frontier territory. By January 1849, Oyanguren obtained a decree from Governor-General Clavería constituting the district as a province by the name of Nueva Guipuzcoa, with its capital, Nueva Bergara (today the city of Davao) named after his native town. In December 1853, another decree of the colonial government divided the territory of Nueva Guipuzcoa into two politico-military districts—Bislig and Davao. The names of Nueva Guipuzcoa and Bergara remained in use until 1862. In time "Davao" came to be used for both the capital and the district.[18]

Nueva Guipuzcoa was the second province named after a Basque province. In 1839, the Basque governor-general Luis Lardizabal created the province of Nueva Vizcaya, which was carved out of the southern portion of the vast Cagayan Province. It possessed a politico-military government whose governor controlled all the administrative functions of government. Ecclesiastically, the province fell under the jurisdiction of the Diocese of Nueva Segovia (Ilocos). The Augustinian and Dominican orders were in charge of its religious missions. By 1850, the province had reached a Christian population of 22,236 and gave tributes amounting to 5,410 pesos.[19] Nueva Guipuzcoa is no longer on Philippine maps, as it later became Davao Province; Nueva Vizcaya, however, still exists.

After a new governor-general, the marquis of Solana, assumed office, Oyanguren was relieved of his post in the territory he bizarrely conquered and was replaced by an army captain. Oyanguren would desperately appeal his case to the Audiencia, spending both time and money, but to no avail. Desolate and financially ruined, he died in October 1859 in Davao and was buried in the "cemetery of Bergara." Ironically, Oyanguren's tormentor turned out to be another Basque, Antonio de Urbiztondo y Eguía.

There was no clear explanation for the action taken by Urbiztondo against Oyanguren. Oyanguren's arrangement with Governor-General Clavería could have been interpreted as coterminus with his term in the colonial government. There could have been strong political differences between Urbiztondo and Oyanguren. Although the Basques often exhibit unity of thought, action, and interests vis-à-vis other groups, their solidarity also ends somewhere. Conflicts among the Basques abound.[20]

But let us go back to our story. Antonio de Urbiztondo himself was an extraordinary man. Throughout his life he amassed honors and titles, including the following: marquis of Solana, Knight Grand Cross of the Royal American Order of Isabel the Catholic, Knight of the Royal Order of San Fernando of the first and third class, and that of San Hermenegildo, lieutenant-general of the National Forces, governor and captain-general of the Philippine Islands, president of the Royal Audiencia of the Philippine Islands, judge-subdelegate of Post Office Revenue, vice-royal patron, and director-general of the troops.

Urbiztondo was born in Donostia, Gipuzkoa, in 1794. While still in the university, a successful revolt in Bizkaia by Basque nationalists inspired him to abandon his studies and join the movement. Later he entered Donostia as a hero and was named governor. It did not take long before he made himself dictator of Gipuzkoa.[21]

Alarmed by the developments in the Basque Country, the Madrid government sent a huge force to subdue the rebellion. Urbiztondo was among those taken to prison in Vitoria where a war council condemned them to death. Thanks to his contacts in the high echelons of the Spanish government, Urbiztondo's sentence was commuted to banishment to the town of Oñati.

In 1822 he went to France, where he organized a military faction and later joined the Carlist forces in the mountains of the Basque Country. He was given the rank of captain as a reward for assembling a military force. Owing to his brilliant performance, he was promoted to lieutenant colonel and became a trusted aid of Carlos, the pretender to the Spanish throne. Urbiztondo was sent to London to procure weapons, but the vessel was shipwrecked along the way. He tried again, but his bad luck continued. His ship was cornered by troops loyal to Isabel II along the coast of Santander. Again Urbiztondo was condemned to death but was instead exiled to Puerto Rico. There he escaped in a British ship and reached London, wisely evading his persecutors. He rejoined the Carlist camp and was quickly elevated to brigadier and later assigned to the general headquarters.

Urbiztondo showed his military genius by winning a series of victories. He later laid plans for the conquest of Catalonia. Jealous of his success and growing influence, the Catalonian generals thwarted his strategy and discredited him to Carlos. Frustrated, Urbiztondo resigned his post. As the defeat of the Carlist forces drew nearer, he joined other generals in pursuing peace with the Spanish crown provided that Basque rights and privileges would be respected. As noted earlier, the efforts were futile.

Urbiztondo was later given a royal amnesty and was named by the Spanish government as military commander in Bizkaia. His outstanding talent as a soldier and shift of allegiance from Carlos to Queen Isabel were handsomely compensated. Urbiztondo was soon awarded a marquisate and was subsequently appointed as governor-general of the Philippines in 1849. Urbiztondo's first task was to organize a military campaign against the Sulu sultanate under the pretext of invading Jolo to claim Sulu's trade.[22]

Early that year, its ruler, Sultan Muhammad Fadl, had entered into a treaty of friendship and commerce with the British government through James Brooke, the ambitious British governor of Labuan, an island off the coast of present-day Brunei, which served as a commercial entrepôt for Borneo and also as a naval base. After an initial campaign in which over a hundred boats and a thousand houses were destroyed, the Spanish forces returned to Zamboanga. There Urbiztondo assembled an expeditionary force consisting of a fleet of steam and sailing ships, as well as native boats, with 142 officers, 2,876 soldiers, and 925 volunteers from Cebu, Iloilo, and Zamboanga.[23] This was an impressive military campaign by the standards of the time.

Practically assured of victory, Urbiztondo led the Spanish troops in their attack on

Jolo on February 28, 1851. Despite a stubborn defense, the sultanate's forces succumbed to the superior Spanish military power. The sultan and his subjects fled to the island's interior, while the Spanish troops sacked all the fortifications and villages of Jolo within two days. Spanish casualties were minimal. As an English chronicler wrote: "The loss of the Spaniards in the whole affair was 34 men killed and 84 wounded. A very unpleasant circumstance to the army was connected to this expedition. Two field officers, both of them acting lieutenant colonels of separate regiments, showed white feather at the moment of danger; for which, I believe, they could have been cashiered or shot, had their chief (Urbiztondo) not been as merciful as he is brave."[24]

The defeat of the Sulu sultanate paved the way for the conclusion of a treaty of incorporation into the Spanish monarchy signed in April 1851 between the military governor of Zamboanga and the sultan and his principal datus (leaders). The treaty, although not enforced, made the Sultanate of Sulu and its dependencies an integral part of the Spanish colony of the Philippines. It nullified the Brooke agreement and stated that no foreign vessel would be allowed to trade in the Sulu archipelago except at a port properly approved for foreign commerce. The treaty also called for the establishment of a trading factory and naval station in Jolo to protect Spain's commercial interests and prevent future traffic in munitions.[25]

Urbiztondo made history not only in the annals of military affairs but also in Philippine business. On August 1, 1851, he founded the first bank in the archipelago. He likewise carried his apostasy to Carlos further when he named it Banco Español-Filipino de Isabel II. It became the official government bank of the Philippines and the sole issuer of bank notes. It is also the oldest bank in Southeast Asia, continuing to this day as the Bank of the Philippine Islands (BPI). Soon after, other Basques, like Antonio de Ayala and Joaquín José de Ynchausti served as its directors. In 1897, the bank opened a branch in Iloilo, obviously to cater to the booming sugar business that was already in the hands of the Basques. After his tour of duty in the Philippines, Urbiztondo asked to be assigned to Araba, a posting that was granted to him. He was summoned to Madrid in 1857, where he died mysteriously, a victim of a political crime.[26]

One of the industries spawned by the agricultural revolution was inter-island and international shipping for the transport of goods and people. This was a boon for the Basques inasmuch as many came to the Philippines as mariners and shipbuilders. Juan Bautista Arrechea from Zumilla (Navarre) arrived in Manila in 1823, settled in Lingayen, in the province of Pangasinan, and initiated a shipbuilding company. A widower, Arrechea started building coastal vessels called *pontin* of twenty-eight cubits of keel in 1826. By 1839, he was already building a brig. Interestingly, his building permits were signed by three Basques: Luís Lardizabal (the governor), Luís Arrejola (the lieutenant governor), and Tiburcio Gorostiza (the treasurer). By 1846, he was evidently doing brisk business, for he was already requesting permits to build ten ships. Arrechea entered into partnerships with other Basques in 1848: José Irribaren from Astitz, Navarre, and Antonio Eguiluz from Vitoria, Araba, both with 3,000 pesos each. In that year Arrechea had an estimated capital of 15,000 pesos.[27]

On Leyte Island, Bizkaian Basques such as Muertegui (Palompon), Urrutia (Tacloban), Larrazabal, Uriarte, and Yrastorza (Ormoc) became established Manila hemp merchants and shipowners. Yrastorza even had a short-lived partnership with the British firm of Brodett and Company. In Iloilo, Ynchausti and Company, owned by José Joaquín de Ynchausti y Gurchategui, was involved in all kinds of business: abaca, tobacco, sugar, shipping, banking, and so on, and employed hundreds of Basques. During the third quarter of the nineteenth century, José Joaquín de Ynchausti was probably the most important Basque in the Philippines.[28] Ynchausti and Company also financed the building of the Puente Colgante (Suspension Bridge), the first suspension bridge over the Pasig River in Manila. The bridge was 110 meters long and 7 meters wide. Its construction was directed by a Basque engineer, Matías Mechacatorre, from 1849 to 1853.

Like Ynchausti and Company, Aldecoa and Company was thriving in the sugar business. In the 1880s, Aldecoa and Company also sponsored the immigration of many Basques, including Antonio de Yturri, Segundo Emaldi, Manuel Laserna Martínez, Francisco Longa Erquiaga, Juan Pedro de Acordagoicoechea, Domingo Aldamiz Erquiaga, Basilio Anduiza, Eusebio Dauden, Juan José Echano Jauregui, Leopoldo Elizalde Isasi, Eulogio Escubi Zuluaga, Ricardo Gallega Elordieta, Gregorio Gamboa Garay, Justo Madariaga Arrasate, Guillermo de Acordagoitia, Antonio Arana Acha, and Jose Manuel Zuluaga Garteiz.[29] The list could go on and on. Basques during the second half of the nineteenth century possessed a solid business network that slowly dominated the economy.

The opening of the Suez Canal in 1869 brought a new wave of Basque settlers to the Philippines. The Second Carlist War (1872–1876) created its own refugees. Furthermore, many young men with business experience were brought out by the Basque companies involved in agriculture and trade. The same companies were buying foreign steamships or constructing boats for the inter-island and international trade. Consequently, 90 percent of the captains and pilots in the inter-island trade and on the Singapore-Manila and Hong Kong–Manila runs were Basques. So were many of the port officials of Manila, Legazpi, Cebu, and Iloilo.[30] But even before the opening of the Suez Canal, Basques were active in shipping. Several boats, including the *Bella Vascongada, Bilbaino, Aurreta, Alavesa, Neurea,* and *Unzueta* were plying the route between the Philippines and Spain.[31]

In the 1870s, the Basque trading firm Olano, Larrrinaga, and Company was also the most important shipping firm and for many years the only link between the Philippines and Europe. Its head office was in Liverpool, the leading commercial city of England. Its ships embarked monthly, stopping at the ports of Cádiz, Barcelona, and finally Manila.[32] In addition, the company also operated the Liverpool-Bilbao-Manila route, as well as the Liverpool–New York and Liverpool-Havana runs.

One of the founders of the company was Ramón de Larrinaga, a Basque merchant marine captain. He was born in the Bizkaian town of Mundaka. His ancestors were also mariners, based in Bilbao since 1773. In 1862 Larrinaga entered into a partnership with José Antonio de Olano, another Basque mariner residing in Liverpool, and a certain Captain Longa to form "Olano, Larrinaga y Cía.," with its office located in 4 Goree Piazza (Liverpool), beginning business as agents and ship suppliers.[33]

The three partners divided the tasks among themselves. Longa piloted their first ship, the *Felix*, a secondhand wooden hauler, while Olano and Larrinaga took care of the land operation. Their company operated mainly with old sailing ships until they ordered three steamships constructed in 1871. The opening of the Suez Canal convinced Larrinaga that the future of navigation was in steamships and that their company's destiny was in plying the Europe-Asia route. However, the three partners quarreled over strategy. Larrinaga maintained his futuristic views, while Olano and Longa opposed them. Finally they decided to settle the matter by tossing a coin while shouting the word "buenaventura" (good fortune). Larrinaga won. The company flag consisted of three hands joined together to symbolize their pact.

Buenaventura was also the name they gave to their first steamship. It made history when it became the first Spanish vessel to cross through Suez Canal. It also had the distinction of being the first Spanish ship captured by the Americans during the initial salvo of the Spanish-American War in April 1898, while discharging its cargo in the port of Pascagoula, Mississippi, in the United States. Despite pleading that the *Buenaventura* was a British ship, being registered in Liverpool, their ship became the property of L. Luckenback Transport and Wrecking Co. of New York. But after several trips along the U.S. eastern seaboard, it was left as a pontoon off Chesapeake Bay.[34]

In April 1873, Olano, Larrinaga, and Company won the contract from the Spanish government to transport to and from the Philippines (via the Suez Canal) all civilian, military, and naval employees as well as administrative corps of the national navy every forty days. In September of the same year, the company was forced to pay a fine of 1,500 to 3,000 duros for the delay of disembarkment, although it later lived up to expectations. Soon it controlled one of the busiest and lucrative routes at the time: Liverpool-Cádiz-Barcelona–Port Said–Suez Canal–Ceylon-Singapore-Manila.

Thus, with its numerous fleet of steam and sailing ships that transported goods and people directly from Spain and the Philippines by the cheapest and fastest way, Olano, Larrinaga, and Company played an essential role in Philippine foreign trade and even internal security. Its importance to the colonial economy and government was described as follows: "that Olano, Larrinaga, and Company, without any subsidy and using its own resources, established a shipping line in such unfavorable circumstances, clearly shows the entrepreneurial genius and the intelligent management that governs the company, which is worthy of public applause and merits the protection of the Spanish government for the great services and savings for the treasury, in the transport of officials, as well as the free services rendered recently to the top authority of the Philippines for the expedition to Jolo, whose patriotic service had employed the magnificent ships *León* and *Buenaventura*, facilitating, with the transport of provision, munitions, and troops, the good success of the expedition."[35]

In November 1879, however, the company lost its preeminence when it lost the monopoly on the Spain-Philippines shipping route to the marquez de Campo, a Valencian shipping magnate. In 1881, the company quit its business in the Philippines and was absorbed by the Cía Transatlantica Española, then the biggest Spanish shipping firm, and became its agent and representative in England. Its ships were diverted to Cuba and Puerto Rico. Olano, Larrinaga, and Company disbanded in 1885 and was succeeded by Larrinaga and Company. Its ships were registered in the port of Bilbao and plied the Antilles until the Spanish-American War. The company also diversified its operation in Liverpool. The English branch actually survived until the 1970s.[36]

The Basques, as an ethnic group, were competing not so much against other Spaniards but against the English, American, and Chinese traders. Aside from Ynchausti and Ayala, Basque businessmen such as Zubiri, Matia, Menchacatorre, Aldecoa, Gorostiza, Marcaida, Menchaca, Eguilúz, Aristegui, Laucirica, Azcona, and Nessi-Arrola[37] competed vigorously against foreign competitors. The English and the Americans did not pose much of a real threat because their interests relied on trade. The main rivals were the more numerous Chinese, who controlled the domestic retail trade and were starting to own land and property.

The other side of Basque emigration to the Philippines consisted of Philippine-born Basques who later settled in Spain to pursue successful careers. This was the case with the Azcárraga brothers, Manuel and Marcelo, the sons of José de Azcárraga, a political dissident who became a member of the Royal Economic Society of the Philippines.

Manuel de Azcárraga was born in Manila in 1830. He studied law at the Universidad de Santo Tomás and continued his studies at the Universidad Central de Madrid, graduating in 1853. He held important positions in the colonial bureaucracy, such as solicitor of the Navy Tribunal in the Philippines, solicitor of the Court of Manila, provincial governor of Cagayan for many years, and civil governor and administrator (*alcalde corregidor*) of the city of Manila.[38]

From 1872 to 1876, Manuel de Azcárraga served as adviser for Philippine affairs in the Overseas Ministry (Ministerio de Ultramar), after which he was elected as a member of congress representing Solsona. In 1891 he was elected senator in the province of Lérida. He was twice director-general of Grace and Justice of the Overseas Ministry; legal counsel of the Superior Board of the Obras Pías (Pious Works) of the Philippines; and a member of different Spanish and foreign corporations. For his achievements, he received numerous awards and, shortly before his death in 1896, he was designated senator for life.[39] Aside from his success in law and politics, Manuel de Azcárraga was also known as a reformer and an economist. His *The Liberty of Commerce in the Philippines* (*La libertad del comercio en las islas Filipinas*), published Madrid in 1871, is an authoritative study of the Philippine economy during the nineteenth century. His other works include *The Reform of the Indigenous Municipality in the Philippines* (*La reforma del municipio indígena en Filipinas*), *Project of the Demonopolization of Tobacco in the Philippines* (*Proyecto del desentanco del tabaco en Filipinas*), and *Vulgar Letters on Our Political Customs* (*Cartas vulgares sobre nuestras costumbres políticas*).

Manuel's brother, Marcelo de Azcárraga, was born in Manila in 1836. He studied in the Colegio de San Juan de Letrán, a Dominican institution, partly doing kitchen chores at the school in exchange for his education. He was a brilliant student, and, while still very young, already spoke of some day becoming a famous general. From Letrán, he went to a preparatory military school that had just opened in Manila, later completed his military training at the Academia de Estado Mayor in Madrid, and was then sent to Cuba. He was a lieutenant at eighteen, a captain at twenty, and a major at twenty-two. During the Carlist revolt in Spain, he fought on the side of the crown and is said never to have lost a battle. In 1871, at thirty-five, he fulfilled his childhood dream and became a brigadier general.[40] In 1872, a street in Manila, Calle Azcárraga, was named in his honor.

Marcelo de Azcárraga was minister of war in three governments headed by Cánovas (in 1890, 1891, and 1895) and in two by Silvela (in 1899 and 1900). He likewise became prime minister of Spain in October 1900. His brief stint as head of government was plagued by public disorder and protests. Owing to the bloody confrontation between the armed forces and civilians during the burial of poet Ramón de Campoamor, a state of war was declared in Madrid. In late February 1901, the Azcárraga government stepped down. Azcárraga would later preside over a transitional government that lasted barely a month (December 1904–January 1905). He died in Madrid in 1915.[41]

During the Philippine revolution against Spain in 1896 and 1898, Basque participation was limited. Some Basque families, such as that of Eusebio and José Ruíz de Luzurriaga in Negros, were actively involved in the independence movement against Spanish control of the area, but many stayed out of politics.[42] José Ruíz de Luzurriaga became the president of congress of the short-lived Federal Republic of Negros (December 1898–March 1899). Another Basque, Agustín Amenabar, became a delegate of Agriculture and Commerce in the first revolutionary government of Negros Occidental.[43] Fernando Zobel y Ayala, whose father Antonio de Ayala was previously imprisoned by the Spanish colonial authorities on suspicion of rebellion, also aided the Filipino revolutionaries.

The principal reason for this noninvolvement was likely that the Basques were thriving in trade and commerce that depended mainly on Spain. It was natural that they maintained their support of the status quo. Another factor was that the new Basque settlers were not yet established enough to manifest a strong desire to be part of an independent country. There was no Philippine equivalent of Simón Bolívar. But although there was no true-to-life Basque liberator, there existed a Basque persona that has become immortalized in Philippine literature.

José Rizal and the Basques

José Rizal (1861–1896), the Philippine national hero, whose writings inspired the Filipinos to revolt against Spanish rule, had an interesting relation with the Basques. Rizal's protagonist in the novel *Noli Me Tangere* (1887),[44] Crisóstomo Ibarra (who became Simoun in the 1891 sequel, *El Filibusterismo*),[45] is a Basque descendant, a tribute to the Basques' ubiquitousness in the Philippines during Rizal's time. Curiously, we find no reference in Rizal's numerous accounts to Basque friends, although he spent a month in a Biarritz villa in the French Basque Country in the spring of 1891. It was there that he completed the draft of *El Filibusterismo.* Undoubtedly, he was very much aware of the emergence of Basque nationalism in his day.

José Rizal was born of an affluent Malay-Filipino family in Calamba, Laguna (about fifty kilometers from Manila), on June 19, 1861.[46] He was an extremely talented writer and a versatile scholar. He also spoke several foreign languages, among them Spanish, Latin, Greek, French, German, Japanese, and English. As a young boy, he saw members of his family suffer political persecution by the Spanish colonial government and ecclesiastical authorities. His elder brother, Paciano, for fear of being implicated in an alleged conspiracy attributed to his native clergy mentor, had to quit his studies in Manila and return to the province. As a result, the young José was forced to use "Rizal" as surname rather than "Mercado," the true family name, to disguise his identity. His mother was falsely charged with attempted poisoning, and, as punishment, the Spanish provincial authorities ordered her to march under the glare of the public through two prominent towns in the province. She was acquitted after suffering much pain and humiliation. Since his family was leasing and working the lands owned by the Dominican order, his father regularly had disputes with the Dominicans over taxes, rentals, and tithes.

In June 1882, at age twenty-one, Rizal left for Spain to continue his studies. He took up medicine (ophthalmology) and philosophy and letters at the same time in the Universidad Central de Madrid. Although he did not formally complete his medical studies, he practiced as an eye doctor when he returned to the Philippines in 1888. A prolific writer and incisive thinker, Rizal formed part of the group of Filipino students and expatriates in Madrid who advocated political reforms in the Philippines. Collectively, they were called the Ilustrados (the Enlightened Ones). They published a nationalist newspaper called *La Solidaridad* (*The Solidarity*) from February 1889 to November 1895 to spread their views and attract supporters to their cause.

Rizal, however, wanted to do more than contribute articles and essays. He decided to write more serious works that would tackle the political and social problems in the Philippines. He therefore thought of writing a novel, *Noli Me Tangere,* as a critique of the abuses of the Spanish friars and the colonial government in the islands. But before we discuss the Basque characters in Rizal's novel, it is important to emphasize that his early writings already showed his admiration for the Basques.

As a high school student in the Jesuit-run Ateneo Municipal of Manila, he wrote two Spanish poems honoring two Basque personalities—Juan Sebastián Elcano and Antonio de Urbiztondo. Rizal paid tribute to Elcano in his poem "And Spain's Elcano Was the First to Round the Globe." He referred to Elcano not as a Basque but a "new titan of the Pyrenees / is this hero of Spain who furiously defies / the obstructing hurricane." Rizal also described the Basque navigator as "unfrightened / by the magnitude of the task" and "immutable as a rock" that "the roaring waters he subdued / with the naval craft of Spain."[47]

In the last two stanzas of the poem, Rizal immortalizes Elcano's feat:

Victorious he rounded
the vast ring of the world
and fearlessly he measured
the wide orb as it whirled

Athlete of Spain, a thousand
laurels crown you now;
and a shining diadem
be on your glorious brow![48]

In the poem "The Combat: Urbiztondo, Terror of Jolo," Rizal describes the valor of Governor-General Antonio de Urbiztondo, whose troops spearheaded the attack against the Muslims of Jolo, earning him the title "conqueror of Jolo." Upon landing on the shores of Jolo, Urbiztondo had only one thing in mind—victory. As Spanish troops prepared for battle, he said: "Friends, the laurel of victory upon your valor depends. I would prefer to perish than to retreat in shame; behold the Nation entrusts you with its holy and noble name."[49]

Rizal, however, called Urbiztondo "the Lion of Castille" and glorified him in mythical proportions:

Fallen are the eight ramparts
of the Moros of Jolo
to the thunder of Mars above
and Urbiztondo below!

Ah, noble Spain, these men
like heroes of Lepanto are;
they are those who were in Pavia
the thunderbolts of war!

Fire consumes the castles
and palaces; and devours
all that Jolo possesses
and in this assault of ours.

Sultan Muhammad flees
Impious tyrant and foe;
And all the valiant warriors,
Singing, enter Jolo.[50]

A summary of *Noli Me Tangere* will help us better appreciate the novel and its Basque characters:

> Crisóstomo Ibarra, the son of a wealthy Creole landlord [he is actually a fourth-generation Basque], is betrothed from early youth to María Clara, the only daughter of Santiago de los Santos (Capitán Tiago). Ibarra is sent to Europe to study; in his absence his father, Rafael, runs afoul of the Spanish authorities by accidentally killing a Spanish tax-collector. He dies in prison and, as a free thinker who had stopped going to confession, is denied Christian burial by Father Dámaso, the Spanish parish priest of their lakeside hometown of San Diego.
>
> When Ibarra returns and learns of his father's fate, he is at first overcome with rage but, dedicated to the uplift of his people through education, he puts aside his plans for revenge in order to secure official approval for the establishment of the town school. But Father Salví, who has replaced Father Dámaso as parish priest, is himself in love with María Clara. At the laying of the school's cornerstone, Ibarra is almost killed in an obviously contrived accident and is saved only by the intervention of Elías, a mysterious boatman whom he had earlier rescued from death during an outing on the lake.
>
> Father Dámaso too is vehemently and openly opposed to the marriage between Ibarra and María Clara. At a public dinner after the school opening ceremony he insults the memory of Ibarra's father; Ibarra loses his head and is about to kill him when María Clara stops his hand. Ibarra, automatically ex-

communicated for laying violent hands on a priest, is forbidden to see María Clara again. Father Dámaso arranges for her marriage instead to Linares, his Spanish relative. Worse is still to happen; Father Salví's head sacristan recruits the desperate and the oppressed of San Diego for an uprising allegedly in the name and money of Ibarra; the plot is denounced by the parish priest to the constabulary and is suppressed; the young liberals of the town, with Ibarra at their head, are arrested and charged with rebellion. There is no proof against Ibarra until María Clara is persuaded to surrender to Father Salví and the authorities some letters of dubious loyalty which Ibarra had written to her from abroad.

Ibarra is found guilty but is liberated from prison by Elías. He confronts María Clara with her treachery and she confesses that she was forced to exchange his letters for some of Father Dámaso, which Father Salví had found in the parish house. The letters would have proved that her real father was the friar. Ibarra, having forgiven María Clara, flees with Elías up to the lake but they are sighted by a constabulary patrol; one of them is killed; who survives remains a mystery until a dying man buries Ibarra's treasure at the foot of his great-grandfather's (Pedro Ibarramendia) grave. María Clara, believing Ibarra dead, refuses to go on with her marriage with Linares; she had planned to run away afterwards to join her lover.

Father Dámaso pleads with her; he had not realized how much she loved Ibarra, he had only opposed their marriage and persecuted Ibarra's family because he could not bear the thought of her becoming a wife of a native (a Basque descendant to be exact), without privileges, without rights. When she threatens to kill herself, Father Dámaso consents at last to her entering the convent of Saint Clare; here the chaplain is Father Salví, who is waiting for the promotion due to him for frustrating the uprising in San Diego. The story ends with a glimpse of a young nun on the roof of the convent bewailing her wrongs amid the thunder and lighting of a storm.[51]

When Rizal chose a Basque descendant as a leading character in his novels, he would have been aware of the division among the Spanish ethnic groups in the Philippines. Rizal's narration of the life of Pedro Eibarramendía, Crisóstomo's great-grandfather also captures developments in the Philippines during the last decades of the eighteenth century. That Pedro Eibarramendía was a member of an economic society; that he cultivated indigo; and that he was actively involved in agriculture and scientific studies clearly alludes to the role played by the Basque-inspired Royal Society of the Friends of the Country during that epoch.

Rizal may also have been cognizant of the Basques' participation in the Carlist wars in Spain and that their independent-mindedness was often viewed with suspicion by the colonial government and the ecclesiastical authorities. As years passed,

Basque descendants, like Crisóstomo and his father, Don Rafael, began identifying themselves first as Filipinos (the term was originally applied to Philippine-born Spaniards) and ended up defending Philippine interests against mother Spain. Crisóstomo's establishment of a school in honor of his father can be considered a manifestation of his nativization and concern for the future of the Philippines and its people. Such is the nature of the transformation of Ibarra from a peace-loving reformist and Spanish loyalist in *Noli Me Tangere* into a fanatical revolutionary in *El Filibusterismo* bent on destroying the establishment at all cost.

Rizal's portrayal of the Ibarra family transcends the simplistic Basque stereotype. While the patriarchs, Don Pedro and Don Saturnino, are hated, despised, and feared, the later generations, Don Rafael and Crisóstomo, are well respected and loved by the town elite and peasants. In fact, the accidental discovery by Elías, the rebel, that Ibarra is of Basque ancestry and the great-grandson of Don Pedro Eibarramendía constitutes the climax of *Noli Me Tangere.*

Let us review the scene. Elias goes to Ibarra's house to inform him of the conspiracy to implicate him as leader of a rebellion against the Spanish authorities and of the threat to his life. Ibarra asks Elias to help him burn the family letters and documents that may compromise him. Rizal writes:

> And the young man [Crisóstomo Ibarra], bewildered, stunned, opened and shut drawers, gathered up papers, read letters hurriedly, tore up some and kept others, took down books and leafed through them. Elías was doing the same thing, in less confusion but with equal zeal. Then he stopped, staring at a paper in his hands, and asked hoarsely:
>
> "Did your family know Don Pedro Eibarramendía?"
>
> "Of course," Ibarra answered, opening a drawer and taking out a bundle of papers, "he was my great grandfather."
>
> "Your great grandfather, Don Pedro Eibarramendía?" Elías asked again, livid, his face distorted.
>
> "Yes," Ibarra replied offhandedly. "We shortened the name; it was too long.
>
> *"Was he Basque?"*
>
> *"A Basque?* [italics added] What's the matter with you?" Ibarra asked, surprised.
>
> Elías pressed his fists against his brow and glared at Ibarra, who fell back at the expression on his face.
>
> "You know who Don Pedro Eibarramendía was?" he asked between clenched teeth. "Don Pedro Eibarramendía was the scoundrel who falsely accused my grandfather and was the cause of all our misfortunes. It was his name I sought. God has delivered you unto me. Render me an accounting for our misfortunes!"

Crisóstomo looked at him terrified, but Elias shook him by the arm and said in a bitter voice burning with hatred:

"Look at me well; judge whether I have suffered; and you are alive, you love, you have wealth, a home, honours—you alive, you live!"

Beside himself, he ran to a small collection of arms, but he had scarcely seized two daggers when he dropped them and stared like a madman at Ibarra, who remained motionless.

"What was I going to do?" he muttered and fled from the house.[52]

This is perhaps the most compelling part of the novel. To get the story straight, Don Pedro Ibarramendía is a rich businessman in Manila, who accused his bookkeeper (Elías's grandfather) of arson when his warehouse was mysteriously gutted by fire. The bookkeeper's reputation was forever ruined, as well as that of all his descendants. Elías is mocked and socially ostracized. His sister commits suicide when her fiancé leaves her after discovering her roots. Marginalized and desperate, Elías resorts to banditry for survival and, together with other outlaws, plots to overthrow the colonial establishment. Had Elías killed Ibarra to revenge his family's misfortune, there would have been no *El Filibusterismo,* the sequel to *Noli Me Tangere.* The fact that Elías verifies that Don Pedro Eibarramendía was indeed a "Basque" reflects the Philippine view of Basques as having a strong ethnic subculture.

The numerous Basque names on the present map of the Philippines is indicative of the presence of Basque explorers and settlers. The saga of three generations of the Ibarra family in *Noli Me Tangere* shows the role of the Basques in the founding of towns and settlements or the expansion of established ones. Rizal depicts this process in the chapter on "San Diego," a once sleepy hamlet that grew into a prosperous town:

When San Diego was only a miserable bunch of huts, and deer and wild pig roamed its grass-grown streets at night, there came to it one day an old Spaniard [it was actually the Basque Pedro Ibarramendía] with deep-set eyes. He spoke Tagalog quite well, and, after going around the neighborhood, he asked for the owners of the forest and acquired it, presumably because it was known to have some hot springs, in exchange for clothes, jewelry, and a certain amount of money, which he handed over to pretenders who really had no title.

Afterwards, no one knew how, he disappeared. The simple peasants were beginning to believe he had been the victim of an enemy's spell when a fetid odor from the forest called the attention of some herdsmen. They traced it to its source and found the body of the old man in a state of putrefaction hanging from the branch of a *balete* tree.

. . . Months after, a young man, a Spanish half-breed to all appearances, arrived and said he was the son of the deceased. He established himself in those parts, dedicating himself to agriculture, especially growing indigo. Don Saturnino was taciturn, with a rather violent character, sometimes cruel, but very active and hard working. He wailed at the grave of his father and visited it from time to time. When he was getting on in years, he married a girl from Manila, by whom he had Don Rafael, the father of Crisóstomo Ibarra.

Don Rafael from an early age made himself loved by the peasants; agriculture, introduced and encouraged by his father, developed rapidly; new settlers came, behind them many Chinese. The hamlet soon became a village with a native priest; then the village became a town.[53]

Before ending this chapter, we have to answer the following questions: Why did Rizal choose a Basque descendant to be the protagonist of his novels? Was Rizal contemplating that the Basque descendants would one day lead the Philippines to independence? Probably yes. Rizal must have been familiar with the exploits of Simón Bolívar, a fifth-generation Basque, who led the liberation of South America from Spanish colonialism.

In the *El Filibusterismo,* the young, idealistic Ibarra becomes the sinister jeweler Simoun. After thirteen years, he comes back to San Diego brilliantly disguised in appearance, speech, and demeanor so that even his enemies do not recognize his true identity. Many people mistake him for "an Indian, a Portuguese, a South American, or a mulatto, the Brown Cardinal, His Black Eminence, the evil spirit of the Governor-General." Ibarra's transformation into Simoun is often compared to the situation in Alexandre Dumas's *Count of Monte Cristo,* but with a more loathsome character. Simoun is more vindictive and zealously plans the destruction of the Spanish establishment. In contrast with Ibarra's gradual, reformist stance, Simoun advocates complete independence for the Philippines by force and violence.

Using his vast wealth, Simoun ingratiates himself with the Spanish governor-general and makes friends with the authorities and religious orders. He avidly supports repressive colonial policies in regard to the Filipinos, but with the intention of inciting them to rebel. In short, he is an agent provocateur. His is not blind radicalism, however, inasmuch as he espouses a nationalism and rejects the Filipinos' dependence on Spanish tutelage. Chastising a young proponent of the establishment of a Spanish academy in the country, Simoun declares:

> You ask parity rights, the Spanish way of life, and you do not realize that what you are asking is death, the destruction of your national identity, the disappearance of your homeland, the ratification of tyranny. What is to become of you? A people without a soul, a nation without freedom; everything in you will be borrowed, even your very defects. You ask for Hispanization, and do not blush for shame when it is denied you. And even if it were given you, what would

> you do with it? What do you have to gain? At best, to become a country of military revolts, a country racked by civil wars, a republic of the greedy and the needy like some republics of South America. Now you ask for the teaching of Spanish, an inspiration that would be ridiculous if it did not entail such deplorable consequences. For you would add one more language to more than forty already spoken in these islands, no doubt so that you may understand one another less and less![54]

Simoun also denounces the teaching of Spanish to the Filipinos and defends the preservation of the native languages:

> Spanish will never be the national language because the people will never speak it. That tongue cannot express their ideas and their emotions. Each people has its own way of speaking just as it has its way of feeling. What will you do with Spanish, the few of you who speak it? You will only kill your individual personality and subject your thoughts to other minds. Instead of making yourselves free, you will make yourselves truly slaves. Nine of ten among you who presume to be educated are renegades of your own country. Whoever among you speaks Spanish is so indifferent to his own language that he can neither write nor understand it. How many have I seen who pretend not to know a single word of their native tongue! Fortunately you have a stupid government. While Russia compels the Poles to study Russian in order to enslave them, while Germany prohibits the use of French in the provinces she has just conquered from France, your government fights to keep alive your native languages, while you, on the other hand, an extraordinary people under an incredible government, struggle to get rid of your national identity. Both of you forget that as long as a people keep its own language, they keep a pledge of liberty, just as a man is free as long as he can think for himself. Language is a people's way of thinking.[55]

Toward the end of the novel, Simoun discovers that his beloved María Clara has died before they can meet again. The tragic news weakens his desire to struggle, and his plan to ignite a revolution fails. Wounded and frustrated, he flees to a house beside the Pacific and commits suicide by drinking poison.

In June 1892, José Rizal founded the Liga Filipina (Philippine League), a patriotic organization, to advocate peaceful political and social reforms in the Philippines. Since the Spanish colonial government and ecclesiastical authorities considered him a dangerous enemy of Spain because of his subversive writings, Rizal was exiled to Dapitan in Mindanao from July 1892 to July 1896. He volunteered to serve as a doctor for the Spanish forces in Cuba, where an insurrection was raging. But before he could leave the Philippines, a rebellion broke out in August 1896. Like Ibarra in *Noli Me Tangere,* Rizal was implicated in a rebellion he did not have knowledge of.

He was tried for sedition and was executed by firing squad on December 30, 1896, at the age of thirty-five.

Marcelo de Azcárraga, the Philippine-born Basque, could have saved Rizal's life. As Spain's minister of war, he is said to have ignored a petition of clemency that could have halted the execution.[56] Rizal's life was inextricably intertwined with the Basques, who were both his heroes and his nemeses.

Chapter Nine

During the American and Japanese Occupations

> The Filipino nation ought to feel great sympathies for the Basques, since its history has developed in constant contact with members of the industrious and indefatigable Basque family.
>
> José Manuel de Zendoya, "El Pueblo Basko"

The United States annexed the Philippines upon the signing of the Treaty of Paris on December 10, 1898, several months after a one-sided victory in the Philippine episode of the Spanish-American War. The United States paid U.S.$20 million as compensation to Spain for developing the archipelago. The Filipinos, who had earlier fought the Spaniards to attain their cherished independence, once again succumbed to a colonial power. Their experiment in self-rule, with the establishment of the Malolos Republic in January 1899, the first constitutional democracy proclaimed in Asia, was short-lived. They resisted valiantly but were no match against the superior American forces. With the capture of General Emilio Aguinaldo, the revolutionary leader, in March 1901, the Filipino struggle for independence was all but lost.

The price of American sovereignty over the Philippines, however, had not been cheap. By the time the Philippines was pacified, the campaign had cost the U.S. government an estimated $300 million.[1] American casualties included 4,234 dead (scarcely any bodies were ever brought home) and 2,818 soldiers wounded, with hundreds more returning home to die of service-related diseases like malaria and dysentery. On the Filipino side of the ledger, the entry was larger. Sixteen thousand rebel corpses (revolutionaries as far as Filipinos are concerned) were counted by the Americans. The true toll exceeded twenty thousand. About two hundred civilians were dead of pestilence and disease.[2]

The Americans moved swiftly to win the support of the people, particularly the Filipino intellectuals and businessmen. They were immensely successful in co-opting these elites, as well as the big landowners, securing their collaboration and, in the process, effecting a satisfactory and enduring compromise between American and Philippine capitalism and nationalism.[3] There was no outright appropriation of the haciendas of the Spaniards (including those of the Basques). Many of the established business were left alone insofar as they professed allegiance to the United States. The U.S. occupation also did not curtail Basque immigration. To the contrary, young

Basque males who wanted to avoid military conscription or who were jobless in Spain joined their relatives in the Philippines.

In Article IV of the Treaty of Paris, the United States agreed to admit Spanish ships and merchandise to Philippine ports "on the same terms as ships and merchandise of the United States" during a ten-year period. This had a stabilizing effect on trade and normalized the flow of business transactions. As a consequence, the Basques found it natural to ally themselves with the Americans. Since the Philippines was now a U.S. colony, all Filipinos, including Philippine-born Basques, were technically American citizens and, in theory, enjoyed the rights and privileges of that nation.

Some influential Basques were given important positions in the incipient colonial bureaucracy. José Ruíz de Luzurriaga, for example, was appointed as a member of the Second Philippine Commission, the civilian legislature headed by William Howard Taft, and later became one of the founders of the Federalista Party in 1901, the first political party in the Philippines whose principal platform was to advocate immediate peace and openly support U.S. statehood.

Economically, American sovereignty provided a big boost to Basque business, as Philippine products such as sugar, abaca, copra, and tobacco received preferential entry into the huge U.S. market. Furthermore, a free trade agreement allowed all Philippine exports unlimited access to the United States and shielded them from foreign competition. Basques in the sugar business made windfall profits. The Luzurriaga-owned Victorias Milling Company transformed itself into one of the world's biggest mills during the American occupation, and its refined sugar was sold straightaway on the shelves of Safeway supermarkets in the United States.

Sugar production shot up. From 1902 to 1938, the area planted to sugar in the Philippines rose from 72,000 hectares to 230,000 hectares, an increase of 320 percent. Many sugar mills financed by the Philippine National Bank were established in the 1920s, and totaled forty-five by 1934. Production had increased so dramatically that U.S. sugar producers lobbied the U.S. Congress to limit competition from Philippine sugar.[4] By this time, sugar accounted for 60 percent of total Philippine exports. However, the Tydings-McDuffie Act of 1934, the law that prepared the Philippines for independence, among other acts, limited the entry of duty-free sugar to the American market and regulated the sugar industry. Its effect was devastating, as sugar export dropped by half.

The most important haciendas and sugar plantations in the country before World War II continued to be Basque-owned: Central San Isidro owned by Bidaurrezaga; Central Palma, managed by Gurrucharri and collectively owned by Federico Soloaga, Carmelo Imaz, and Donato Inchausti; Grandes Haciendas of the Uriarte brothers under the direction of Hilario Zamacona and others; Hacienda Navarra of the Oquinena family; Carmen Grande and Carmen Chica, administered by Eugenio and Santi de Enchanojauregui; haciendas and coconut plantations of the Aldecoa,

Isasi, and Erquiaga families; haciendas of Arraza and Salutregui; Hacienda San Antonio, managed by Tomás Sagastasoloa; Hacienda San José of Celestino Mendiola and Hermogenes Inunciaga; Hacienda Euskara and Baskonia of Marino Gamboa; Hacienda Domingo Menchaca, administered by his political protégé, Roberto Llantada Larrasquitu, later by the Txomin brothers, Andrés and Isaías, and Antonio Menchaca.[5]

It was during the first decade of the American occupation that Basque nationalism reached the Philippines. It was a powerful force that united the Philippine Basques with their motherland. Before the foundation of the Basque Nationalist Party by Sabino de Arana in 1895, the Basques, although very aware of their distinct identity, did not attempt to unite into an independent state or organize themselves as an ethnic group.

Sabino de Arana y Goiri was born in 1865 in a suburb of Bilbao.[6] He came from a family of industrialists engaged in shipbuilding. His father, a Carlist supporter, went into exile in southern France to escape persecution. Sabino later studied in Barcelona, where he was greatly impressed by Catalonian nationalism. Though he spoke only Spanish, he realized that Basque nationalism would not prosper unless Euskara was given the special status it deserved. Hence, he painstakingly learned the Basque language and started writing and publishing his political ideas in it. He even invented new words to further his movement, among them the word "Euskadi," to refer to the Basque fatherland, a nonexistent concept at that time. In 1894, Arana and his brother Luis founded the first Centro Vasco, a cultural propaganda office that also served as a sort of folklore center and informal club for nationalists. In just a few years, Centros Vascos had spread not only throughout the Basque Provinces, but also to cities in North and South America and the Philippines where Basques had migrated.[7]

Arana also designed the red, green, and white flag that is now used officially by the Basque Country's government. Many Basques rallied behind Arana, and the Basque political movement was born in 1895. He died prematurely of the rare Addison's disease in 1903, at age thirty-eight, but his work lived on. The political party he founded continues to dominate Basque politics to this day. The famous Basque writer Miguel de Unamuno, in his epilogue to Wenceslao Retana's *Vida y escritos del Dr. José Rizal* (*Life and Writings of Dr. José Rizal*), published in Madrid in 1907, made an interesting comparison between the nationalisms of José Rizal and Sabino de Arana. Unamuno remarked: "Arana has a close relation with Rizal, and like Rizal, he died misunderstood by his own people and others. And like the filibuster Rizal, Arana was also called filibuster or something similar. They were the same even in trivial details, although they were highly significant. . . . Arana started the reform of the Basque orthography and Rizal did the same in Tagalog."[8]

On July 31, 1909, the feast day of the Basque patron saint Ignatius of Loyola, some Basques in Iloilo, inspired by the ideas of Sabino Arana, founded the

Euzkeldun Batzokija, the first Basque nationalist society in the Philippines. The board of directors consisted of Cornelio de Elordi, president; Juan Tomás de Elordi, vice president; Julio de Salutregui, treasurer; and Elías de Goñi, board member. The Basque club aimed to create a strong sense of nationalism and ethnic solidarity among the Philippine Basques. In fact, as early as 1907, pro-nationalist Basque sentiment in Iloilo ran high. A baptismal record book in Saint Joseph Church has a Basque language entry, "Marco ta Barandiaran' tar Erinea" (it would normally have been written as "Marco de Barandiaran y Erinea"). This nationalist mode of registering a birth was used by a Navarrese couple from Lizarra and is possibly the earliest usage of its kind anywhere in the world.[9]

The Basque society was located in the Hotel Bilbao, which had been established by the Elordi brothers, Cornelio and Juan Tomás, in the early 1900s. Famous for its good food, the hotel began as a boarding house for the many Basque bachelors in Iloilo and *hacenderos* of Negros. As the organization expanded, the Euzkeldun Batzokija's activities moved to the English Club building and later to the Panay Club, previously the American Club. The hotel was closed after World War II.[10]

The Basque society, which was known by the name of Euskadi (accented on the *u*) by non-Basques, collected money to help Basques in distress pay their hospital bills or their way back to the Basque Country. Every year the members celebrated Saint Ignatius's day with a mass in Basque, followed by a banquet with singing and dancing in the Hotel Bilbao. This religious feast day was observed in the Basque communities of Manila, Legazpi, and Cebu as well.[11]

Saint Ignatius is more the patron of the Bizkaians and Gipuzkoans. The Navarrese were inclined to celebrate the feast of their patron, San Fermín, on July 17. However, at one time many Navarrese participated in the Saint Ignatius Day proceedings as well. For instance, of the group of eight dancers that performed during the festivities in Manila in 1932, two were Navarrese. At the following banquet of Basque nationalists, of the seventeen bachelors, five were Navarrese and the rest Bizkaians. However, with the beginning of the Spanish civil war in 1936, during which Navarre supported General Franco's revolt against the Spanish Republic, political tensions developed between the two groups. In a photograph taken in 1939 on Saint Ignatius Day at the Hacienda La Euskara in San Carlos (Negros Occidental), only one of the twenty-four celebrants is Navarrese.[12]

On March 31, 1937, Franco launched the military offensive against Bizkaia. The air force—whose core group was composed of German and Italian pilots—pounded the cities of Eibar, Durango, Gernika, Zornotza, Mungia, and Bilbao, causing hundreds of deaths. As depicted in the famous painting of Pablo Picasso, Gernika was razed. In fact, the town had no military installation and was not sheltering combatants. It became a prime target because it was the place where the fueros of the Basques were traditionally renewed by the Spanish monarchs. It was therefore a symbol of Basque autonomy. The destruction of Gernika was meant to crush the

Basque spirit of resistance. The Basque residents in the Philippines were divided. Those from Bizkaia and Gipuzkoa loathed Franco, while those from Navarre backed him. In fact, Navarre was the first province in Spain to throw its support to Franco and supplied troops to the nationalist cause. One of Franco's able military commanders, General Emilio Mola, was Navarrese.

When the Spanish civil war broke out in 1936, Basque exiles like Saturnino de Uriarte and Estanislao Garovilla settled in Cebu and established the most important fish-canning factory in the country, the Cebu Fishing Corporation. Uriarte was previously a partner in Garovilla Hermanos y Compañia, a canning factory in Bermeo (Bizkaia). Basque philanthropists such as Marino de Gamboa and Manuel María de Ynchausti, and companies, like Aldecoa-Erquiaga and Company, extended assistance to Basque refugees.[13]

Although the Basques in the Philippines were concerned about the Spanish civil war, they were more preoccupied with the imminent war in the Pacific. Japan had invaded China in 1939, and its relations with the United States had become antagonistic and bellicose. The Philippine Commonwealth government under President Manuel L. Quezon hired General Douglas MacArthur, the newly retired chairman of the Joint Chiefs of Staff of the U.S. Army, as field marshal to prepare the Philippine defense in the event of war.

On December 8, 1941, Pearl Harbor was attacked and destroyed by the Japanese Imperial Navy. Days after, Manila was declared an open city to spare it from destruction. The American air force bases in Clark (Pampanga) and Iba (Zambales)) in central Luzon were destroyed. The Japanese forces entered Manila on January 2, 1942, without a fight. The combined American and Filipino forces defended Bataan in a last-ditch effort to halt the Japanese advances. On April 9, Bataan fell, and Japan became the new colonial master of the Philippines. But the resistance movement continued.

During the war, Spaniards, including the Basques, were viewed with suspicion and hostility by many Filipinos. Some Spaniards collaborated outright with the Japanese and openly rejoiced over the initial defeat of the Americans, believing naively that the Japanese would return the Philippines to Spain. All the *castilas* (Spaniards), therefore, became the target of resentment and were vilified as the "Fifth Column," a derogatory term meaning opportunists, potential traitors, and outright collaborationists. In fact, assets of Basque families and companies, such as Aboitiz, Ayala, Elizalde, were frozen by the Philippine Commonwealth government, although they supported the American military. For instance, the vessels of La Naviera, a shipping firm partly owned by the Aboitiz and Company, were put at the disposition of the American forces. Aboitiz and Company was singled out because it had had a Japanese director on its board and exported large quantities of copra to Japan in the 1930s, obviously used to fuel Japan's war machine.[14]

The hatred against the Spaniards was further exacerbated by the fact that General

Francisco Franco, the *caudillo* (supreme ruler) of Spain, sent a congratulatory message to the Japanese command immediately after the fall of Corregidor and Bataan. Spain was one of the eleven nations aligned with the Axis powers that recognized the puppet government established by the Japanese military forces in the Philippines.[15]

Most Basques were fiercely opposed to the Japanese occupation. Many Basque families, like the Elizaldes, the Luzurriagas, and the Legarretas, contributed indirectly and directly to the Philippine guerrilla movement. Others, like the Uriartes, the Bilbaos, and the Elordis, joined the resistance movement in Negros and the Visayas region. Basques in the Bicol peninsula, such as Garchitorena, Oturbe, and Ormaechea, also became guerrillas. KZRH, a radio station owned by the Elizalde family of Manila, continued to broadcast pro-Allied programs until it was shut down by the Japanese army. The Elizalde brothers, Juan and Manuel, were incarcerated in Fort Santiago because of their anti-Japanese activities. Juan was later killed by the Japanese in prison.

Basque participation in the resistance movement against the Japanese imperial forces in the Philippines is depicted vividly in the accounts of Higinio de Uriarte, a third-generation Basque, in his book *A Basque Among the Guerrillas of Negros.*[16] The book narrates his war experiences as an operative for the Allied Intelligence Bureau (AIB). One of his outstanding contributions, although kept secret for security reasons even after the war, was the setting up of two radio transmitters, the only ones operational in the Philippines prior to the return of the American forces in October 1944.

Higinio de Uriarte was born in January 1917 of Basque parents, Pedro de Uriarte and Candida Zamacona, in the town of La Carlota in Negros, an island about six hundred kilometers south of Manila. He was popularly known as "Castila," the generic term used by native Filipinos for Spaniards. As an enlisted man, he held the rank of captain (ASNO 47952) and used the nom de guerre "Gudari," the Basque word for soldier. He had an elder brother, Juan Antonio, and his parents were residing in Bilbao when the war in the Pacific broke out in December 1941.

The battles of Bataan and Corregidor has overshadowed the heroism and valor of guerrilla warfare waged by Filipino civilians in other parts of the archipelago, including the saga of the people of Negros recounted in Uriarte's book. He claimed that the intelligence reports on the activities of Japanese forces in the Visayas that they forwarded to General MacArthur's headquarters in Australia hastened the end of Japanese occupation of the Philippines.

He explained the cause of his involvement in the guerrilla movement in an emotional fashion:

> I, an outsider—an alien in a manner of speaking—was drawn into the conflict of the Filipinos for the same reasons that prompt all men who love freedom to resist

> tyranny. I made the Filipino cause against the Japanese my own. I was not only a witness but a participant in their fight for freedom. I speak of my humble share of the struggle to give testimony to their courage and patriotism, and to what they were able to accomplish in the face of insurmountable difficulties.
>
> . . . I have come to realize that one does not have to be a native Filipino to be a good Filipino. You will note in this book that there were many Basques and Spaniards who made common cause with their Filipino brothers.
>
> We, an alien race, who joined the Resistance Movement, look upon the Philippines as our second Fatherland. Many of us were born and raised in this country. It is here we have built our homes and created our families. In this soil we have sunk deeper roots because we have faith in the greatness of the Philippines.[17]

Higinio de Uriarte staunchly claimed that, as a Basque, his political convictions were completely antitotalitarian. He added that his sympathies and loyalties were with and for the Filipinos and the Philippines, which, for two generations, had given the Uriarte family protection and shelter. The Uriartes had arrived in Negros around 1840, among the first wave of Basque immigrants who settled and developed the land in the Visayan Islands.

A hundred years later, in the 1940s, the Uriarte family owned shares in various corporations and possessed three haciendas, named Fe, Vizcaya, and Candelaria. The three haciendas, measuring 1,700 hectares, were planted to sugar and rice and had a pre-war annual yield of 5,000 tons of sugar and 2,000 sacks of unmilled rice. Bizkaian Basques like the Uriartes looked on the Franco regime with disdain. The Spanish civil war (1936–1939), still fresh in their minds, had resulted in the destruction of Gernika and other cities in Bizkaia, and the eventual suppression of Basque language and culture.

Uriarte himself was not taken seriously when he sought membership in the resistance movement, given that many of the landed elite of Spanish descent collaborated with the Japanese Imperial Army in order to retain their properties and protect their families. As he admitted:

> My brother and I took a stand that was directly opposite of that taken by some of our race, our fellow Spaniards. For these people, I am sorry to say, the Japanese invasion was a rich opportunity for personal and selfish advantages. They thought they would be better off under the Japanese than under the Americans. It was only gradually as events unfolded that they realized to their dismay and consternation that they had been miserably deceived and misled. Those who welcomed and catered to the new regime or compromised with the invaders were ignored and regarded all the same as "whites" and consequently hostile to the Japanese policy of "Asia for the Asians."[18]

José Francisco Castaño, the Spanish consul in Manila, corroborated Ugarte's observation and admitted that many Spaniards were indeed close to the Japanese and that a number of them took the opportunity to enrich themselves with the help of the Japanese invaders. Some Spaniards and Basques were murdered or executed by the guerrillas in Camarines (Bicol) and in the Visayas. In some cases, the killings had overtones of personal vendettas or class resentments, such as with the landowning Basque family of Toribio Echarri of Hacienda Izarra.

According to Spanish Consul Castaño, the killings were more for political than ethnic reasons. He further noted: "The truth surfaced that there was no single 'Basque separatist' who was killed, as many of the Basques make up the Spanish colony in Negros. This group is composed mostly of Basque nationalists, supporters of the Republic, and were against the policies of the Falange [Franco regime], that is why some of them decided to join the resistance movement."[19]

On joining the guerrillas, Uriarte's main task was to contribute and solicit funds for the operations. Because of his civilian status and Caucasian features, he was not readily suspected of aiding the resistance movement against Japanese rule. Later, when Uriarte joined the Allied Intelligence Bureau, considered "the elite of the guerrillas," since it was in direct contact with the headquarters of General MacArthur, he was assigned to Luzon. This was a dangerous mission since Luzon was under strong Japanese control.

Uriarte had to use different identities in order to elude detection and, from time to time, had to invoke Spanish nationality to avoid arrest. His unit was instrumental in providing intelligence reports on the Japanese air defenses. With this intelligence, the American air force was able to cripple the Japanese forces in the Visayas, allowing General MacArthur to land almost unopposed in Leyte on October 20, 1944.[20]

In January 1945, the Allied forces advanced northward to retake Luzon. Uriarte's comrades guided the Americans in liberating Manila. Incidentally, the U.S. Cavalry Division's tank brigade was spearheaded by a unit called the "Fighting Basques" from Idaho.[21] One can imagine the dramatic reaction of Philippine Basques when they met the Idaho Basques who formed part of the American forces.

The liberation of Manila proved bloody and destructive. Only Warsaw, Poland, suffered greater devastation in World War II. There were thousands of civilian casualties. Japanese forces committed all sorts of atrocities and went on a killing spree as they prepared to die to the last man. This was a system called *senko-seisaku,* a three-part paradigm of "kill all, burn all, and destroy all." Spaniards and Basques were not exempted from the massacre. It is estimated that about 235 Spanish nationals died. One consular official wrapped himself in the Spanish flag to emphasize his neutrality. Nonetheless, he was shot dead in the street by the Japanese. So intense had their xenophobia become that any Caucasian, or anybody resembling one, became a target for extermination.[22]

Basque religious were not spared, as we can appreciate from the memoir of Fray Bienvenido de Arbeiza, a Basque Capuchin friar. He took over the Capuchin mission after the death of other Capuchin fathers, six of whom were Navarrese, along with two Gipuzkoans and one Bizkaian. The following is Fray Arbeiza's summary of the tragedy of Intramuros, the old district of Manila:

> On February 5, 1945, the Japanese forced the people of Intramuros to gather in Hollywood cinema, the churches of San Agustin and San Francisco, and in the cathedral and closed the gates of the walled city. Meanwhile the American artillery continued to bombard the city walls until they opened breaches. On the night of February 19, Japanese soldiers took the Spanish priests and laymen from the San Agustin church and brought them to the cathedral, where a refuge was built by the Japanese at the right hand of the temple's entrance.
>
> Two Filipino assistants of the Capuchins were pulled out, sprayed with gasoline, and burnt alive. Before entering a larger refuge, a Japanese soldier ordered them to squeeze themselves together as many as possible. They were told to remain standing since they would not stay there for a long time. Following the soldier's orders, about eighty of them stood and jammed together. Among them were our friars of Intramuros: M. R. P. Florencio de Lezáun, superior of the mission; Fr. Félix de Iguzquiza, discrete; Fr. Ladislao de Busturia and Brethren Fr. Valentín Azcoitia, Fr. Elzeario de Sarasate and Fr. Ignacio de Vidania. Once inside, they were suspicious and concerned but they kept silent. A priest invited them to an act of contrition and gave them the funeral absolution. Soon the slaughter began, as bombs and grenades were launched through the refuge's skylights. Those who rushed to the doors to escape met rifle and machine-gun fire. Only the Augustinian priest, Belarmino Celis, and the layman Rocamora escaped alive, who, seriously injured, waited until the American vanguard entered. Capuchin fathers Santiago de Ibiricu and Raimundo de Labiano, and Pacífico de Villatuerta, a parish priest and coadjutor of the Singalong church in Manila, had been pulled out of their church by the Japanese and were beheaded in a nearby brook.
>
> Out of the twenty churches of the walled city of Manila, only that of San Agustin remained standing but devastated. Dr. Jesús Arocena had survived the massacre, but was later assassinated by a Japanese soldier, while holding a white flag, in a procession of women and children.[23]

Other Basque religious who died during the massacre were Juan Cavanas, an Augustinian brother, and Fray Mariano Alegria and Fray Hernán Biurrun and Brother Juan Machicote of the Recollects. Fray Bienvenido de Arbeiza later took charge of the management of the Capuchin mission. The house of Claudio Luzurriaga of Manila, one of the few left standing, became an asylum for numerous refugees. The valuable crown of the Virgin of Lourdes of the Capuchin church in Manila, together with its treasure, was saved while kept in the vault of Raimundo Soloaga's office in Binondo (Manila). This treasure was sold at the end of the war to build a new church in Quezon City. The images of the Virgins of La Guía and Lourdes were also saved. In 1948, Fray Blas de Guernica raised the walls of the church of Ermita parish with temporary construction materials. A few years later, Fathers Alberto de Urdiain and Carlos de Urzainqui would initiate the construction of a concrete church. In 1950, Salvador Araneta (descendant of Basques from Gipuzkoa) donated the grounds for the new chruch of Lourdes. At the inauguration the Capuchin bishop Miguel Angel Olano Urteaga was in attendance.[24]

After the war, the Basques struggled to rebuild their fortunes, many of them starting from scratch. But the scars and wounds of battle took time to heal. The issue of collaboration still divided the nation. The testimonies of guerrillas such as Higinio de Uriarte were sought after to determine the culprits. His reluctance to vindicate the guilty would earn him many powerful enemies, and he and his family became targets of harassment. On July 4, 1946, the United States granted the country its independence, and the Republic of the Philippines was inaugurated. For many Basques there was the choice of whether to stay or leave the Philippines.

Chapter Ten

Descendants in Philippine Society

The Philippines is my home.

Jaime Zobel de Ayala, former chair and president, Ayala Corporation

Since World War II there has been an exodus of Basques from the Philippines to Australia, Latin America, the United States, and Europe. The ones who remain are likely to send their children to Europe or the United States to be educated. Some of those return to take care of a family business. However, it is easy to detect a nervousness among the Philippine Basques regarding their future.[1] The Basques who decided to stay in the Philippines after World War II had to downplay their ethnicity. They had to embrace Philippine nationality either by choice or out of sheer necessity. For some, like Higinio de Uriarte, the process of naturalization was a legal nightmare. Being a Spanish subject also became an irritant in his application for naturalization.

Uriarte's petition for Filipino citizenship was initially denied, notwithstanding his services in the resistance movement and his demonstrated loyalty to the Philippines. In its ruling, dated November 2, 1946, the court of First Instance of Negros Occidental cited two reasons: that his petition "is not accompanied by a declaration of intention which is required of the petitioner to file one year prior to the filing of his petition of admission to Philippine citizenship with the Bureau of Justice his intention to become a citizen of the Philippines as provided under Section 5 of the Naturalization Law"; and "that under Section 4 of the same Act, paragraph H, the petitioner being a Spanish subject or citizen other than of the United States, no documentary evidence is filed to establish the fact that laws of Spain grant Filipinos the right to become naturalized citizens of said country."[2] After a long delay, Uriarte was granted Filipino citizenship in 1962.

The sugar barons of Negros, the majority of whom were Basques, collectively enjoyed economic and, by extension, political clout. The boom in sugar export was one of the driving forces of the economy, making the Philippines the second most prosperous country in Asia after Japan. Basque hacienda owners, however, had to contend with social unrest as the Communist ideology swept the countryside. The new republic ushered in a new conflict, this time not between Filipinos and invaders but between the rich and the poor. Communism began to take root among oppressed peasants and laborers and attracted radical adherents. Disgruntled tenant farmers and peasants resented the prevailing feudal system. They demanded that the government carry out land reform. Manuel María de Ynchausti's voluntary land divestiture in the 1930s had been the rare exception. Notwithstanding the insurgency problems that beset Negros and the waning of the sugar industry, particularly during the 1970s, the Basques and their descendants tenaciously held on. They had made the Philippines their home.

Some Basques enthusiastically joined the government service of the fledgling republic. Joaquin Miguel Elizalde became the first Philippine ambassador to Washington from 1946 to 1951 and later served as secretary of foreign affairs from 1952 to 1953 during the administration of President Elpidio Quirino. Mariano Garchitorena became the secretary of agriculture in the same cabinet. Salvador Z. Araneta, whose roots could be traced to Gipuzkoa, was also a prominent politician and nationalist. He served in numerous positions in government: secretary of economic coordination under President Elpidio Quirino, secretary of agriculture and member of the National Economic Council under President Ramon Magsaysay, and member of the Constitutional Convention in 1933 and 1971. He was known as an ardent nationalist who fought the interventionist and economic policies favorable to the United States. He advocated protectionism for the welfare of infant industries and local retailers. He founded the NEPA (National Economic Protectionism Association) in the 1930s. He was a major proponent of a federal system of government of the Philippines and collective leadership. His ideas on many aspects of governance still resonate today. He was "a man ahead of his time."[3]

A multifaceted man, Araneta also founded the Feati Institute of Technology in 1946 to serve the needs of the Far Eastern Air Transport Inc. (FEATI), the first carrier in the Philippines after the war. It flew to Hong Kong, Shanghai, and San Francisco. Araneta also established the Gregorio Araneta University foundation. As an industrialist, he established Republic Flour Mills (RFM), still one of the country's profitable companies, Republic Soya, Feati Industries (electric motors), AIA Feed Mills (animal feeds), and AIA Biological Laboratories (animal vaccines).[4]

Nowadays Basque descendants stay away from politics and do what they have done best—business.[5] Many of them have flourished. For instance, Francisco Eizmendi Jr. was for many years the president of San Miguel Corporation, the Philippines' biggest beverage and food company. At present, Xavier Loinaz is the president of the Bank of the Philippine Islands, the largest and oldest private commercial bank in the country; and Fred Elizalde acts as chairman of the Manila Broadcasting Company, the biggest radio broadcasting company in the Philippines.

Some Basques also made names in Philippine sports. Carlos Loyzaga became the country's dominant basketball player during the 1950s and early 1960s. He is considered the greatest Filipino basketball player of all time.[6] Born on the island of Mindoro in 1930, Loyzaga stood six foot three, a towering height for a Filipino cager.

With his shooting and rebounding prowess, not to mention his handsome European looks, he easily became a superstar.

With Loyzaga on the team, the Philippines dominated the Asian Games, winning four straight championships—New Delhi in 1951, Manila in 1954, Tokyo in 1958, and Jakarta in 1962. Loyzaga also played in the 1952 Helsinki Olympics and the 1956 Melbourne Olympics. One of his teammates in the Melbourne Games was another Basque Filipino, Martin Urra.

Loyzaga's most memorable achievement was in 1954 as a member of the amazing Philippine team that placed third in the second World Basketball Championship in Rio de Janeiro, Brazil. Loyzaga was also named to the all-tournament team. The United States won the championship by beating host Brazil, 62–41 in the finals. The Philippines took third place by beating the highly favored Uruguay team, 67–63. Loyzaga also played for the Philippine team that placed eighth in the world basketball tournament in Chile in 1959.[7]

Loyzaga would again lead the Philippines to championships in the ABC tournament in Manila in 1960 and in Taipei in 1963. He also coached the Philippine team that won the 1967 ABC championship in Seoul in 1967.

One sport in which Basques made a great impact on Philippine society was their own game of pelota. Popularly known as jai alai, which means "happy feast" in Basque, the game was initially the sport of Manila's elite. In fact, the proceeds of the competitions were donated to charities and other philanthropic works. Jai alai is touted as the world's fastest ball game, with the missile reaching a speed of 250 kph. During its heyday, it was described in the Philippines as the "game of a thousand thrills."

According to some accounts, Basque pelota was first introduced in the Philippines in 1899 by a group of aficionados headed by the Elizalde brothers, Tiburcio, Santiago, and Joaquín. They organized friendly matches with other Basques such as Navascues, Arregui, Matute, Nieto, Soloaga, Pascual, Larranaga, Inchusti, and Garriz.[8] This version, however, is *pelota a mano,* which is played with the bare hand. There was also a small fronton in the compound of the Casino Español, constructed in 1918, where *cesta punta* (wicker basket) was played.

The second wave of aficionados included José Arriola, Juan Tellechea, Dionisio Leguizamon, Martín de Eiguren, Nestor Gamechogoicoechea, the brothers Sarasola, Zabaljauregui, Cincunegui, and Azparren, Jose Egozcua, L. Garteiz, L. Garriz, Angel and Juan Miguel Elizalde, Rafael Iturralde, and Pedro Uriarte.[9]

The Manila fronton was constructed in 1939. It was designed by Welton Beckett, a famous American architect. With its sleek and streamlined design fashionable in the 1930s, the structure became an icon. The games were formally inaugurated on October 17, 1940, by a team of Basque *pelotaris* composed of Urrutia, Agirre, Arana, Unanue, Salsamendi, Girasola, and Aranzibia. Jai alai became an instant hit among Manila's elite. It slowly evolved into a exclusive sport for the rich, much like golf nowadays.

Manila old-timers nostalgically remember jai alai matches as a social event that the Spanish, Basque, or mestizo gentry attended in nineteenth-century coat and tie, drinking, dancing, and generally making merry at any of the three full-band nightclubs overlooking the fronton. The games were mostly holiday and weekend happenings at that time. Spectators placed bets on the numbered players through gofers.[10]

The Japanese invasion in January 1942 disrupted the sport. Some Basque pelotaris, such as Garriz, Catro, and Soucheiron, died during the Japanese occupation. The fronton was also damaged during the liberation of Manila. Other pelotaris, like José María Aranzibia, resorted to selling whiskey and Tanduay rum, procured from the Navarrese Manolo Elizalde, to the American soldiers.[11]

A small group of Basque pelotaris that remained in the Philippines after the war revived jai alai in 1948. These included Nieto, Dampierre, Olaso, Aguirre, Egozcue, Uriarte, and Gamecho. The games were managed by A. Argarate, while the organizing committee was presided over by Manuel Elizalde. These were the golden years for the Basque pelotaris. Since jai alai became a prosperous betting game, they received celebrity status. In the 1950s the Filipino pelotaris participated in various world championships. Despite being new in the sport, the Filipinos made a good showing. In 1967, a second fronton was opened in Cebu that catered to the Basques from Cebu and Negros. These aficionados would troop to Manila just to watch the inter-island competition.

Jai alai became so popular that the former few-days-a-week schedule expanded to six days. As the game shed its elitist origins, more and more Filipinos became hooked. It became so profitable that the government started regulating jai alai in 1951. During the initial years of the game, the aficionados could bet on a single player (win) or on several (forecast) among the six players.

In 1972, a new innovation, called *special llave*, was introduced. This meant that one could simply bet on the top three winning players in the order of first to third place. It also promised a huge return: a two-peso bet could win as much as a 13,000-peso jackpot. As a result, jai alai earnings skyrocketed. By 1977, the Manila fronton's average monthly earnings were 40 million pesos (U.S.$5.7 million at the exchange rate of the time).

The fronton also had three exclusive nightclub-restaurants that became the hub of the rich and famous. The best bands in the country would normally play in the Skyroom, then the most popular nightspot in Manila. During the Marcos regime, the Philippine Jai Alai and Amusement Corporation, owned by the Romualdez family, managed the fronton. But then jai alai slowly become notorious for game-fixing and massive gambling problems. Opposition to the game, particularly from the Catholic Church, grew stronger.

When Marcos was toppled by a peaceful revolution in 1986, the Manila fronton was closed. The building was converted into a passport office from 1989 to 1991, after the Foreign Affairs building was gutted by fire in 1988. Attempts were made to revive the popular betting game during the Aquino and Ramos administrations but to no avail. After the election of President Joseph Estrada in May 1998, jai alai was resurrected. But it has not recovered its former glory. Rampant game-fixing and sloppy play did not help. After a year, the venture failed. Some pelotaris imported from the Basque Country even got deported in the process. Finally in September 2000, the city government of Manila ordered the fronton demolished to make way for construction of a new hall of justice. Many people held demonstrations and petitioned the city mayor to spare the building—not because they like Basque pelota, but because the fronton's architectural design had gained fans among conservationists and history buffs. But all was in vain. One concrete manifestation of Basque culture vanished forever in the capital's landscape.

How does one explain the good fortune and prominence of the Basques in the Philippines? They are so few yet so influential. The answer perhaps lies in their character. The Basques, in general, are hardworking, thrifty, proud, determined, and obsessed with winning. More importantly, once in a foreign country and among other nationalities, ethnic consciousness among them becomes stronger and translates into a high degree of cooperation that contributes to their collective success. They are tenacious, sometimes bordering on stubbornness. They are quick to take advantage of opportunities, to the point of opportunism their critics would say. But they are also fast to abandon a losing venture and start anew. Other factors, such as political acumen and keen knowledge of the workings of the society, may also play a role. Basques have also demonstrated an ability to adapt to and take advantage of opportunities in an alien environment. But as a minority, they have always maintained a low profile.

Let us now take a look at some Basque descendants in the Philippines—Aboitiz, Ayala, Elizalde, and Ynchausti—whose stories are intimately connected with their family business. I selected these families because of their prominence. By coincidence they also represent the four provinces of the Basque Country in Spain, namely Araba, Bizkaia, Gipuzkoa, and Navarre.

Aboitiz

The patriarch of the Aboitiz family, Paulino Aboitiz, was a Basque mariner who came to the Philippines in the 1870s. Known as Txarton after his familial house "Txarton Torre,"[12] he was the second son of a farmer living near Lekeitio, Bizkaia. By custom in his town, the eldest son inherited the land, while the second took to the sea. Thus, Txarton was sent to a nearby mariners' school that had been set up by a rich sailor and where students paid no tuition.[13]

It was not unusual for young men in this land, where life was as rugged as the soil, to seek greener pastures in Spain's far-flung empire. When Paulino left the Basque Country to fulfill his required time at sea, he opted for a better life in another land. Arriving in the Philippines, he found work piloting a sailboat for a portly Leyte shipowner named Gregorio Yrastorza. Gregorio was born on the way to the Philippines, where his Basque parents were going as immigrants.[14]

Paulino eventually married Gregorio's daughter, Emilia. Guadalupe, Emilia's sister, married another Basque, Angel Moraza, who was a farmer from Vitoria, Araba. He came to the Philippines in 1868 as an *alferez cuadrillero* (petty officer) with the Spanish army. Paulino Aboitiz settled in Ormoc and Angel Moraza in Baybay. Paulino took up abaca (Manila hemp) trading and became rich. Once or twice a year he would visit his relatives in the Basque Country.

Paulino and Emilia had nine children: Guillermo, Ana, Antonia, Ramón, Carmen, Dolores, Vidal, Paulino Jr., Luis. One son, Francisco, died in early childhood. Guillermo, the oldest, was sent to his father's mariner's school. Ramón, the second son, born on November 16, 1887, helped in his father's business. The Aboitiz family had a quiet life until the Philippine revolution of 1898. When violence against Spaniards erupted in Ormoc, the Aboitiz family packed up for Cebu and then to Malitbog, where they took refuge in the home of Fernando Escaño together with the Morazas and other Spanish families. After two months, they embarked on the streamer *Escaño* for Manila, where the Morazas and Aboitizes found a house. Meanwhile, fighting between the Filipinos and Americans raged. The Aboitizes decided to return to the Basque Country to wait out the hostilities. They went back to the Philippines in 1901.

Earlier, in 1898, Ramón, who was then ten years old, was sent to Lekeitio for further schooling. His parents were worried for his future as he was getting more and more interested in cockfighting, gambling, and other vices. Sending him to the Basque Country was also a way of disciplining him. Ramón stayed in Lekeitio and Gernika for three years, finishing his first year of high school (*bachiller*) at a college run by Augustinian fathers. He was sent to England for two years to learn English and also attended the Liverpool Institute, a first-rate public school.[15]

Completely transformed in outlook, Ramón returned to the Philippines on July 8, 1903, at the age of fifteen. He briefly worked as a clerk in a Basque shipping firm, Aldecoa y Compañía in Cebu. His newly acquired knowledge from Europe would be put to good use. Two years before, in 1901, his father joined another Basque, José Muertegui, an abaca dealer from Palompon (Leyte) in a business partnership—the Muertegui y Aboitiz Compañía. Muertegui originally came from Ea, Bizkaia.

The Muertegui y Aboitiz Compañía engaged in the abaca trade at a time when it was the principal export of the Philippines. It also had investments in copra, sugar, timber, and lumber. In Manila the company contracted another Basque firm, Urrutia y Compañía, as its commissioned agents. By 1907, Muertegui y Aboitiz acquired *Picket*, a twin-screw steam launch with 120 gross tonnage and two-engine streamers from the Bureau of Navigation. To utilize their vessel, Muertegui and Aboitiz took to selling their abaca again in Cebu with the *Picket* as their mode of transport. Since Aldecoa and Company had closed shop, the partners dealt with another Basque firm, Oquinena and Company (owned by Sandalio Oquinena and Anastacio de Aldecoa). The company also operated a hardware and grocery store in Cebu.[16]

Since Cebu was the bustling center of trade and commerce of the Visayas, Muertegui y Aboitiz thought of establishing business there. But this would mean tougher competition from both local and foreign companies. It would take another five years before the plan was implemented. In March 1910, Ramon Aboitiz and his cousin Joaquín Yrastorza, who worked as a clerk, opened a small office in Cebu to sell abaca, also starting a merchandise business that sold rice and cooking oil as well as horses and cows.

In 1912 Ramón Aboitiz married Dolores Sidebottom, the pretty daughter of the Manila manager of Smith Bell, a British trading firm. She had graduated from the Philippine Normal School and also studied in a finishing school in England. Later Ramón and his elder brother, Guillermo, formed their own company, G. y R. Aboitiz, to sell general merchandise in areas not covered by Muertegui y Aboitiz. Ramón also acted as an agent for the insurer Filipinas Compañía de Seguros and for El Hogar Filipino, a building and loan association in Manila.[17]

The year 1912 was also a tragic one for the Aboitiz family. Paulino Aboitiz, who was then sixty-two years old, died of anemia and dysentery shortly after arriving in Barcelona. Ramón assumed his father's role in the family business. But Muertegui & Aboitiz did not last long. After José Muertegui decided to return to Spain, the company was eventually dissolved. The Aboitiz brothers acquired Muertegui's share for 95,000 pesos in May 1916, purchased on installment. Ramón turned to John Talbot Knowles, manager of Smith Bell, for financial assistance. Knowles loaned him 30,000 pesos at a low interest rate.

The Aboitiz family formed another company called Viuda e Hijos de P. Aboitiz, which also included the Basque sons-in-law Marcelino Ugarte (husband of Ana) and Pedro Garamendi (husband of Antonia). Although both Viuda e Hijos de P. Aboitiz and G. y R. Aboitiz became profitable, Ramón was fatigued. In 1919, he sold his shares of the abaca and general merchandise business to his brothers Guillermo and Vidal and to Arnaldo F. Silva, a Portuguese mestizo.

Ramón then founded the Aboitiz y Compañía Incorporada on January 31, 1920. It was approved by the Bureau of Commerce and Industry a week later. The company, whose name was changed to Aboitiz and Company, Inc. in 1935, continues to this day. It started with a capital of 1,250,000 pesos. The main shareholders were Guillermo, Vidal, and Silva with 650 shares; Manuel Moraza with 300 shares; Paulino and Luis, Ramón's younger brothers, with 100; and Joaquin Yrastorza, their cousin, with 50 shares. Silva became president and general manager, while Guillermo served as assistant.

Aboitiz and Company then diversified into copra and other cash crops that were either sold to foreign companies in the Philippines or exported abroad. This activity naturally led to the company's development of its interest in inter-island shipping. After the war, the management of Aboitiz and Company passed to another generation of businessmen. Among them were Enrique, Luis Jr., and Eduardo, sons of Vidal Aboitiz and Ana Moraza. They were among the first Aboitizes to be educated in the United States rather than Europe. Enrique, for example, studied at the University of California in Berkeley and Harvard University. Together, the three brothers expanded their business to shipping, heavy equipment and machinery, power generation and electricity distribution, realty development, marketing, and manufacturing. Enrique Aboitiz, as described by many, "is a good, fair, and smart businessman with consistent desire for growth and advancement in the business world."[18]

After the war, the core business of Aboitiz and Company was shipping, but it continued to expand its interest in banking, energy, and real estate. Eduardo Aboitiz took over from Enrique Aboitiz in 1968. From 1978 to 1990, the company was presided over by Luis Aboitiz Jr. At present, Jon R. Aboitiz is the CEO of Aboitiz and Company, Inc.

By 1989, the different companies under the Aboitiz group of companies created a publicly listed holding and management company called the Aboitiz Equity Venture Corporation. Its business interests range from multibillion-peso stakes in eight electricity power firms to banking, flour milling, shipping, transport and distribution, construction, tourism, real estate, and other industries.

The Aboitizes control the country's second and third largest power distribution companies, namely Visayan Electric and Davao Light and Power, which serve the Visayas and Mindanao. In 1993, they joined two Chinese business groups, the Chongbians and the Gothongs, to form WG&A, the Philippines' largest shipping company. WG&A's current president is Endika Aboitiz. The Aboitiz clan also owns 52 percent of Union Bank, one of the country's most profitable banks, and has a controlling stake in City Savings Bank in Cebu.

In 1996 the Aboitiz group also formed a joint venture with Tsuneishi Holdings, Inc., a Japanese shipbuilding conglomerate, the fourth largest in the world, in the development of Cebu Industrial Park Developers, Inc., (CIPDI). The project is located in the town of Balamban, about sixty-three kilometers from Cebu City. The once sleepy town was converted overnight into an industrial zone. It also became the site of FBM, the Aboitiz shipbuilding facility that makes fast boats and ferries.

Although one of the best-managed conglomerates in the Philippines, the company is not immune to crisis and downturns. For instance, during the Asian financial turmoil in 1997, the Aboitizes were forced to sell their stakes in certain businesses in order to focus on core areas. Years of success caused the group to overexpand in a wide array of business, some of which turned out to be losers in the long term. Thus, in 1998, the clan sold its shares in Pilipinas Kao, Inc., a cosmetics firm, to its Japanese partners. In 1999, the Aboitizes sold Consolidated Industrial Gases, Inc. (CIGI), the country's biggest producer of industrial gases, to British Oxygen Co. (BOC). This was followed by the sale of Southern Industrial Gases to BOC. In the same year, the Aboitiz interests sold the country's largest insurance brokerage, Jardine Aboitiz Insurance Brokers, Inc., to the British-owned Jardine Group. Other sales of noncore investments include the billion-peso Republic Cement, shares in World Finance Plaza in Ortigas Center, and South Western Cement.[19]

The present generation of Aboitizes that manages the family's business empire is highly educated, cosmopolitan in outlook, and very talented in business. They learn from the best practices of both West and East. While some members of the clan are normally sent to the United States to study, others are now also studying in Beijing. The Aboitizes are well respected by partners and competitors alike. The family maintains a strong Basque identity. Many members of the Aboitiz clan carry Basque names such as Jon, Endika, Andoni, Erramon, and Iñaki. More importantly, they are proud of their Basque origins, a trait unfortunately no longer shared by some other Basque descendants in the Philippines.

Ayala

Antonio de Ayala, the patriarch of the Ayala clan, was born in Hueto Abajo, Araba, in 1804. He sailed to Manila when his uncle, Monsignor José Segui, was the archbishop. He eventually got a job with the commercial house of Domingo Roxas and became a trusted employee. In 1834, at age twenty-nine, Antonio de Ayala entered into partnership with Domingo Roxas to form the Casa Roxas. While all the other commercial houses were engaged in the lucrative foreign commission business, Casa Roxas invested the bulk of its assets in a crude, but efficient distillery factory. It was located in Manila's Quiapo District overlooking the Pasig River. Its products included gin, rum, whiskey, and cognac.[20] When it began, the Roxas distillery depended wholly on a primitive still made of a hollow log with bamboo tubing and operated by fire. The finished product was poured into jugs that were transported to the market on flat cargo boats. It was only in 1876 that the factory acquired modern equipment from France. Another Basque manager at Casa Roxas was José Zabarte, son of Pedro Zabarte from Vitoria, who came to Manila with Antonio de Ayala.

In 1843, a mutiny in the military garrison in Fort Santiago broke out. Domingo Roxas and Antonio de Ayala were arrested on suspicion of aiding the rebellion. Roxas died in prison. In 1844, upon his release, Antonio married Margarita, the daughter of Roxas. Their principal sponsor was José de Azcárraga, a prominent businessman and member of the Royal Economic Society. Azcárraga's two sons, Marcelo and Manuel, as we previously learned, gained prominence in Spain as a general and economist-politician, respectively.

Casa Roxas later became known as Destillería y Licorería de Ayala when Antonio and Margarita became owners. The Ayala distillery became the largest in East Asia at that time. The Quiapo plant, however, was sold in June 1924 to the Palancas, a Filipino-Chinese family, who changed its name to La Tondeña.

Ayala decided to diversify into agriculture by purchasing croplands in Panay, as well as into mining by acquiring coal mines in Bicol and Cebu. He also opened a plant to make commercial dyes from indigo. On April 7, 1851, Antonio bought a vast tract of grassland in San Pedro de Makati for 52,000 pesos—the present site of the Makati Central Business District.

In the same year, Antonio became a director and later auditor of the Banco Español-Filipino de Isabel II, the first bank in the Philippines, founded by the Basque governor-general Antonio de Urbiztondo. The Banco Español-Filipino issued *pesos fuertes* (strong pesos), the first paper money in the country. Aside from being legal tender, the pesos fuertes were also redeemable in Mexican pesos, the strongest currency in the Philippines at that time. The Banco Español-Filipino circulated the first coins and opened its first branch in Iloilo. The bank became heavily involved in the country's infrastructure development, financing the first telephone system, the first electric power utility, and first steamship service. In 1912, the bank's name was changed to Bank of the Philippine Islands, the name it has kept to this day. In 1969, the Ayala family took over the bank's ownership when Ayala Corporation became its single biggest shareholder.[21]

Antonio de Ayala made a successful shift in the world of finance. He got into the insurance business as a director of La Esperanza, a shipping insurance company, as well as a director of a bonding company, the Sociedad Filipina de Finanzas. He served as treasurer or collector (*síndico procurador*) for the city of Manila. He was also a member of the Junta de Comercio, a quasi-judicial body that governed insular trade and navigation. Owing to his avid interest in maritime activities, he received the title *alférez,* or naval lieutenant. He prodded the Junta de Comercio to sponsor classes in English and French for businessmen and merchants. He was also among the founders of the exclusive Manila Jockey Club. Ayala lost his wife Margarita in 1869. He himself passed away in 1876.

María Trinidad, daughter of Antonio de Ayala and Margarita Roxas, married Jacobo Zobel Zangróniz in 1876. Ana María Zangróniz y Arrieta, the mother of Jacobo, was the daughter of a justice in the Royal Audiencia of Manila and came from a prominent family in Navarre. María Trinidad's sister, María Camilla, married the Basque Andrés Ortíz de Zarate, who was actually her first cousin. Upon the death of their parents, the ownership of Ayala y Compañia passed to María Trinidad, which she held until her death in 1917. The marriage of María Trinidad and Jacobo produced five children: Fernando Antonio, the twins Enrique and Alfonso, Margarita, and Gloria. Gloria died several months after birth, while Alfonso died at five years of age.[22]

Jacobo Zobel Zangróniz was described as a visionary of his time. He studied land transportation in Europe, and when he returned to Manila he prepared the plan for the tramcar service, known as "tranvía." Together with Adolfo Bayon, Jacobo organized the Compañia de los Tranvías de Filipinas, which operated the first tramcar service in Manila. The earliest tramcars were modest-sized carriages of steel and wood, each drawn by a single pony.[23]

María Trinidad's son, Fernando Antonio Zobel y Ayala, convinced his relatives and friends to support General Emilio Aguinaldo's fight for independence. It paid off with the inauguration of the first Philippine Republic in Malolos in 1899. Fernando later helped fight the American forces. He, together with Enrique Zobel y Ayala, would continue the family business during the American occupation. Fernando Antonio remained a bachelor until his death in 1949. Enrique would marry twice: first with Consuelo Roxas, who died in 1908 (Consuelo was actually his first cousin); and second to Fermina Montojo. With Consuelo, Enrique had three children: Jacobo, Alfonso, and Mercedes. With Fermina, he had four: Matilde, Consuelo, Gloria, and Fernando. The present day Zobel-Ayala family actually descends from the branch of Enrique and Consuelo. Jacobo would serve as a colonel in the Philippine army during the the war, while Mercedes would marry Joseph McMicking Jr., a Basque-British businessman, who would later lay the foundation for the development of the Ayala business center in Makati. McMicking's mother, Angelina de Ynchausti, was Basque and a scion of the prominent Ynchausti family of Manila. Continuing the family tree, Alfonso would marry Carmen Pfitz and have three children: María Victoria, Jaime, and Alfonso Jr. Jaime Zobel y Pfitz would be better know as Jaime Zobel de Ayala, the corporate genius who transformed the Ayala Corporation into the Philippines' largest conglomerate.

During World War II, the assets of the Ayala y Compañia were frozen by the Japanese Army. After Bataan fell, Colonel Jacobo Zobel became a prisoner of war and joined the "death march" to Tarlac. Alfonso's house in Roxas Boulevard was confiscated by the Japanese, and his family fled to their farm in Calatagan, Batangas, and stayed there until the war ended. As Jaime Zobel de Ayala said: "That was a blessing in itself because, had we stayed in Manila, we could have all been killed. As it was, we lived comfortably in Calatagan where we were never short of food."[24]

Alfonso, who in his early years had undergone a major operation, felt that he needed some time to rest and recover from the war. He took his family to Spain. There, Jaime enrolled in a Christian Brothers School from which eight years later he earned a baccalaureate degree. After that he was admitted to Harvard University where he studied architecture and graduated in 1957. He returned to the Philippines and started working for Ayala Corporation, making 400 pesos (U.S.$200) a month.[25] Before his return, however, he married his Spanish girlfriend, Beatriz Miranda. They had seven children: Jaime Augusto, Fernando, Beatriz Susana, Patrishia, Cristina, Monica, and Sofia. In 1970, Jaime was appointed as Philippine ambassador to the Court of Saint James at the age of thirty-six.

Ayala Corporation was a conservatively run firm with little interest in lines of business outside of insurance, finance, and real estate until 1965, when it entered the food business by acquiring Purefoods. After Jaime Zobel de Ayala's diplomatic tour of duty, he assumed the leadership of Ayala Corporation. It was during his stewardship that the company expanded. It became heavily involved in real estate development.

The name Ayala became synonymous with the development of Makati. The Makati of today owes its glowing success to the brilliant management of the Ayala family. Among the outstanding projects they undertook were Forbes Park, Dasmariñas Village, Urdaneta Village, San Lorenzo Village, Legazpi Village, Salcedo Village, Bel-Air Village, Magallanes Village, Ayala Alabang Subdivision, Makati Commercial Center, and so forth. The Ayala group's phenomenal success came when the large tracts of swamplands they acquired in the 1850s were successfully developed.[26]

Jaime Zobel de Ayala is modest about his personal success: "I became CEO of Ayala when Makati was practically fully developed. So the task was to simply continue keeping Makati as a dynamic city and a prime financial district in the country and to provide the services that a vibrant city like Makati deserves. The 25-year-old plan that was set by my predecessors was obviously excellent as a starting point, but developments in urban design have changed considerably and the idea has been to constantly reinvent ourselves according to the new standards of modern urban design."[27]

In the beginning of the 1990s the family further diversified into information technology (IT) and telecommunications. After several years, the Ayala group became a major provider of IT products and services through its subsidiaries, such as Integrated Microelectronics, Ayala Systems Technology, and EDINet Phils. In March 1998, Ayala Corporation and Microsoft, the world's largest software producer, signed an agreement to explore several areas of partnership in the field of information technology.

In the competitive field of telecommunications, the Ayala group forged a partnership with Singapore Telecom to create Globe Telecom (GT). A survey done during the first half of 2001 by *Asiamoney*, a Hong Kong-based publication, rated Ayala Corporation as one of the best-managed firms in the Asia-Pacific region. The current head of the Ayala Corporation, Jaime Augusto Zobel de Ayala, a Harvard MBA graduate, has set his sights on overseas expansion. "We feel it's important to be part of the broader ASEAN (Association of Southeast Asian Nations) community, and the way we intend to do that is by attracting partners from overseas. Secondly, we plan to invest with partners in these countries. We hope that that would blossom into relationships that can be cross-cultural in nature and encourage the flow of goods within the region."[28]

The Ayala Corporation is also an avid patron of arts and culture in the Philippines. It runs the Ayala Museum, which houses the famous dioramas of the Philippines, and the Filipinas Heritage Library.

Elizalde

The founder of the Elizalde dynasty in the Philippines is Joaquín Marcelino Elizalde e Irrisarri. *Elizalde* means "churchyard" in Basque. He was born in Elizondo in the Valley of Baztan in Navarre in 1833. At the tender age of thirteen, he emigrated to the Philippines at the request of his uncle, Juan Bautista Irrisarri,[29] who arrived in the islands at the beginning of the nineteenth century, probably attracted by the opportunities offered by the opening of the Philippines to international trade. Other relatives of Joaquín Marcelino who obtained permission to emigrate to the Philippines were Jaime Venutia e Irrisarri[30] and Valentín Teus e Irrisarri,[31] thirteen and fifteen years old, respectively.

It is interesting to note the young age of emigrants at that time; many were practically children. One reason they petitioned to emigrate at such a young age was to escape military service and to do so before reaching the age of eligibility when they would have to pay for an exemption. In addition, voluntary exiles were prevalent because of war or for political reasons, as was the case after each of the Carlist wars. There was also the traditional resistance of young Basques to joining an army that they considered foreign.[32]

Joaquín Marcelino found a job at Ynchausti y Compañia and later became a minority partner in the firm because he was "honest, hardworking, and competent."[33] By 1877, he already figured as a respectable businessman in Manila.[34] In 1892, Marcelino became chairman of the commission that presented the construction project for a monument to honor of the Basques Legazpi and Urdaneta.[35] The statue survived the destruction of Intramuros during World War II, and it currently stands in Rizal Park.

José Joaquín, the second-generation Elizalde, took over his father's business. He later married Carmen Díaz Monreau from Spain. They had six children: Joaquin Miguel (Mike), Juan Miguel, Angel, Manuel (popularly known as Manolo), Federico, and Carmenchu. They were educated in various parts of the globe—Spain, England, United States, and Switzerland.[36] In 1933, the Elizalde family acquired some of the assets of Ynchausti y Compañia when it was dissolved by Manuel María de Ynchausti. Among them were the La Carlota and Pilar sugar mills. The Elizaldes also owned a shipping firm, the Manila Steamship Company, an insurance firm, the Metropolitan Insurance Company, and a mining company, Samar Mining Co., Inc., before the war.

Manolo Elizalde also founded the first radio station, KZRH, in the Philippines in 1940, which became the nucleus of Manila Broadcasting Company (MBC), the oldest broadcasting company in the country. The station announced that Pearl Harbor had been bombed and that the war in Europe had already reached the Far East. The station played a crucial role during the war by continuing to broadcast pro-Allied forces' news. As one writer said: "In the darkest hour of the nation's struggle for independence, KZRH was the only station left fighting the war through the airwaves. It provided a glimmer of hope, as KZRH managed to broadcast the message of Douglas MacArthur from Australia: 'The President of the United States has ordered me to break through ranks from Corregidor to Australia . . . I came through and I shall return.'"[37] Because of their anti-Japanese activities, Juan and Manolo Elizalde were incarcerated in Fort Santiago. Juan, in fact, was killed by the Japanese.[38]

The Japanese Imperial Army closed down KZRH for four years during World War II. After the war, Manolo begun rebuilding the family fortune. While he continued its traditional interest in sugar, he saw the potential for expanding the family business in the media, first in broadcasting and later in print. Radio broadcasting was a fast-growing medium at that time. He set up the Manila Broadcasting Company to be a leader in the field. He hired some Americans soldiers who stayed on in the Philippines after the liberation to manage the company. One of them was William Dunn, who arrived with General Douglas MacArthur in Leyte. Dunn served as general manager of MBC until 1956. MBC flourished under Dunn's tutelage. He hired professional announcers and made sure they trained their Filipino counterparts. When he joined the advertising firm of J. Walter Thompson, his young assistant, Ira Davis, succeeded him.[39]

After the liberation, KZRH scrambled for the best U.S.-based suppliers of broadcasting equipment, and within forty days a new studio was erected on the top floor of the Insular Life building in Plaza Cervantes. On July 4, 1946, KZRH was ready for the inauguration of Manuel Roxas as the first president of the second Philippine Republic. That same year, MBC also established sister station DYRC in Cebu, which quickly became the leading news and drama station in the Visayas and Mindanao.[40] The Elizaldes also bought the Philippine Broadcasting System from the Soriano family.

For the next two years, the Elizaldes pumped every cent of profit back into the operations. On July 15, 1949, KZRH went on simultaneous nationwide broadcast, becoming the first station to reach audiences from as far north as Basco to as far south as Jolo. That same year, Swiss Radio Commission officials joined in an international project with the Philippine government, replacing the "K" in all local radio stations with "D." Thus was born DZRH.[41] The station remains today as one of the top radio stations in the country.

After the war, Manolo Elizalde took over the presidency of Elizalde and Company. He replaced Joaquin "Mike" Elizalde, who then became chairman. Mike previously served as vice president and then company president in 1936 at the age of thirty-six. President Manuel L. Quezon, however, appointed him as resident commissioner to the United States, and he became the first Philippine ambassador extraordinary and plenipotentiary to the United States from 1946 to 1951. He also served briefly as secretary of foreign affairs (1952–53) during the administration of President Elpidio Quirino and as chairman of the Philippine delegation to the United Nations from 1952 to 1955.

With Manolo at the helm, Elizalde's rope factory began to recover, and soon La

Carlota and Pilar's Sugar Central Azucareras. Tanduay Distillery picked up and regained stability and is today one of the country's largest distilling firms. Utilizing only the most modern facilities in wine and liquor production and continually introducing major improvements in this field, Tanduay's products became a byword. Tanduay rum is still one of the largest selling rums in the Philippines today.[42] On May 10, 1988, Twin Ace Holdings Corp. of the Lucio Tan Group purchased Tanduay.

During the 1950s, the Elizalde family was invariably associated with sports. Manolo Elizalde was greatly involved in sports enterprises. His interest spanned a number of sports—swimming, tennis, boxing, horsemanship, pelota, basketball, marksmanship, football, yachting, gymnastics, chess, and bowling. No wonder he was called the "Patron Saint of Local Sports" (1954) by the Philippine Free Press, "Sportsman of the Year" (1954) by the *Philippines Herald*, and "Patron of Sports" by the Sports Writers Association.[43]

The Elizalde brothers were all excellent horsemen. Before the war, they attained such skill in polo that they carried a heavy twenty-goal handicap, at that time the highest total in Philippine polo. By 1934, they ruled the sport. Some of their rivals were high-ranking officers from the U.S. Armed Forces as well as international stars. So huge was polo's following at the time that the Elizaldes built Los Tamaraws Polo Club, an elegant site of many international matches, making 1939 one of the greatest polo seasons in the country.[44]

Manolo Elizalde was also known as the owner of the YCO Painters amateur basketball team, which he established in 1934. It was discontinued during the war, but was revived in 1952 and dominated the country's basketball league during the 1950s and 1960s. One of its most popular players was Mike Bilbao, a Philippine Basque. Manolo Elizalde also supported a number of Filipino tennis players, who swept junior crowns in Japan, won the Asian singles championship, reached Wimbledon's round of sixteen in doubles play, won matches in Sydney, Melbourne, and Forest Hills, and helped with Olympic and world honors in basketball. Manolo also sponsored the 1957 Australia-Mexico tennis championship in the Philippines. He brought to the country international and Olympic tennis and swimming champions while they were still in their prime. He likewise subsidized foreign coaches and imported boxers. He even brought a bullfighter once. All this because he wanted the Philippines to see the best and to know more about other sports.[45]

In 1962, Fred J. Elizalde joined the family firm. Fred had just returned from Harvard, where he graduated magna cum laude in social relations. He also studied architecture at Magdalen College in England. He was a member of the Philippine swimming team during the Rome Olympics in 1960. While at Harvard, he was with the All-American swimming team and was also a junior swimming champion in the United States.[46]

Fred expanded the family business in the print media. He started acquiring important publications such as the *Evening News*, the *Daily News International* (a newspaper for expatriates), the *Philippine Sun* (a bilingual newspaper in English and Tagalog), the *Bulaklák* (a Tagalog magazine), and a tourist magazine called the *Manila Guide Fortnightly*.

In 1972 President Ferdinand Marcos declared martial law, and all the media entities were closed down. DZRH survived, but only under strict government censorship. All Elizalde publications folded. Fred concentrated his energies on managing the family's sugar mills, Central Azucarera La Carlota and Central Azucarera de Pilar (now Capiz Sugar Central). Within two years of taking over management, Fred bought a new Farrell mill to replace the aging ones.

Moreover, he concentrated on increasing cane supply. Traditionally cane could come only from the "milling districts," (nondistrict cane being marginal). Fred changed this with La Carlota's purchase and/or lease of farms to ensure continuous supply and achieve greater milling efficiency. In 1994, however, Fred Elizalde sold La Carlota to the Roxas y Compañía group that already owned the Central Azucarera de Don Pedro in Batangas.[47]

During the Marcos years, one of the Elizaldes, Jose Manuel Elizalde Jr., popularly known as "Manda," was named presidential assistant on national minorities. He is closely associated with the discovery of the Tasadays, a "lost" tribe in Mindanao that still lived in the Stone Age.[48] Supposedly they had been isolated from modern civilization until being discovered in the late 1960s. However, anthropologists later denounced the tribe a hoax. Manda fled abroad after the scandal. He is reportedly now living in Latin America.

Meanwhile, Fred Elizalde won the presidency of the Philippine Chamber of Commerce and Industry and served for three consecutive terms. He was also its chairman from 1983 to 1985. He was elected as assemblyman in the Batasang Pambansa (National Assembly). Here, too, he devoted his efforts to the liberalization of business in general and the concerns of the sugar and broadcast industries in particular.[49]

During the People Power revolution at EDSA (Epifanio de los Santos Avenue)[50] in February 1986, DZRH was at the forefront in covering the historic event. As Fred Elizalde recalls: "Everyone else had been knocked off the air, including Radio Veritas, whose transmitter was bombed. On the last two days, we were the only ones doing fearless radio coverage."[51] Today the Manila Broadcasting Company is a publicly listed company, although the Elizaldes still own 40 percent and Fred Elizalde sits as its president. MBC operates more than 180 stations in the country, making it the largest radio network, with coverage in 97 percent of the country.

Ynchausti

The Ynchaustis' roots can be traced to Andoain and Zumarraga in the Basque province of Gipuzkoa. The patriarch of the clan, José Antonio de Ynchausti, was a shipowner and captain who navigated to the Philippines, Venezuela, and Europe. "He was shipwrecked three times, and three times he started from scratch."[52] His son, José Joaquín de Ynchausti, settled in the Philippines in the second quarter of the nineteenth century. He was born on September 26, 1815, in Cádiz. His mother was also a Basque, Martina Gregoria Gurruchategui.[53] In 1854, at the age of thirty-five, he founded Ynchausti y Compañia (Ynchausti and Company) in Manila to consolidate all the commercial activities of the Ynchaustis. While the main activity of Ynchausti y Compañia was trade and shipping with its own fleet under Ynchausti Naviera (Ynchausti Steamship Company), it branched out into industry and agriculture. It grew to become one of the biggest companies in the Philippines during the second half of the nineteenth century, with offices in Manila, Iloilo, Gubat, and Sorsogon. The company had branches in Hong Kong, Shanghai, San Francisco, and New York.

Ynchausti y Compañia owned Sicogon Island and vast haciendas in Bicol, Negros, and Panay. La Carlota Sugar Central, one of the first modern sugar mills in Negros, was to process sugar cane from its plantations. The company was also one of the first to import locomotives. The railroad network covered more than 120 kilometers and linked the municipalities of La Carlota, La Castellana, and the seaport of Pontevedra. Ynchausti y Compañia also established the YCO paint factory, Destilería Tanduay, which made quality rum, a cement factory in Binangonan, Rizal, and a rope factory at the Muelle de la Industria in Manila. The rope that the company manufactured became known worldwide as Manila hemp and was the first Philippine industrial product to gain international acceptance owing to its high quality.[54]

José Joaquín de Ynchausti also became one of the principal stockholders and consequently managing director of the Banco Español-Filipino de Isabel II (later renamed Bank of the Philippine Islands) for fifteen years, from 1868 to 1873 and from 1876 to 1884. He also served as a member of the board (consejo de administración) of the Monte de Piedad y Caja de Ahorros de Manila (Monte Piedad and Savings Bank of Manila) when the bank was established by the Catholic Church and the Spanish colonial government in 1880. The other Basque members of the board were Tomás Aguirre and Andrés Ortíz de Zarate.[55]

One of the clear symbols of the commercial success of Ynchausti y Compañia was the Puente Colgante on the Pasig River. When commerce at that time was increasingly being conducted in the Binondo area, José Joaquín de Ynchausti commissioned the Basque engineer Matias Mechacatorre to design and build the bridge that would connect Intramuros to the Ynchausti y Compañia hemp factory in the Muelle de la Industria in Binondo, across the Pasig River. The bridge was started in 1849 and finished in 1852. This was not only the first bridge over the Pasig River but the first steel suspension bridge in Asia.

In 1879, the *Emuy,* one of the ships of the Ynchausti fleet, rescued *La Vencedora,* a vessel of the Spanish Royal Navy and towed it to Manila free of charge. In recognition of his service, King Alfonso XII of Spain bestowed on José Joaquín a medal, the Gran Cruz del Mérito Naval.[56]

José Joaquín married Isabel Gonzalez Y Ferrer, marquesa de Viademonte, and they had three children: Clothilde, Joaquín José, and Rafael. When José Joaquín died in September 1889, his son, Joaquín José, led Ynchausti and Company, then the biggest firm in the Philippines. He also became a managing director of the Bank of the Philippine Islands from 1902 to 1907. When Joaquín José died of a heart attack in Madrid in September 1920, the helm of the family business passed to his son, Manuel María de Ynchausti (1900–1961), who was only twenty at that time and completing his law studies at the University of Madrid.

Manuel met his wife, Ana Belén de Larrauri, in Donostia while on vacation in Gipuzkoa. The Larrauri family had extensive holdings in the Basque Country, and her grandfather, Miguel Larrauri y Azcue, was mayor of Donostia during the 1880s. A Capuchin father introduced them. Ana Belén was a pious and generous woman. After they married in Donostia in 1926, Ana Belén took the citizenship of Manuel, and they traveled home to Manila. They had five children: Antonio, Joachim, Miren, Arantza, and Anna.

Manuel was very religious and a firm believer in social justice. He advocated that wealth be shared with those that helped create it and the less fortunate. In the late 1920s he parceled the haciendas and gave them to the tillers of the soil and to the Catholic Church. All this was done quietly and without publicity. He also gave away to the Capuchin fathers several properties on Dewey (now Roxas) Boulevard in Pasay. He can be therefore be considered an exponent of voluntary land reform in the Philippines.

In 1927 Manuel founded in Manila the Patronato de Nuestra Señora de Lourdes, a free medical clinic for the poor that was run by the Sisters of Saint Paul de Chartres. The Ynchausti family funded its operations until 1948. This institution still exists today in Saint Anthony's Parish in Singalong, Manila. For all Manuel's extraordinary achievements, in May 1927 in a private audience at the Vatican, Pope Pious XI bestowed on him the Knighthood of Saint Gregory. In 1945, the Jesuits in New York awarded him the gold medal for outstanding missionary distinction. The Ynchausti family, in fact, had a tradition of philanthropy. In 1894, for instance, Manuel's father, Joaquín, and his brother, Rafael, donated funds and lands to the Capuchin fathers in Panay for the construction of health clinics.[57]

Manuel also developed strong ties with the American colonial establishment. He became a close friend of Frank Murphy, the American governor of the islands, and later U.S. attorney general, and Henry Taft, the brother of William H. Taft, also former governor of the Philippines and later president of the United States. These connections would prove invaluable later when Ynchausti organized the American chapter of the International League of the Friends of the Basques in New York toward the end of the 1930s.

In 1933, Manuel decided to expand to Europe, by establishing a base in the Basque Country. He sold some of the company's assets to the Elizalde family and invested in real estate development in Donostia, since his wife's family already had holdings there. He bought a house in the neighborhood of Ondarreta, where he stayed with his young wife and son Antonio.

During the Commonwealth government in the Philippines, the Ynchausti family traveled on U.S. passports and enjoyed the rights and privileges of U.S. nationals. In July 1936 while the family was staying in Donostia, the Spanish civil war broke out. The city was surrounded by the troops of General Francisco Franco. Manuel de Ynchausti made a U.S. flag and displayed it outside their house. The U.S. ambassador to Spain, Claude Bowers, came with a navy ship, the USS *Cayuga*, to evacuate the Ynchausti family. From their residence the Ynchaustis were escorted to the port by the Basque forces. Manuel María, as a sign of gratitude, gave his two cars, a Ford and a Buick with Manila license plates, to Commander Saseta, head of the Basque resistance forces. Franco was said to be fuming when he found out about the incident. The USS *Cayuga* took the Ynchausti family to Saint-Jean-de-Luz (Donibane Lohizune) on the French side of the Basque Country.[58] Manuel also actively aided refugee Basque children of the Spanish civil war. For two years, he and his wife, Ana Belén, adopted thirty children whom they housed, clothed, fed, and educated.[59] This was the start of Manuel's numerous philanthropic activities for the Basque Country.

In December 1938, Manuel cofounded the International League of the Friends of the Basques in Paris to gather the support of friends and sympathizers of the Basques to promote assistance to Basque exiles. He supported resistance against the invading Nazis by donating funds and other medical aid for the French army. In 1948 he was one of the principal organizers of the Seventh and Eighth Congress of Basque Studies, in Biarritz, wherein he also headed the section Basques in the World. Manuel was described by his colleagues as a man of culture, generous without ostentation, who retained a childlike enthusiasm for any new initiative.[60]

In October 1939, Manuel conceived the idea of creating a World Basque Union (Ludiko Euzko Bazkuna) to gather all Basques around the globe, whether Euskadi-born or with foreign citizenship, to extend mutual help among the Basques, to promote knowledge of the diversity of lives and characteristics of the Basque race, and to support the interests of Euskadi and the Basque people. Many Basque leaders, among them José Antonio de Aguirre, the *lehendakari* (president) of the Basque government in exile, lauded and supported the project.[61]

During this period, Manuel and his family traveled extensively and lived in Donostia, Paris, and Ustaritze. However,, Manuel had to return to the Philippines to oversee the family's business interests. On August 5, 1939, the Ynchaustis started their trip back to Manila. From Cherbourg (France), they first traveled to Canada and the United States. Toward the end of 1941, they were set to leave New York for

Manila when news of the Japanese attack on Pearl Harbor caught them. They were forced to stay in the United States until 1947.

While in Quebec, Manuel initiated the establishment of the International Catholic Emergency Relief (Socorro Católico International) with Cardinal Villeneuve of Quebec and later with Archbishop Spellman of New York. The organization's proposed main purpose was to extend assistance to all victims of wars, epidemics, earthquakes, conflagration, floods, and other calamities.

In 1941 when José Antonio Aguirre, then president of the Basque government-in-exile, was escaping the Nazis, it was Manuel María de Ynchausti who planned and assisted his departure from Europe. This entailed top-level diplomatic negotiations, even reaching the office of President Roosevelt. When Aguirre arrived in New York with his family, he stayed at the Ynchausti home in White Plains. Manuel also donated a professorial chair to Columbia University so that Aguirre could teach there.[62]

At the start of the war, Manuel loaned their ancestral home on Roxas (formerly Dewey) Boulevard to the Philippine Red Cross. For a time, the Japanese army detained Lieutenant General Jonathan Wainwright, one of General MacArthur's commanders, and his staff there. Later, the Japanese admiral took over the property and set up his headquarters. Unfortunately, the house was destroyed during the liberation of Manila.[63]

After the war, Manuel was offered U.S. citizenship, but he chose to keep his Philippine one. He always wanted to return home to the Philippines, but because health concerns he was unable to do so. Meanwhile, the family's business interests in the Philippines were being handled by Salvador Z. Araneta, a lawyer and close friend of Manuel de Ynchausti. Salvador's father, Gregorio Araneta, was also a good friend of Joaquín José de Ynchausti, and he too came from Gipuzkoa. Unfortunately, with Manuel's health failing, he was unable to travel back to the Philippines. This was left to his son Antonio María. Manuel died in April 1961 in Ustaritze (French Basque Country).

Antonio María de Ynchausti was the fourth-generation Ynchausti in the Philippines. He was born in their ancestral home on Dewey Boulevard, Manila, a stone's throw away from Malate Church. He attended grade school and part of high school at the Iona School run by the Christian Brothers of Ireland in New Rochelle, New York. In 1947, he continued his studies at the Collège Saint François-Xavier in Ustaritze, taking up philosophy. He later went to the University of Paris and took up business administration at the École des Hautes Études Commerciales. Afterwards, he studied economics at the École de Sciences Politiques and sociology at the Institut d'Études Sociales run by the Jesuits at the Institut Catholique (Catholic University of Paris). He did his postgraduate work in town planning and construction at the Bouwcentrum in Rotterdam.[64]

After his studies, Antonio was tasked by his father with overseeing their real estate holdings in Donostia. In 1959, he founded together with his younger brother, Joachim José, the International Center of Information and Documentation for the Construction Industry in Southwestern Europe (ETXEGINTZA) with offices in one of the Ynchausti buildings. The objective of the center was to prepare Basque industry for the European Common Market.

In August 1960, Antonio was appointed as Philippine honorary consul in Donostia by Felixberto M. Serrano, Philippine secretary of foreign affairs. Later, Philippine Ambassador to France Salvador P. Lopez also appointed Antonio *chargé de mission*. At the time, he organized exhibits of Philippine products and crafts. He was also instrumental in the reciprocal removal of visa requirements for Filipinos traveling to France and Spain.[65]

In 1964, Antonio quietly returned to Manila to oversee, along with Salvador Z. Araneta, the Ynchausti interests in the Philippines. Though majority of the Ynchaustis already lived in the Basque Country, France, and Spain, the Ynchaustis still had ties in the Philippines through Rafael de Ynchausti y Gonzalez, younger brother of Joaquín José, where the Ortigas branch of the Ynchaustis began. Rafael had a daughter, Consuelo, who married Dr. Ignacio R. Ortigas. They had eight children: Rafael, Miguel, Joaquín José, Elena, María Luisa, Arturo, and José Mari. After the war, the Ortigas clan began developing their vast real estate holdings in Mandaluyong, then one of the suburbs of Manila, into one of the most successful residential, commercial, and business centers in the Philippines today.

After Franco died in 1975, Spain underwent significant political changes, one of which was the granting of autonomy to the different regions in 1979. The Basque Country established its own autonomous government in 1980 under the Statute of Gernika. Antonio's brother, Joachim José de Ynchausti was appointed as minister of culture and tourism of the autonomous Basque government. He visited Basque collectivities in North and South America to intensify relations between the different Basque centers in the world and the Basque government (Eusko Jaurlaritza). He was the first and only Filipino citizen to hold such a high-ranking position in the Basque Government.

In February 1986, Joachim visited the Elko Basque Club in Nevada. It was part of a tour of Basque centers and clubs in the western part of the United States. During a press conference, he said that he hoped to be able to assist Basque groups abroad in the teaching of the Basque language, as well as the preservation of Basque culture, folklore, and sports. He stated that teachers from the Basque Country were to be provided and films would be made available to assist in cultural efforts. His duties as minister of culture and tourism included the establishment of contacts with the Basque centers around the world and the development of ties with other nations of the world.[66] Unfortunately, later in 1986, Joachim died of a cerebral hemorrhage at the age of fifty. Had he lived, there is little doubt he could have initiated efforts to establish links with the Basque diaspora in the Philippines.

Meanwhile in the Philippines, aside from looking after the family's business interests, Antonio continued the family's tradition of philanthropy and service through his involvement in numerous foundations and causes. Having survived the Spanish civil war, World War II in Europe and the Philippines, and forty-five years of the Franco dictatorship, with its virulent repression of the Basque Country, the family also became staunch supporters of nonviolence. In 1987, Antonio spearheaded with Christopher and Ramon Carreon peace talks with Dimas Pundatu, head of the Moro National Liberation Front Reformist Group (MNLF-RG) in Mindanao, introducing the Basque Statute of Autonomy as the model for autonomy in Mindanao. On August 27, 1987, a peace treaty was signed with the MNLF-RG, together with the government representatives, former vice president Emanuel Pelaez and then chief of staff General Fidel Ramos, who later became president of the Philippines. This was reported in *DEIA* of August 28, 1987, the February 17 *El Diario Vasco,* a Basque daily, and the February 11, 1988 *El País,* a Madrid daily.

Nowadays, the members of the Ynchausti family understandably maintain a low profile. Antonio, who divides his time between the Philippines and Europe, is currently the chairman and president of Ynchausti Development Corporation, a firm that oversees the business interests of the family. He is married to a Filipina, María Teresa Tamayo de Lara, who is also of Basque descent.

Understandably, the families I have discussed briefly in this chapter are only four among the most famous, powerful, and prosperous. Other famous families of Basque ancestry in the Philippines include the Aldecoas, the Garchitorenas, the Isasis, the Mondragons, the Ormaecheas, the Urrutias, the Zuluagas, and the Zubiris. These names regularly appear in the headlines and society pages of major dailies in the Philippines.

Most Basques immigrants in the Philippines enjoyed only modest success. However, it is evident that the accomplishments of the Basques in the Philippines are disproportionately greater than their numbers. The Basques are clearly among the nation's most successful groups.

Conclusion

Today most Filipinos are very familiar with two things related to Basque culture, though without knowing it—*chorizo de Bilbao,* a kind of sausage, and jai alai. At the same time, the Basque legacy in the Philippines is perhaps manifested most obviously in the number of Basque place-names. Many of Manila's streets still have Basque names, though many more have been erased and changed in recent years for the sake of modernization and nationalism. The most obvious example is Avenida Azcárraga, which was renamed Claro M. Recto Avenue in honor of the great Filipino nationalist and senator. Among the surviving Basque street names are Ayala, Arlegui, Barrengoa, Bilbao, Gaztambide, Ozcariz, Elizondo, Guernica, Durango, Echague, Goiti, and Mendiola. In Makati, the posh residential and business enclaves are called Legazpi, Salcedo, and Urdaneta.

The current map of the Philippines is still replete with provinces, towns, and cities that bear Basque names, such as Anda, Arteche, Azpeita, Lavezares, Legazpi, Loyola, Mondragon, Nueva Vizcaya, Oroquieta, Oteiza, Pamplona, Urbistondo, Urdaneta, Zarraga, and Zumarraga.

The Basques' outstanding achievements and the high status enjoyed by their descendants in contemporary Philippine society must be considered against the backdrop of the future of Basque-Philippine identity. We should first answer the following questions: How do Basque descendants view their ethnicity? Do they still regard themselves as unique? To what extent have they assimilated into the local culture?

The new generation of Basque descendants have little contact with the Basque Country. Some are still proud of their Basque heritage, although compared to their counterparts in Latin America, they are fast losing their ethnic consciousness, if in fact it is not already lost. This is in part a function of the vast distance that separates the Philippines and the Basque Country, as well as a function of the limited number of Basque settlers in the Philippines at any time. Such demographic paucity makes it impossible for a strong Basque-Philippine culture and identity to flourish. Except for some articles that are published occasionally about a few families of Basque origin, many third- and fourth-generation Basques lack ethnic awareness and are oblivious to their roots. And even when they are vaguely aware of their origins, they lack a deeper knowledge, appreciation, and understanding of things Basques. Only a handful have ever been to the Basque Country. As Andoni F. Aboitiz, a fourth-generation Basque has said: "We really think of ourselves as Filipinos first and of Basque descent second."[1] Even if some descendants are proud of their Basque roots, they seem to prefer not to talk about them. As Robert Laxalt, an American novelist of Basque origin, has observed: "Reticence has always been the deeper mark of the Basque character."[2]

Intermarriage is another factor that has weakened the Basques' ethnicity. Although it was often the practice for newly arrived Basques during the nineteenth century to marry among themselves, succeeding generations did not follow suit. Many took Spanish and American spouses, while others married mestizos and Malay Filipinos. The Ayala family, example, has practically lost its Basqueness, except for its name, and that could still be lost since the current heirs of the Ayala clan carry the surname "Zobel." The most Basque among the present Basque-Filipinos today seem to be the Aboitizes. Looking at their family tree, it is evident that intermarriage with other Basques has been encouraged. A majority of the Aboitiz clan carry a second Basque name such as Arrizaleta, Luzurriaga, Mendieta, Moraza, Mendezona, Ugarte, Uriarte, and Yrastorza.

In the Philippines, there is no equivalent of the *eusko etxea,* or Basque center, that is maintained by Basque descendants in Latin America and the American West (particularly in the states of California, Idaho, and Nevada). The United States also has the NABO (North American Basque Organizations, Inc.), the umbrella organization that oversees nearly thirty Basque clubs and provides them with common cause and activity. There is also an Argentinian FEVA (Federación de las Entidades Vascas de la Argentina, or Federation of Basque Entities of Argentina), which links more than sixty Basque centers and institutions. In the Philippines, there is not a single Basque club at present.

Philippine Basque descendants no longer speak Euskara. The predominance of regional languages, such as Ilonggo, Bicolano, and Cebuano; the promotion of Filipino, the Tagalog-based national language; and the strong influence of American culture with a corresponding extensive use of English in education, business, and government in the Philippines have together wreaked havoc on the vestiges of Spanish tradition, not to mention the Basque one. The Spanish language, which was still dominant among the Philippine elite during the American occupation, slowly waned in influence. By the 1960s, Spanish lost its premier status, and, although it was included as an official language in the 1973 Philippine constitution, its decline was irreversible. It was finally eliminated as an official language in 1987.

Even as an academic subject, Spanish has dwindled to nothing. Constituting twenty-four required units in the school system in the early 1950s, it was demoted to twelve units in the 1980s. It was subsequently abolished as a requirement. Many Basque descendants today cannot even speak Spanish—considered the language of the aristocracy and landed gentry in the Philippines—let alone Basque.

The new generation is simply too assimilated to the mainstream of Philippine society and culture. As English Basque scholar Rodney Gallop noted in his famous work *A Book of the Basques,* first published in 1930: "When a Basque emigrates to South America or Mexico, and is no longer under the influence of his own racial environment, he becomes a different man. He throws off his clogging conservatism, responds to the call of progress, and develops unsuspected qualities of energy and initiative. But there is a risk that he may cease, to all intents and purposes, to be a Basque."[3]

It would also be unfair to compare the Basques in the Philippines with their brethren and cousins in Latin America and the American West. The Philippine Basques had to adjust, sometimes painfully, to changing historical and political developments. Spanish America, for example, had only one colonial master (Spain), while the Philippines has been occupied by a number of colonial powers (Spain, the United States, and Japan). In addition, the surge of Filipino nationalism after independence in 1946 left little room to assert one's foreign ethnic identity.

The Basques, whether they liked it or not, were lumped with the Spaniards, who were unfairly viewed with contempt (although this is changing) in contrast to the relatively favorable treatment of the Americans (although ardent Filipino nationalists will never agree). Since the United States continues to be a world power, many Basque families send their children to that country for schooling since the English language and an American diploma are highly valued and useful in the Philippines. Given the sizable number of Filipinos in the United States (about two million at present), we can paraphrase Pierre Lhande's definition of a Basque as "having an uncle in the Americas" and define Filipinos as "having a relative in America."

Given all this, is there any hope for the revival of Basque ethnic consciousness in the Philippines? The answer is not clear. In 1991 a delegation of officials from Zumarraga, the birthplace of Miguel López de Legazpi, visited Tagbilaran City in Leyte Province to renew the ties of friendship between the Basques and the Filipinos. Juan José Sagarna, Zumarraga's councilor for culture, after witnessing the reenactment of the *sanduguan*, the blood compact, that Legazpi and the local chief Sikatuna performed to seal their alliance in 1565, said the visit was "memorable and marked the beginning of a new relationship." Two years later, in 1993, the Filipinos returned the visit. This time the mayor of Tagbilaran City, Jose Maria Rocha, accompanied by the Philippine ambassador to Spain, Isabel Wilson, went to the Basque Country. Mayor Rocha, together with his counterpart from Zumarraga, Mayor Aitor Gabilondo, signed a sister-city agreement.[4]

In 1998 the Philippines celebrated the 100th anniversary of the declaration of independence from Spain. Many historical studies and projects were undertaken. Antonio María de Ynchausti together with Fray Pedro G. Galende, O.S.A., the curator of the Museum of San Agustin Monastery in Intramuros, curated an exhibit in the museum dedicated exclusively to Basque pioneers in the Philippines. They obtained paintings, books, and other articles from José Mari Agirre, vice minister of culture of the Basque Government (Eusko Jaurlaritza). They were assisted by relatives and friends from the Basque Country, such as Txabier de Irala, the then president of Iberia Airlines, the Spanish flag carrier, who also happens to be a graduate of the prestigious De La Salle University in Manila.

In the same year, three TV and print journalists from Bilbao went to the Philippines to make a documentary on the Basques there. However, certain Basque-Filipinos that still maintain strong ties with the Basque Country were reluctant to appear on the program, fearing possible reprisal from the Basque separatist group ETA. A spate of kidnappings, brutal assassinations, and other forms of violent activities was attributed to the group at that time.

Even in this era of globalization characterized by high-speed transportation and communication, there is still hope that Basque-Philippine identity can be reinforced. Although I do not expect a new wave of Basques settlers in the Philippines, cultural and business links between the Philippines and the Basque Country could be gradually revived. The Internet provides resources and opportunities for maintaining Basque identity. Travel between the Basque Country and the Philippines can now be of the virtual variety.

As the Basque Country embarks on an aggressive program to draw investment and to engage in business with East Asia, it seems that Basque officialdom has forgotten that the Philippines could serve as its doorway to that region. So far, Basque trade with, and investment in, the Philippines is negligible compared to that in other Asian nations. As the Philippine economy recovers from the Asian financial turmoil, it could offer more opportunities to Basque business. Indeed, the Philippines could be the missing link in the advancement of Basque economic interests in Asia. Traditional ties and partnerships might be strengthened by new networks among Basque businessmen and the Basque descendants in the Philippines. After all, the Basques came to the Philippines mainly for economic reasons. In the future, the same motive could underpin a new kind of Basque-Philippine relationship.

The Basque legacy in the Philippines will continue if the Basques themselves wish it and take steps to at least reinforce interest in Basque history and culture and its impact on the Philippines. It is also up to Basque descendants to provide the thread of continuity to this important heritage. If nothing is done, the Basque legacy will remain a mere footnote in Philippine history. Nothing will be left in the collective memory of the Filipinos but the popular dish chorizo de Bilbao and jai alai, rather than the struggles and successes of a brave, proud, and industrious people from the Basque Country.

Appendix

BASQUE CREW IN THE MAGELLAN EXPEDITION, 1519–1522: ORIGINAL SHIP ASSIGNMENT AND POSITIONS

Concepción

Juan Sebastián Elcano, master; Juan de Acurio from Bermeo, warrant officer; Antonio de Basozabal, also from Bermeo, caulker; Domingo de Ycaza from Deba, carpenter; Lorenzo de Iruña from Gipuzkoa; Joan Navarro from Iruñea; Pedro de Muguertegui from Markina; Juan de Aguirre, Martin de Isaurraga, and Pedro de Chindurza, all sailors from Bermeo.

San Antonio

Juan de Elorriaga, master, from Gipuzkoa; Pedro de Olabarrieta, barber, from Galdako; Juan Ortiz Goperi, quartermaster, from Bilbao; Pedro de Bilbao, caulker; Pedro de Sabatua from Bermeo, carpenter; Juan de Segura from Gipuzkoa; Pedro de Laredo from Poblete; Martín de Aguirre from Arrigorriaga; Joanes Iranzo from Irun and Juan de Orue from Mungia, all sailors; and Juan de Menchaca, crossbowman, from Bilbao.

Santiago

Martín de Barrena and Juan de Santelices from Somorrostro, both cabin boys, from Gipuzkoa; Juan de Aroca, carpenter, from Bizkaia; Perucho from Bermeo and Martin de Hurrira (origin unknown) did not have a fixed position in any of the ships.

Trinidad

Domingo de Urrutia, a mate, native of Lekeitio; and León de Espeleta, scribe.

Victoria

Martín de Gárate, carpenter, from Deba; Juanico (also called Vizcaino), cabin boy, from Somorrostro; Juan de Arratia, cabin boy, from Bilbao; Ochote de Erando, cabin boy, from Bilbao; Pedro de Tolosa, cabin boy, from Gipuzkoa; and Juan Zubileta, page, from Barakaldo; and Lope Navarro from Tudela.

Source: Enciclopedia General Ilustrada del País Vasco (San Sebastián: Editorial Auñamendi, 1982).

BASQUE GOVERNORS-GENERAL DURING THE SPANISH REGIME, 1565–1898

Miguel López de Legazpi,* 1565–1572
*Guido de Lavezares,** 1572–1575
Francisco de Sande, 1575–1580
Gonzalo Ronquillo de Peñalosa, 1580–1583
Diego Ronquillo, 1583–1584
Santiago de Vera, 1584–1590
Gómez Pérez Dasmariñas, 1590–1593
Pedro de Rojas, 1593
Luis Pérez Dasmariñas, 1593–1595
*Antonio de Morga,** 1595–1596
Francisco Tello de Guzmán, 1596–1602
Pedro Bravo de Acuña, 1602–1606
Cristóbal Téllez de Almansa, 1606–1608
Rodrigo de Vivero, 1608–1609
Juan de Silva, 1609–1616
Andrés Alcázar, 1616
Jerónimo de Silva, 1616–1618
Alonso Fajardo y Tenza, 1613–1624
Fernando de Silva, 1624–1625
Juan Niño de Tabora, 1625–1632
Lorenzo de Olaso, 1632–1633
Juan Cerezo de Salamanca, 1633–1635
Sebastián Hurtado de Corcuera, 1635–1644
Diego Fajardo y Chacón, 1644–1653
Sabiniano Manrique de Lara, 1653–1663
Diego Salcedo, 1663–1668
Juan Manuel de la Peña Bonifaz, 1668–1669
Manuel de León, 1669–1677
Francisco Montemayor y Mansilla, 1677–1678
Francisco Coloma, 1677–1678
Juan Vargas Hurtado, 1678–1684
Gabriel Curuzalaegui y Arriola,* 1684–1689
Alonzo de Avila Fuertes, 1689–1690
Fausto Cruzat y Góngora,* 1690–1701
Domingo Zabálburu y Echeverri,* 1701–1709
Martín de Ursúa y Arizmendi,* 1709–1715
José de Torralba, 1715–1717
Fernando Manuel de Bustamante y Bustillo, 1717–1719
Archbishop Francisco de la Cuesta, 1719–1721
Toribio José de Cosio y Campo, 1721–1729
Fernando de Valdés y Tamón, 1729–1739
Gaspar de la Torre, 1739–1745
*Bishop Juan de Arechederra,** 1745–1750
Francisco José de Ovando y Solís, 1750–1754
Pedro Manuel de Arandía y Santisteban,* 1754–1759
*Bishop Miguel Lino de Espeleta,** 1759–1761
Archbishop Manuel Rojo del Río, 1761–1762
*Simón de Anda y Salazar,** 1762–1764
Francisco Javier de la Torre, 1764–1765
José Raón, 1765–1770
Simón de Anda y Salazar,* 1770–1776
Pedro Sarrio, 1776–1778
José de Basco y Vargas, 1778–1787
Pedro Sarrio, 1787–1788
Felix Berenguer de Marquina, 1788–1793
Rafael María de Aguilar y Ponce de León, 1793–1806
Mariano Fernández de Folgueras, 1806–1810
Manuel González de Aguilar, 1810–1813
José de Gardoqui Jaraveitia,* 1813–1816
Mariano Fernández de Folgueras, 1816–1822
Juan Antonio Martinez, 1822–1825
Mariano Ricafort Palacín y Abarca, 1825–1830
Pascual Enrile y Alcedo, 1830–1835
Gabriel de Torres, 1835
Juan Cramer, 1835

Pedro Antonio Salazar Castillo y Varona, 1835–1837
Andrés Garcia Camba, 1837–1838
Luís Lardizabal y Montojo,* 1838–1841
Marcelino de Oraá Lecumberri,* 1841–1843
Francisco de Paula Alcalá de la Torre, 1843–1844
Narciso Clavería y Zaldúa, 1844–1849
Antonio María Blanco, 1849–1850
Antonio de Urbiztondo y Eguía,* 1850–1853
Ramón Montero y Blandino, 1853–1854
Manuel Pavía y Lay, 1854
Ramón Montero y Blandino, 1854
Manuel Crespo y Cebrián, 1854–1856
Ramón Montero y Blandino, 1856–1857
Fernando Norzagaray y Escudero,* 1857–1860
Ramón Solano y Llanderal, 1860
Juan Herrera Dávila, 1860–1861
José Lémery e Ibarrola, 1861–1862
Salvador Valdés, 1862
Rafael de Echagüe y Berminghám,* 1862–1865
Joaquin del Solar e Ibañez, 1865
Juan de Lara e Irigoyen,* 1865–1866
José Laureano Sanz y Possé, 1866
Antonio Osorio, 1866
Joaquín del Solar e Ibañez, 1866
José de la Gándara y Navarro, 1866–1869
Manuel Maldonado, 1869
Carlos María de la Torre y Navacerrada, 1869–1871
Rafael de Izquierdo y Gutiérrez, 1871–1873
Manuel Macrohon, 1873
Juan Alaminos y Vivar, 1873–1874
Manuel Blanco Valderrama, 1874
José Malcampo y Monje, 1874–1877
Domingo Moriones y Murillo, 1877–1880
Rafael Rodríguez Arias, 1880
Fernando Primo de Rivera, 1880–1883
Emilio de Molins, 1883
Joaquín Jovellar y Soler, 1883–1885
Emilio de Molins, 1885
Emilio Terrero y Perinát, 1885–1888
Antonio Molto, 1888
Federico Lobatón, 1888
Valeriano Weyler y Nicolao, 1888–1891
Eulogio Despujol y Dusay, 1891–1893
Federico Ochando, 1893
Ramón Blanco y Erenas, 1893–1896
Camilo G. de Polavieja, 1896–1897
José de Lachambre y Dominguez, 1897
Fernando Primo de Rivera, 1897–1898
Basilio Augustin, 1898
Fermin Jaídenes y Alvarez, 1898
Francisco Rizzo, 1898
Diego de los Ríos, 1898

Source: Based on the list by Dr. Domingo Abella, former director of the Philippine Bureau of Records, published in *Cedulario de Manila.*

* denotes Basques; names in italics are those who held the position of governor-general in an ad interim capacity.

BASQUE-OWNED HACIENDAS IN NEGROS AND ILOILO

Alarcon (La Carlota, Negros Oc.)
Algorta
Anilao
Batea
Begonia (Manapla, Negros Oc.)
Bilbao (Manapla, Negros Oc.)
Boubon* (Kabalkan, Negros. Oc.)
Buena Vista (Bulacan)
Carinaman
Camanug (La Carlota, Negros Oc.)
Candelaria
Canhagan (Capiz, Panay)
Canlaon (Pontevedra, Negros Oc.)
Caridad
Carmelin (Isabela, Negros Oc.)
Carmen (La Carlota, Negros Oc.)
Casa Mata (Cebu)
Central Bearin (Kabankalan, Negros Oc.)
Central Palma (Kabalkan, Negros Oc.)
Central San Isidro (Kabankalan, Negros Oc.)
Central Santa Eugenia (Kabankalan, Negros Oc.)
Clementina (Kabankalanan, Negros Oc.)
Constancia
Consuelo
Cristina
Durango
Elena (La Carlota, Negros Oc.)
Encarnacion (Talisay, Negros Oc.)
Esperanza* (La Carlota, Negros Oc.)
Euskara (San Carlos, Negros Oc.)
Fe (La Carlota, Negros Oc.)
Flora (Kabalakan, Negros Oc.)
Grande (La Castellana, Negros Oc.)
Guadalupe (Janinay, Iloilo)
Isabel
Kagaui (La Carlota, Negros Oc.)
Lanjagan (Capiz, Panay)
Maria (La Carlota, Negros Oc.)
Merced
Naga
Najalin* (La Carlota, Negros Oc.)
Pacol (Valladolid, Negros Oc.)
Pilar* (La Carlota, Negros Oc.)
Pilar* (Saravia, Negros Oc.)
Pilarica (Pontevedra, Negros Oc.)
Pinantan* (La Carlota, Negros Oc.)
Refugio (San Carlos, Negros Oc.)
Rosalia
Salamanca* (La Carlota, Negros Oc.)
San Agustin (Negros Oc.)
San Antonio (La Carlota, Negros Oc.)
San Bonifacio (Negros Oc.)
San Gabriel (Lagayon, Pontevedra, Negros Oc.)
San Ignacio (La Carlota, Negros Oc.)
San Isidro (Kabankalan, Negros Oc.)
San Jose* (La Carlota, Negros Oc.)
San Jose (San Carlos, Negros Oc.)
San Juan (Kabankalan, Negros Oc.)
San Luis (Valladolid, Negros Oc.)
San Miguel (La Carlota, Negros Oc.)
San Rafael (Silay, Negros Oc.)
San Ramon (Saravia, Negros Oc.)
San Vicente Sangay (Manapla, Negros, Oc.)
Santa Filomena (San Carlos, Negros Oc.)
Santa Rita
Santa Rosalia
Santo Tomas*
Socorro
Talabaan (San Carlos, Negros Oc.)
Togbac (Manapla, Negros, Oc.)
Tortosa
Valencia* (Dumaguete, Negros Or.)

Vasconia (San Carlos, Negros Oc.)
Velez-Malaga (La Castellana, Negros Oc.)
Vizcaya (La Carlota-Pontevedra, Negros Oc.)

Source: Jon Bilbao, *Basque Emigration Studies, Working Papers I. Philippine Islands (1830–1910)* (Reno, Nev.: Basque Studies Program, University of Nevada, 1979).
* denotes ownership by Ynchausti & Company.

BASQUE-OWNED/OPERATED SHIPS

Macleod (steamer)*
Abeja (lorcha)*
Aeolus (steamer)*
Alabama (steamer)*
Alava (lorcha)*
Alavés (brig)
Alavesa (frigate)
Alola (motorboat)*
América (frigate)
Amigos (brig)
Andalusa (schooner)
Antonia (lorcha)*
Arizona (frigate)
Asunción (bark)
Atanasio (lorcha)*
Aurrera (lorcha)*
Aurrera (steamer)
Barcelona (steamer)
Bauan (steamer)*
Begona (lorcha)*
Belgika (steamer) *
Bella Gallega (frigate)
Betis (brig)
Bilbaino (brig)
Bilbao (lorcha)*
Bilbao (steamer)*
Bisayas (steamer)*
Bolinao (steamer)*
Brutus (steamer) *
Butuan (steamer)*
Cádiz (steamer)
Calupasa (brig)
Caridad (lorcha)*
Carmencita (lorcha)*
Casaysay (brig)
Castellano (steamer)*
Católico (pailebot)
Ceanuri (lorcha)*
Cebuana (bark)
Cervantes (frigate)
Chicago (steamer)*
Chisone (steamer)*
Chispa (steamer)*
Churruca (steamer)*
Churruca (bark)
Circe (warship)
Ciudad Condal (steamer)
Colombian (steamer)
Colón (frigate)
Cometa (brig)
Concepción (motorboat)*
Conchita (lorcha)*
Cornelio (steamer)
Darocana (brig)
Diederichsen (steamer)*
Dominga (brig)
Don José (steamer)*
Dos Hermanas (steamer)*
Dos Hermanos (brig)
Elcano (steamer)*
Emigrante (frigate)
Emilia (brig)
Emmy (steamer)
Encarnación (bark)
España (steamer)*
Estella (lorcha)*
Eusebia (motorboat)*
F. Pleguezuelo (steamer)*
Felisa (steamer)*
Filipina (motorboat)*
Filipino (steamer)*
Flor (lorcha)*
Flora (lorcha)*
Francisco Reyes (steamer)*
Fritz (steamer)*
Gloria (steamer)
Gordejuela (lorcha)
Governor Forbes (steamer)*
Guipúzcoa (lorcha)*
Heredia (bark)
Herminia (steamer)*
Hispano-Filipina (frigate)
Hospicio (lorcha)*
Iruna (steamer)*
Irurita (lorcha)*
Irusquiza (brig)
Isabel (lorcha)*
Isabelita (bark)
Isla de Luzon (steamer)
Isla de Panay (steamer)
J. Diederichsen (steamer)*
Jesus (motorboat)*
Jos Mariia (lorcha)*
Josefina (steamer)*
Julia (lorcha)*
Julia (schooner)
Julian de Unzueta (frigate)
Juno (steamer)
León XIII (steamer)
Leonidas (brig)
Lola (bark)

BASQUE-OWNED/OPERATED SHIPS (*continued*)

L'Orient (frigate)
Luna (motorboat)*
Luzuriaga (lorcha)*
Magallanes (steamer)*
Man (motorboat)*
Manapla (motorboat)*
Manila (bark)
Manila (motorboat)
Maria (bark)
Mariveles (bark)
Matilde (frigate)
Mayon (steamer)*
Medusa (frigate)
Melleza (motorboat)*
Melliza (steamer)*
Mundaca (steamer)*
Navarra (lorcha)*
Navarrete (pilot's boat)
Negros (steamer)*
Neguri (motorboat)*
Neurea (brig)
Nuestra Señora del Carmen (steamer)*
Nuestra Senora de Lourdes (steamer)*
Nuestra Señora del Rosario (steamer)*
Nuestro (lorcha)
Nueva Engracia (bark)
Nueva Victoria (bark)
Nueva Zafiro (frigate)
Neptuno (brig)
Ojo (lorcha)*
Olga (motorboat)*
Olite (lorcha)
Palma (motorboat)*
Paz (lorcha)*
Paz (lorcha)*
Perla (bark)
Perla del Oceano (brig)
Provincia de Santander (frigate)
Querida (frigate)
Rafaela (lorcha)*
Rafaela (motorboat)*
Reginito (steamer)*
Reina de los Angeles (frigate)
Reina Mercedes (steamer)
Romulus (steamer)*
Rosa (lorcha)*
Rudecindo Melliza (steamer)*
Sales (bark)
Salvadora (steamer)*
Samos (bark)
San Carlos (steamer)*
San Francisco (steamer)
San Jose (lorcha)*
San Juan (steamer)*
Santísima Trinidad (frigate)
Santo Domingo (motorboat)*
Santo Domingo (steamer)
Saturnina (steamer)*
Saturnus (steamer)*
Serafina (frigate)
Shanghay (bark)
Sofía (bark)
Steipner (steamer)*
Tafalla (lorcha)*
Teresa (pilot's boat)*
Texaco (motorboat)*
Trajano (brig)
Trinidad (lorcha)*
Trueno (towboat)*
Ulataya (lorcha)*
Unión (steamer)*
Uranus (steamer)*
Venus (lorcha)*
Venus (steamer)*
Victoria (frigate)
Victoria (steamer)
Villa de Rivadavia (frigate)
Visayas (steamer)
Vizcaya (lorcha)*
Vizcaya (steamer)*
Yahiko Maru (motorboat)*
Ynchausti (motorboat)*
Yug-an (steamer)*
Zafiro (frigate)
Zoilo Ibañez de Aldecoa (steamer)*

Source: Jon Bilbao, "Philippine Islands (1830–1910)," unpublished monograph, Basque Emigration Studies, Working Papers 1 (Reno: Basque Studies Program, University of Nevada, 1979, photocopy).

* denotes accounts with Ynchausti & Company.

Notes

CHAPTER ONE. THE BASQUE PEOPLE

Epigraph: "Pour être un Basque authentique, trois choses sont requisées: porter un nom sonnant qui dise l'origine; parler la langue des fils d'Aitor, et . . . avoir un oncle en Amérique." Unless otherwise indicated all translations are mine. Aitor is the legendary patriarch of the Basques.

1. Robert Gallop, *A Book of the Basques* (Reno: University of Nevada Press, 1998), 80.
2. "La langue basque est une patrie, j'ai presque dit une religion" (Victor Hugo). Quoted in Vicente de Amézaga Aresti, *El hombre vasco* (Buenos Aires: Editorial Vasca Ekin S.R.L., 1987), 78.
3. Robert P. Clark, *The Basques: The Franco Years and Beyond* (Reno: University of Nevada Press, 1979), 20.
4. Julio Caro Baroja, *Los vascos,* 3rd ed. (Madrid: Istmo, 1970), 195.
5. Ibid.
6. Ibid., 201.
7. Ibid., 196.
8. John Lynch, *España bajo los Austias: Imperio y absolutismo (1516–1598),* trans. Joseph Maria Bernardas (Barcelona: Ediciones Península, 1989), 1:217.
9. Amézaga Aresti, *El hombre vasco,* 44.
10. Ibid., 62–63.
11. Gallop, *A Book of the Basques,* 212.
12. William A. Douglass and Jon Bilbao, *Amerikanuak: Basques in the New World* (Reno: University of Nevada Press, 1975), 111.
13. Juan José Alzugaray, *Vascos universales del siglo XVI* (Madrid: Ediciones Encuentro, 1988), 50.

CHAPTER TWO. INITIAL CONTACTS

Epigraph: "Las Islas del mar Océano oriental, adyacentes a Asia ulterior, de la corona de España, son llamadas comunmente, de los navegan a ellas: por la demarcación de Castilla, y sus mares y tierras de América, las Islas del Poniete, porque, desde que se sale de España, se navega hasta llegar a ellas, por el camino que el sol hace, de Oriente a Poniente. Y por la misma razón son llamadas orientales, de los que hacen la navegación por la India de Portugal, del Occidente al Oriente; dando vuelta unos y otros, por viajes contrarios al mundo, hasta venirse a juntar en estas islas; que son muchas, mayores y menores, las que propiamente son llamadas Filipinas. . . ." Antonio de Morga, *Sucesos de las Islas Filipinas* (México: 1609). Republished and annotated by José Rizal (Paris: Librería de Garnier Hermanos, 1890), 255.

1. Accounts disagree on the exact number of the crew of the Magellan expedition. The figures given are 237, 265, and 275.

2. Historians still disagree about how to write his name. Some prefer "del Cano," others use "Delcano," and so on. I will use "Elcano" throughout this book.

3. José Arteche, *Elcano* (Madrid: Espasa-Calpe S.A., 1972), 49.

4. Ibid., 20, 49.

5. V. M. de Sola, "Juan Sebastián Elcano," in *Los vascos en la hispanidad,* ed. J. R. Madaria (Bilbao: Diputación de Vizcaya, 1964), 161. See also Wenceslao Retana, *Índice bibliográfico de los que asistieron al descubrimento de las Islas Filipinas* (Madrid: 1921).

6. The foremost proponent of this claim is the noted Filipino historian Carlos Quirino. He proposed that, since Enrique was the first Malay to circumnavigate the world in the company of Magellan, he should therefore be in the patheon of Philippine heroes. Sketchy accounts suggest that Enrique was a native of Palawan.

7. Stefan Zweig, *Magallanes: El homre y su gesta,* 3rd ed. (Barcelona: Editorial Juventud, S.A., 1981), 196–97. The book was first published in German in 1957.

8. *Enciclopedia general ilustrada del País Vasco,* s.v. "Filipinas," 13:468.

9. Zweig, *Magallanes,* 198.

10. J. Ybarra, *Gestas Vascongadas* (San Sebastián: Editorial Ichaparonal, 1952), 67.

11. Antonio Pigafetta, *Primer viaje alrededor del mundo* (1522). I refer to the edition published by Historia 16 (Madrid), 1988.

12. Zweig, *Magallanes,* 206–7.

13. Mitchell Mairin, *Elcano: The First Circumnavigator* (London: Herder, 1958), 161.

14. Pierre Lhande, *La emigración vasca* (San Sebastián: Editorial Auñamendi, 1971), 85.

15. Ybarra, *Gestas Vascongadas,* 68.

16. J. R. Madaria, ed., *Los vascos en la hispanidad* (Bilbao: Diputación de Vizcaya, 1964), 201–2.

CHAPTER THREE. THE LEGAZPI-URDANETA EXPEDITION

Epigraph: "Il est clair que les Basques ont contribué, dans une large mesure, a propager la culture et religion occidentales, jouant un role important dans l'élaboration historique de notre peuple." Quoted in Antonio M. de Ynchausti, "Quelque Basques qui ont contribué au développement des Philippines," *Gurre Herria* 31 (1959): 127.

1. "Monumento a Legazpi y Urdaneta," *Euskal Erria* 31 (1892): 221–22. Joaquín Marcelino Elizalde was the chairman of the commission that implemented the project.

2. *Enciclopedia general ilustrada,* s.v. "Filipinas," 39:475.

3. Description of the Legazpi-Urdandeta Monument at the pictorial catalogue of the Filipinas Heritage Library (Makati City, Philippines).

4. Segundo de Ispízua, *Historia de los vascos en el descubrimiento, conquista y civilización de América* (Bilbao, 1915), 2:227.

5. *Enciclopedia general ilustrada*, s.v. "Filipinas," 8:470–71.

6. Ispízua, *Historia de los vascos*, 230–31.

7. Carmelo de Corta Echegaray, "Legazpi y Urdaneta en la colonización de Filipinas," *Euskalerrian Alde* 12 (1923): 21.

8. The cost of outfitting the expedition exceeded 400,000 Mexican pesos.

9. *Enciclopedia general ilustrada*, s.v. "Filipinas," 13:471; and Ybarra, *Gestas Vascongadas*, 70.

10. Ispízua, *Historia de los vascos*, 236.

11. Nicolas Cushner, *Spain in the Philippines: From Conquest to Revolution* (Quezon City: Ateneo de Manila University Press, 1972), 42.

12. For an in-depth account in English of the Legazpi expedition's crossing of the north Pacific, see Andrew Sharp, *Adventurous Armada: The Story of Legazpi's Expedition* (New Zealand: Whitcombe and Tombs, 1961).

13. Joaquín Martínez de Zuñiga, *Historia de las Islas Filipinas* (Sampaloc, 1803), 65. Martínez de Zuñiga was a Navarrese Augustinian friar.

14. Ibid. 70.

15. Ibid., 66–67.

16. Ibid., 72.

17. José Arteche, *Urdaneta, el dominador de los espacios del Océano Pacifico* (Madrid: Espasa-Calpe S.A., 1943), 176.

18. Morga, *Sucesos de las Islas Filipinas*, 9.

19. Somehow Alonso de Arellano avoided being sent to the Philippines to face the wrath of Legazpi. Thus Lope Martín was the only one who embarked on the *San Gerónimo* to the Philippines. However, he conspired with a Basque, Rodrigo de Ataguren, in recruiting the crew that would later help him stage a mutiny at sea. While crossing the Pacific, Martín took over the ship with the help of other conspirators, among them a Basque called Bartolome de Lara. Martín tried to eliminate those who were not loyal to him by leaving them to starve on a barren island. Sensing his plans, the other crew, led by Rodgrigo del Angle, successfully wrestled the ship from the mutineers. Martín and his companion, Felipe de Ocampo, were the ones abandoned instead. When the *San Gerónimo* reached Cebu, Legazpi ordered the execution of other deserters and traitors, among them the Basque scribe Juan de Zaldívar. See Martínez de Zuñiga, *Historia de las Islas Filipinas*, 82.

20. Taken from Mitchell Mairin, *Friar Andres de Urdaneta, O.S.A.* (London: Macdonalds and Evans, 1964), 5.

21. Manila's approval as a city was granted on June 21, 1574, but it took more than twenty-four years after its founding (November 19, 1595) before King Philip II finally approved the designation of Manila as the capital of the Philippines. Four months later, the official seal of the city also got official approval from Philip by virtue of a *cedula* (order) dated March 20, 1596. The seal of the city of Manila, which is still used, consists of a gold castle with closed blue gate and window with a red background on the upper part and a half-dolphin half-lion with its feet holding a sword and its tail wagging the sea

on the lower part. Interestingly, the king's secretary at the time was a Basque, Juan de Ybarra. *Cedulario de la Insigne, Muy Noble y Siempre Leal Ciudad de Manila* (Manila: Imprenta de José María Dayot, 1834), 3–7.

22. Historical Conservation Society, *The Christianization of the Philippines, trans.* Rafael Lopez and Alfonso Felix Jr. (Manila: 1965). From Benito J. Legarda Jr., *After the Galleons: Foreign Trade, Economic Change, and Entrepreneurship in the Nineteenth Century Philippines* (Quezon City: Ateneo de Manila University Press, 1999), 31.

23. *Enciclopedia general ilustrada,* s.v. "Filipinas," 8:475.

24. Ispízua, *Historia de los vascos,* 260–61.

25. Alzugaray, *Vascos universales del siglo XVI,* 210–11.

26. Legarda, *After the Galleons,* 17.

27. Looking at the instructions from the Real Audiencia, Legazpi had indeed faithfully executed it to the letter. "Upon reaching the Philippines and other islands adjascent to them," the instructions said, "you shall endeavor to discover and explore what ports they have and to obtain accurate information regarding their inhabitants and resources, the character and way of life of the people, what trade and commerce they engage in and with what nations, at what prices spices are valued among them and what kind of spice they have, what the selling price is of the merchandise and trade goods you are bringing hence with you, and what other articles may profitably be sold. You shall make every effort to enter into and maintain friendly and peaceful terms with the natives, informing them of the good will and affection which His Majesty bears them, giving them suitable presents and treating them as well as possible. You shall barter the trade goods and merchandise you are bringing with spices, drugs, gold, and any other articles of value and in demand which they may have; and if the land should seem to you so well provided that you ought to settle there, you shall found a settlement in the region and place that appear to you most suitable and when the inhabitants are most friendly, and this friendship you shall cultivate and faithfully keep." From Horacio de la Costa, *Readings in Philippine History* (Manila: Bookmark, 1965), 16.

28. Gaspar de San Agustín, *Conquista espiritual y temporal de Filipinas* (Madrid: 1698). Also see Martínez de Zuñiga, *Historia de las Islas Filipinas,* 55; Morga, *Sucesos de las Islas Filipinas,* 7. Urdaneta was correct in his assessment that the Philippines belonged to the Portuguese by virtue of the Treaty of Zaragosa of 1529. Earlier, he argued to Philip II that Spain's purpose in sending an expedition to the Philippines was to rescue possible survivors of the previous expeditions and that Spanish settlements must not be built there but in New Guinea. Fearful of Urdaneta's refusal to sail to the Philippines, the Real Audiencia furtively concealed the real order of the Spanish monarch by ordering that its instruction was not to be opened before disembarking but only upon reaching the high seas where the Augustinian friar would have no choice but to continue with the voyage.

CHAPTER FOUR. CONQUERORS

Epigraph: "Las armas que usan son lanzas, paveses terciados, esto de diario, y en la guerra un manojo de varas tiraderas, coseletes de palo, escupiles de nudillo, y algunos, arco y flecha. Usan tratar poca verdad, son inconstantes y algunas tienen guerras entre sí, en las cuales se matan y cautivan. Mostraron tener grandísimo miedo a nuestras naves." From a letter of Miguel López de Legazpi to the duke of Alba dated March 30, 1566, *De los documentos escogidos de la Casa de Alba* (Madrid, 1891). Quoted in Segundo de Ispízua, *Historia de los vascos,* 2:240–41.

1. Quoted in O. D. Corpuz, *The Roots of the Filipino Nation* (Quezon City, Philippines, 1989, AKLAHI Foundation), 1:55.

2. This man's surname has been spelled in ten different ways in various historical accounts and documents. Labazarri, Labazarris, Labezares, Labezarri, Labezarii, Lavazares, Lavezares, Lavesares, Lavezari, and Lauzaris. The most common is Lavezares, which still exists as the name of a river and a town in the island province of Samar, a living memory to the work of the man who consolidated Spanish hegemony in the Philippines. J. R. Madaria, "El navegante vizcaino Guido de Labazarri," in *Los vascos en la Hispanidad,* ed. J. R. Madaria (Bilbao: Diputación de Vizcaya, 1964), 200.

3. San Agustín, *Conquista espiritual y temporal de Filipinas,* 396.

4. This is why early historians, even Basque ones like Rodrigo Aganduru Móriz, author of the *Historia general de las Islas Occidentales a la Asia adyacente* (Madrid: 1882), thought that Lavezares was a *sevillano,* since he was a resident of Seville.

5. Ispízua, *Historia de los vascos,* 2:265.

6. Ibid., 2:266.

7. Morga, *Sucesos de las Islas Filipinas,* 13.

8. Martínez de Zuñiga, *Historia de las Islas Philipinas,* 117.

9. San Agustín, *Conquista espiritual y temporal de Filipinas,* 11–12.

10. Juan Caro y Mora, *Ataque de Limahong en Manila en 1574* (Manila: 1894), 11–12.

11. Ibid., 23.

12. Martínez de Zuñiga, *Historia de las Islas Philipinas,* 120. Cesar V. Callanta, in his book *The Limahong Invasion* (Quezon City: New Day Publishers, 1989), estimated that Limahong's forces consisted only of about 1,500–2,000 soldiers and 2,000 women, with the rest being a supporting workforce. Many of the women were kidnapped from China's coastal communities to serve as slaves.

13. Ispízua, *Historia de los vascos,* 2:270.

14. Martínez de Zuñiga, *Historia de las Islas Philipinas,* 122. See also Ispízua, *Historia de los vascos,* 2:270.

15. Martínez de Zuñiga, *Historia de las Islas Philipinas,* 123.

16. Ispízua, *Historia de los vascos,* 2:271.

17. As a young soldier, Goiti had seen combat in Spain's military campaigns in Italy. He was originally the captain of artillery and arms expert of the Legazpi-Urdaneta expedition and rose to become Legazpi's military commander. In the Philippines, he spearheaded the crucial reconnaissance missions that ensured the military victories of the Spaniards, including the capture of Manila. He led the conquest of Pampanga in late 1571. The following year he repeated his success in Zambales, Pangasinan, and parts of Ilocos. His last campaign won him a handful of gold washed by the Igorots, an ethic group from the Mountain Province. Joaquín Martínez de Zuñiga, *Estadismo de Filipinas*

(Sampaloc: 1803), 2:587. Ilocos at that time encompassed what is now called the Mountain Province where the Igorots live.

18. Ispizua, *Historia de los vascos,* 2:275.

19. Callanta, *The Limahong Invasion,* 35. Early Spanish historians, however, never mention a third attack by Limahong's reserves.

20. Ispízua, *Historia de los vascos,* 2:273.

21. According to Gaspar de San Agustín, Salcedo was accompanied by 1,500 friendly native troops from Cebu, Bohoy, Leyte, and Panay, aside from those who manned the Spanish ships and transported cargos. Chief Lacandula and his sons and relatives also joined with 200 Visayans. The natives of Pangasinan also enlisted in the campaign against Limahong. See Morga, *Sucesos de las Islas Filipinas,* 13.

22. Ispízua, *Historia de los vascos,* 2:276.

23. Morga, *Sucesos de las Islas Filipinas,* 21.

24. Sinsay was said to be a Chinese resident of Manila. He also served as an interpreter for Salcedo during the siege of Limahong's fort in Lingayen.

25. Ybarra, *Gestas Vascongadas,* 70–71.

26. Ispízua, *Historia de los vascos,* 2:277.

27. Comment of Gaspar de San Agustín, in Morga, *Sucesos de las Islas Filipinas,* 12.

28. Carlos Quirino, "El primer mexicano en Filipinas," in *Filipinas y México* (Manila: Comité del Año de Amistad Filipino-Mexicana, 1965), 62.

29. Ispízua, *Historia de los vascos,* 2:254–55.

30. Ibid., 2:256–57.

31. Ibid., 2:257–58.

32. Quirino, "El primer mexicano en Filipinas," 66.

33. Martínez de Zuñiga, *Historia de las Islas Philipinas,* 117.

34. Annotation of José Rizal in Morga, *Sucesos de las Islas Filipinas,* 12.

35. Isacio Rodríguez, *Historia de la provincia agustina del Santísimo Nombre de Jesús de Filipinas* (Manila: 1978), 171–72.

CHAPTER FIVE. MISSIONARIES

Epigraph: Jose Burniol, *History of the Philippines* (Manila: 1912), 12.

1. Fray Miguel Coco in his foreword to Juan de Medina's *Historia de los sucesos de la Orden de San Agustín de estas Islas Filipinas* (Manila: 1893), i.

2. Francis Xavier was born in 1500 in the Castle of Xavier in Navarre. His wealthy upbringing and princely background, however, never deterred the young Francis from pursuing the ascetic life of a missionary. It was during his studies in Paris that he met Ignatius of Loyola, the founder of the Society of Jesus. Legend has it that the two only spoke in Basque to one another and always played Basque pelota together. Shortly thereafter, Xavier became a Jesuit and sailed to India under the auspices of the Portuguese crown. In 1534, Saint Francis arrived in Ternate in the Moluccas.

The story of the evangelization of the island of Mindanao by Francis Xavier, and his visit to the Portuguese missions in the Philippines, is rejected by some, defended by others. Among those to reject it were Father Pio P. Reti and Father Jorge Schuhammer, an eminent Xavierologist. On the other hand, Father Pastells as well as the Filipinologist Wenceslao Retana attributed the evangelization of Mindanao to Francis Xavier, arguing that, since he was a functionary of the Portuguese king, he tried to conceal his involvement in the Mindanao mission to avoid the wrath of the Spanish crown. Father Pastells claimed that the letters of Francis Xavier, which describe the scenery, mountains, ethnography, and languages, actually refer to the shores of Davao, the southeastern part of the island of Mindanao.

Other proponents of this theory such as Father Guillermo Ubillos, s.j., claimed that Francis Xavier, in effect, preached in Mindanao, which appears in the saint's diary as the "island of the Moors." This happened before he proceeded to China and Japan.

Father Jorge Schuhammer, however, countered that "no primitive document exists in the archives of the Society of Jesus that mentions the name of Saint Francis Xavier in the Philippines." In response, Father Ubillos said: "This is true but outside the Jesuit archives there are two primitive documents that state the Xavier tradition—the Bull of the Canonization of Pope Urban VIII and the letters of Saint Francis Xavier dated January 20, 1548." The Xavier letters dated May 10, 1546, and May 20, 1548, led Father Ubillos to conclude that the Jesuit saint indeed preached in Mindanao. His conclusion was supported by other Xavier scholars, such as Father Marcelo Mastrilli, founder of the Novena Gracia (Ninth Grace) and martyred in Japan; Father Antonio Astrain, who wrote the *History of the Society of Jesus in the Province of Castille;* and Father Francisco Apalategui. What is certain is that the debate will continue. See *Enciclopedia general ilustrada,* s.v. "Filipinas," 13:479.

3. Medina, *Historia de los sucesos,* 14–15.

4. Pedro Chirino, *Relación de las Islas Filipinas y lo que en ellas han trabajado los Padres de la Compañía de Jesús,* 2nd ed. (Manila: 1890), 9–10. The book was first published in Rome in 1604.

5. Antonio Pigafetta, *First Voyage Around the World* (Manila: Filipiniana Book Guild, 1969), 40.

6. Martínez de Zuñiga, *Historia de las Islas Philipinas,* 63.

7. Nick Joaquin, "Culture Hero: The Santo Niño de Cebu," in *Culture and History: Occasional Notes on the Process of Philippine Becoming* (Manila: Solar, 1988), 69.

8. Ibid. Thus, the first church in the Philippines was in honor of the Santo Niño, and the first city and capital of Spanish Philippines, Cebu, bears the liturgical title of the child: La Villa del Santísimo Nombre de Jesús.

9. Chirino, *Relación de las Islas Filipinas,* 9–10.

10. Medina, *Historia de los sucesos,* 53–54.

11. Martínez de Zuñiga, *Historia de las Islas Philipinas,* 118.

12. Arteche, *Urdaneta,* 176.

13. Medina, *Historia de los sucesos,* 51–52.

14. Juan de la Concepción, *Historia general de Philipinas* (Manila: 1788), 1:419.

15. Ibid., 1:65.

16. Teodoro Aparicio López, *Misioneros y colonizadores agustinos en Filipinas* (Valladolid: 1965), 75.

17. Martínez de Zuñiga, *Historia de las Islas Philipinas,* 111.

18. Ispízua, *Historia de los vascos,* 2:261.

19. *Enciclopedia general ilustrada,* s.v. "Filipinas," 13:477–78.

20. Ibid.

21. Ispízua, *Historia de los vascos,* 2:277–78.

22. Ibid., 2:279–80.

23. Ibid.

24. Medina, *Historia de los sucesos,* 120.

25. Ispízua, *Historia de los vascos,* 2:288–89.

26. Diego de Aduarte, *Historia de la Provincia del Santo Rosario de Filipinas, Japón y China* (Zaragoza: 1693), 1:169. Aduarte, however, wrote that Salazar was a native of La Rioja in Castilla. See also Alberto Martínez Salazar, *Presencia alavesa en América y Filipinas (1700–1825)* (Vitoria: Diputación Foral de Alava, 1988).

27. Ibid.

28. J. Fernando, *Historia de los padres domínicos en las Islas Filipinas,* 6 vols. (Madrid, 1870–1872), 1:208.

29. Costa, *Readings in Philippine History,* 25.

30. Concepcion, *Historia general de Philipinas,* 2:48.

31. Ibid., 2:53–54.

32. Aduarte, *Historia,* 174.

33. Costa, *Readings in Philippine History,* 30.

34. Morga, *Sucesos de las Islas Filipinas,* 323.

35. Juan Toribio Medina, *El Tribunal de Santo Oficio de Inquisición en las Islas Filipinas* (Santiago de Chile, 1899), 11–13.

36. Ibid., 15.

37. Ibid., 18.

38. Ibid., 24–27.

39. Ibid., 27.

40. Ibid., 27–30.

41. Aduarte, *Historia,* 180–81.

42. The profile of Fray Cristobal de Salvatierra is based mainly on the accounts of Diego de Aduarte, *Historia de la Provincia del Santo Rosario de Filipinas, Japón y China.*

43. Ibid., 183.

44. Ynchausti, "Quelque Basques," 128.

45. *Enciclopedia general ilustrada,* s.v. "Filipinas," 13:479.

46. See John Leddy Phelan, *Hispanization of the Philippines: Spanish Aims and Filipino Responses* (Madison: University of Wisconsin Press, 1959).

47. "Si creyéramos alguna facilidad en poseer lo mismo que podíamos, enderezaríamos las violaciones contra los señores Padres de las Religiones, a cuya persuación y fidelidad se debe la mantención de estos estados. . . . Es cierto que el Dr. Salazar ha obrado como caballero, alabaremos su magnanimidad y amor a su Rey, pues sólo con la protección de los señores Padres venció las dificultades mayores para sostener el edificio de la fidelidad

de los indios." Fray Miguel Coco in his foreword to Juan de Medina's *Historia de los sucesos de la Orden de San Agustín de estas Islas Filipinas,* viii.

48. Carlos Recur, *Filipinas: Estudios administrativos y comerciales* (Madrid: Moreno y Rojas, 1879), 12.

CHAPTER SIX. GALLEON TRADERS AND MERCHANTS

Epigraph: "Cómo no vivir y prosperar en Filipinas, el pueblo que más que los demás de la nación, tan maravillosamente se presta a la adaptación en las tierras nuevas del planeta?" From Pedro Feced, "¿Hay Bascongados en Filipinas?" *Euskal Herria* 27 (1892): 106.

1. Morga, *Sucesos de las Islas Filipinas,* 325.
2. Williman Schurz, *The Manila Galleon* (Manila: Historical Conservation Society, 1985), 28.
3. Martínez de Zúñiga, *Historia de las Islas Philipinas,* 82.
4. María Teresa Martín de Palma, *El Consulado de Manila* (Granada: Universidad de Granada, 1981), 9.
5. Ibid., 9–10.
6. Schurz, *The Manila Galleon,* 39.
7. Morga, *Sucesos de las Islas Filipinas,* 351–52; English translation from Costa, *Readings in Philippine History,* 34–35.
8. Legarda, *After the Galleons,* 38.
9. Costa, *Readings in Philippine History,* 64.
10. Ibid.
11. Vicente Rodríguez García, *El gobierno de Don Gaspar Antonio de la Torre y Ayala en las Islas Filipinas* (Granada: Universidad de Granada, 1976), 102–3.
12. Dennis O. Flynn, Arturo Giráldez, and James Sobredo, eds., *European Entry into the Pacific: Spain and the Acapulco-Manila Galleons* (Aldershot: Ashgate, 2001), xxxii–xxxiii.
13. Expediente que acompaña la carta de Don Gaspar de la Torre al Rey, Manila, 12 de junio de 1745 (A.I.G. Filipinas, 151); fols. 40v–42. Taken from Rodríguez García, *El gobierno de Don Gaspar Antonio,* 105.
14. Martínez Salazar, *Presencia alavesa en América y Filipinas,* 67.
15. Ibid.
16. Ibid., 70.
17. Ibid.
18. Legarda, *After the Galleons,* 54.
19. Ibid., 55.
20. Ibid.
21. *Exposición de la Compañía de Filipinas* (Cadiz, 1813), 6.
22. Ibid., 39–40.
23. Martínez Salazar, *Presencia alavesa en América y Filipinas,* 67.
24. Corpuz, *The Roots of the Filipino Nation,* 1:403–4.
25. *Hoja Informativa de la Real Sociedad Bascongada de Amigos del País,* 13–14.
26. Maria Lourdes Díaz-Trechuelo, "Eighteenth-Century Philippine Economy: Com-

merce," in *European Entry into the Pacific: Spain and the Acapulco-Manila Galleons*, edited by Flynn, Giráldez, and Sobredo, 285.

27. Robert MacMicking, *Recollections of Manilla and the Philippines during the 1848, 1849, and 1850* (London: 1851), 1.

28. Douglass and Bilbao, *Amerikanuak*, 105.

29. Ibid., 109.

30. Ibid., 109, 107.

31. Ibid., 109–11.

32. See Ed. C. de Jesus, *The Tobacco Monopoly in the Philippines: Bureaucratic Enterprise and Social Change, 1766–1880* (Quezon City: Ateneo de Manila University Press, 1980).

33. Costa, *Readings in Philippine History*, 102.

34. Legarda, *After the Galleons*, 75.

35. Rafael Díaz Arenas, *Memorias históricas y estadísticas de Filipinas* (Manila: 1850). See dedication and chapter 1.

36. Ibid., 8th ed.

37. Bangko Sentral ng Pilipinas Web site.

38. Bambi Harper, "Sociedad Económica de Amigos del País," *Philippine Daily Inquirer*, 29 May 2001, p. A7.

39. María Lourdes Díaz-Trechuelo, "De la Compañia Guipuzcoana de Caracas a Compañia de Filipinas," in *Los Vascos y América* (Bilbao: Fundación Banco Bilbao Vizcaya, 1989), 361.

40. *Enciclopedia general ilustrada*, "Real Compañía de Filipinas," 40:100.

41. María Lourdes Díaz-Trechuelo, *La Real Compañia de Filipinas* (Sevilla: Escuela de Estudios Hispano-Americanos de Sevilla, Consejo Superior de Investigaciones Científicas, 1965), 3.

42. L. Garante Ojanguren, "La Real Compañia Guipuzcoana de Caracas," in *Los Vascos y América*, 156.

43. *Enciclopedia general ilustrada*, "Real Compañía de Filipinas," 40:102.

44. Ibid.

45. *Exposición de la Compañía de Filipinas*, 17.

46. Ibid., 105–6.

47. Ibid., 18.

48. Douglass and Bilbao, *Amerikanuak*, 197.

49. Tomás de Comyn, *Estado de las Islas Filipinas en 1810* (Madrid: Imprenta de República, 1820), 62–63.

50. Manuel Buzeta, *Diccionario geográfico, estadístico e histórico de las Islas Filipinas* (Madrid: 1850), 1:223.

51. *Exposición de la Compañía de Filipinas*, 94.

52. Ibid., 114.

53. Díaz Arenas, *Memorias históricas y estadísticas de Filipinas*. See 15th ed.

54. Douglass and Bilbao, *Amerikanuak*, 197.

55. The nonrenewal of the Philippine Company's license could have been politically

motivated since Spain was engulfed in a civil war, namely, the First Carlist War (1833–1839), and the Basques were the main supporters of the Carlist cause.

CHAPTER SEVEN. IN DEFENSE OF SPANISH SOVEREIGNTY

Epigraph: "Si el rey de España abandonara las Islas Filipinas sería lo mismo que arrojar de su corona las dos Américas abiertas y desemparadas totalmente por la parte del Sur." Quoted in Díaz-Trechuelo, "Fortificaciones en las Islas Filipinas (1565–1800)," in *Puertos y Fortificaciones en América y Filipinas* (Madrid: Comisión de Estudios Históricos de Obras Públicas y Urbanismo, 1985), 263. Simón de Anda considered the Philippines a vital cog in the defense of the Spanish empire in the Americas.

1. Wenceslao E. Retana, *Breve Diccionario Biográfico de ingenieros militares que han estado en Filipinas desde 1565 hasta 1898* (Madrid, 1923), 79. Quoted in Díaz-Trechuelo, "Fortificaciones en las Islas Filipinas," 262.

2. Corpuz, *The Roots of the Filipino Nation*, 1:113.

3. Wenceslao Retana, *Indice de personas nobles y otros de calidad que han estado en Filipinas* (Madrid: 1921), 5–6.

4. Maria Lourdes Díaz-Trechuelo, "Defensa de Filipinas en el último cuarto de siglo XVIII," *Anuario de Estudios Americanos* 21 (1964): 157.

5. Ibid., 158.

6. Milagros C. Guerrero, "The Chinese in the Philippines, 1570–1770," in *The Chinese in the Philippines, 1570–1770*, ed. Alberto Felix Jr. (Manila: Solidaridad, 1966), 25.

7. Costa, *Readings in Philippine History*, 35–36.

8. Morga, *Sucesos de las Islas Filipinas*, xxxv.

9. Ibid., 155.

10. Ibid., see prologue.

11. Martínez de Zúñiga, *Historia de las Islas Philipinas*, 286.

12. Ibid., 288–89.

13. Costa, *Readings in Philippine History*, 48.

14. C. R. Boxer, *Jan Compagnie in War and Peace, 1602–1799: A Short History of the Dutch East-India Company* (Hong Kong: Heinemann Asia, 1979), 23. Quoted in Legarda, *After the Galleons*, 37.

15. Costa, *Readings in Philippine History*, 61.

16. Ibid., 165–66.

17. Ibid., 88.

18. Martínez Salazar, *Presencia alavesa en América y Filipinas*, 58–67.

19. Rafael Bernal, "The Chinese Colony in the Philippines, 1570–1770," in *The Chinese in the Philippines, 1570–1770*, ed. Alberto Felix Jr., 57.

20. Costa, *Readings in Philippine History*, 94.

21. The reforms were cited in Anda's famous memorandum "Abusos or desórdenes que se han criado en Filipinas. . . ." See T. H. Pardo de Tavera, *Una Memoria de Anda y Salazar* (Manila: 1899).

CHAPTER EIGHT. NINETEENTH-CENTURY SETTLERS AND ENTREPRENEURS

Epigraph: "¡Bascongados en Filipinas! En todos los órdenes, todas las categorías, todos las actividades y por todos los rincones de aquella constelación de islas." From Pedro Feced (aka Quioquiap), "¿Hay Bascongados en Filipinas?" *Euskal Erria* 27 (1892): 106. Feced, a Basque journalist, was regarded as anti-Filipino because he was critical of the Filipinos reform and propaganda movement in the 1880s to the 1890s. He was also notorious for his open hatred of the Filipinos, as shown in his *Filipinas: Esbozos y pinceladas* (*The Philippines: Outlines and images*), published in Manila in 1888. Thelma B. Kintanar, *U.P. Cultural Dictionary for Filipinos* (Quezon City: University of Philippines Press, 1996), 451.

1. Douglass and Bilbao, *Amerikanuak*, 117–18.

2. Ibid., 118.

3. Ibid., 130. The head of the Carlist force was the Basque Tomás de Zumalacárregui, while other top generals were Uranga and Zaratiegui. The Carlist troops were in fact victorious during the initial phase of the war. But Zumalacárregui died of bullet wound sustained during the Battle of Bilbao in May 1835.

4. Ibid., 131.

5. Jon Bilbao, "Basques in the Philippine Islands," *Basque Studies Program Newsletter*, no. 20 (July 1979), 4.

6. Manuel Azcárraga y Palmero, *La libertad del comercio en las Islas Filipinas* (Madrid: Imprenta de José Noguera, 1871). Quoted in Legarda, *After the Galleons*, 103.

7. Díaz Arenas, *Memorias, históricas y estadísticas de Filipinas*, 5th ed.

8. Buzeta, *Diccionario geográfico, estadístico, histórico*, 1:230.

9. Bilbao, "Basques in the Philippine Islands," 4.

10. Jon Bilbao, "Philippine Islands (1830–1910)," unpublished monograph, Basque Emigration Studies, Working Papers 1 (Reno: Basque Studies Program, University of Nevada, 1979, photocopy).

11. Bilbao, "Basques in the Philippine Islands."

12. Bilbao, "Philippine Islands," entry 172.

13. Bilbao, "Basques in the Philippine Islands," 4.

14. Corpuz, *The Roots of the Filipino Nation*, 1:493.

15. *Enciclopedia universal ilustrada Europeo-Americana* (Madrid: Espasa-Calpe S.A., 1966), s.v. "Oyanguren, Jose," 1247–48.

16. *Catálogo Alfabético de Apellidos* (Manila, 21 November 1849), Philippine National Archives Publication No. D-3, viii.

17. Costa, *Readings in Philippine History*, 175.

18. Bilbao, "Basques in the Philippine Islands," 4.

19. Manuel Buzeta, *Diccionario geográfico, estadístico, histórico*, 2:568–69.

20. According to William A. Douglass, a noted American anthropologist and Basque expert, even within the Basque worldview there are characterological distinctions between Basques of different regions. Other Basques characterize Bizkaians as being extroverted and haughty. Navarrese are frequently described as introverted and distrustful. Persons from Araba are seen as aloof and severe; peasants from the interior of Bizkaia

refer to the coastal people as loud, pretentious busybodies, while the fishermen view the farmers as sullen, shrewd, and tight-lipped. People from northern Navarre call southern Navarrese *ribereños* and see them as violent and hot-blooded; the city dwellers see the rural Basques as rustic and backward; while the Basque peasants depict the urbanites as shiftless and untrustworthy. Douglass and Bilbao, *Amerikanuak*, 15–16.

21. Eduardo de Urritia, "Antonio Urbiztondo," *Euskalerrianen Alde* 19 (1923): 352.

22. James Francis Warren, *The Sulu Zone 1768–1898* (Quezon City: New Day Publishers, 1985), 105.

23. Ibid.

24. MacMicking, *Recollections of Manilla*, 253.

25. Ibid., 106.

26. Urritia, "Antonio Urbiztondo," 354.

27. Bilbao, "Philippine Islands," entry 225.

28. Ibid., entry 839.

29. Ibid., entry 88.

30. Bilbao, "Basques in the Philippine Islands," 5.

31. Ibid., 4.

32. Miguel A. Luzurraga, *Comercio y navegación de Europa y Filipinas* (Santander: 1876), 2–3.

33. Francisco Garay Unibaso, Correos Marítimos Españoles, vol. 3, A Filipinas (Indias Orientales) de 1521 a 1884 y también a Marianas e Indochina (Bilbao: Ediciones Mensajero, 1991), 296–97.

34. Ibid., 298–99.

35. Luzurraga, *Comercio y navegación*, 30.

36. Ibid., 302.

37. Bilbao, "Basques in the Philippine Islands," 4.

38. *Enciclopedia universal ilustrad*, s.v. "Azcarraga, Manuel de," 1367.

39. Ibid.

40. Quijano de Manila [Nick Joaquin], "Calle Azcarraga," in *Language of the Streets and Other Essays* (Manila: National Bookstore, 1980), 92–93.

41. *Enciclopedia universal ilustrada*, s.v. "Azcarraga, Manuel de," 1048.

42. Bilbao, "Basques in the Philippine Islands," 5.

43. Bilbao, "Philippine Islands," entry 132.

44. *Noli Me Tangere*, literally "Touch Me Not," was written in Spanish and published in Berlin in 1887. The words are taken from John 20.17, and are spoken by the risen Christ to Mary Magdalen. Leon Ma. Guerrero, a former Philippine ambassador to London and an eminent scholar on Rizal, has said that Monsignor Knox's translation of the passage to English that renders the phrase as "Do not cling to me thus" would be more appropriate to contemporary readers. Rizal himself explained to a friend that he had chosen the title to suggest that he would write of things as yet unwritten because untouchable, and his dedication expresses the same thought. Preface of Leon Ma. Guerrero to his translation of *Noli Me Tangere* (London: Longmans, 1961), xv–xvii.

45. *El Filibusterismo* (*Subversion*) was also written in Spanish, and was published in Ghent, Belgium, in 1891.

46. For a detailed study of the life of José Rizal, see Leon Ma. Guerrero, *The First Filipino: A Biography of José Rizal* (Manila: National Heroes Commission, 1963) and Wenceslao Emilio Retana y Gamboa, *Vida y escritos del Dr. Rizal* (Madrid: 1907).

47. *The Complete Poems of Jose Rizal,* trans. Nick Joaquin (Manila: Far Eastern University, 1976), 38–41.

48. Ibid.

49. Ibid., 42–45.

50. Ibid.

51. Preface of Leon Ma. Guerrero to his translation of José Rizal's *El Filibusterismo* (London: Longmans, 1961), viii–ix.

52. Rizal, *Noli Me Tangere,* 313–14.

53. Ibid., 48–49.

54. Rizal, *El Filibusterismo,* 39.

55. Ibid.

56. Quijano de Manila, "Calle Azcarraga," 91.

CHAPTER NINE. DURING THE AMERICAN AND JAPANESE OCCUPATIONS

Epigraph: "El Pueblo Filipino debe sentir grandes simpatías por los Baskos, porque ha visto desarrolarse su historia en roce constante con miembros de la industriosa e infatigable familia Baska."

1. Corpuz, *The Roots of the Filipino Nation,* 2:348. The sum of $300 million was based on the *Congressional Record* (6 February 1907) and the *New York Evening Post* (6 March 1907).

2. Leon Wolff, *Little Brown Brother: America's Forgotten Bid for Empire Which Cost 350,000 Lives* (Manila: Erehwon Publishing House, 1968), 360. Later studies, however, revealed more Filipino casualties. See Luzviminda Francisco, "The Philippine-American War," in *The Philippine Reader,* ed. Daniel Schirmer and Stephen Rosskam Shalom (Quezon City: KEN, 1989), 8–19. Francisco mentions that no records on the killings of Filipinos were kept because the American government feared that knowledge of the number of casualties might provoke anti-imperialist protests. She adds that according to estimates made by U.S. General Bell, based on a *New York Times* interview in May 1901, over 600,000 people died in Luzon alone and at least 100,000 in Batangas. There are no figures from the other provinces that also resisted American occupation.

3. See Bonifacio Salamanca, *The Filipino Reaction to American Rule, 1901–1913* (Hamden, Conn.: Shoe String Press, 1968).

4. Resil B. Mojares, *Aboitiz: Family and Firm in the Philippines* (Cebu City: Aboitiz & Company, 1998), 75.

5. *Enciclopedia general ilustrada,* s.v. "Filipinas," 13:483.

6. For a thorough discussion of the life of Sabino Arana y Goiri and the foundation of Basque National Party, refer to Stanley Payne, *Basque Nationalism* (Reno: University of Nevada, 1975).

7. Robert P. Clark, *The Basques: The Franco Years and Beyond* (Reno: University of Nevada Press, 1979.

8. Epilogue by Miguel de Unamuno in Retana, *Vida y escritos del Dr. José Rizal.* The full citation is "Y saco a colación a Sabino Arana, alma ardiente, poética y soñadora, porque tiene un íntimo parentesco con Rizal, como Rizal murió incomprendido por los suyos y por los otros. Y como Rizal filibustero, filibustero o algo parecido fue llamado Arana. Parecíanse hasta en detalles que se muestran nimios y que son, sin embargo, altamente signifacativos. Si no temiera alargar demasiano este ensayo, diría lo que creo significa el que Arana emprendiese la reforma de la ortografía eusquérica o del vascuense y Rizal la del tagalo." Could it be that Arana read Rizal's novels, particularly *El Filibusterismo,* and was influenced by him?

9. Bilbao, "Basques in Philippine Islands," 5.

10. Bilbao, "Philippine Islands," entry 816.

11. Bilbao, "Basques in the Philippine Islands," 5–6.

12. Ibid. 6.

13. *Enciclopedia general ilustrada,* s.v. "Filipinas," 13:483.

14. Mojares, *Aboitiz,* 105.

15. The other ten countries were Germany, Italy, France, Denmark, Bulgaria, Finland, Romania, Slovakia, Burma, and China.

16. Higinio de Uriarte, *A Basque Among the Guerrillas of Negros* (Bacolod City, Philippines, Editor of Civismo Weekly, 1962).

17. Ibid., 18.

18. Ibid., 30–31.

19. Secret letter of Francisco Jose Castaño to G. Méndez Vigo, Manila, 9 October 1943, AMAE, leg. 2910., exp. 9. Quoted in Florentino Rodao, "The Falange in the Philippines, 1935–1945," in *Pagbabalik sa Bayan* (Return to homeland), ed. Fernando Llanes (Manila: Rex Bookstore, 1993), 146. Castaño was a national delegate of the Spanish government in the Philippines from 1937 to 1940 and later was consul in the Spanish consulate in Manila. Méndez Vigo was a minister in the Spanish embassy in Tokyo.

20. Uriarte, *A Basque Among the Guerillas of Negros,* 163.

21. Ibid. 208. "At least 350 Idaho Basques, both European- and American-born, served in the United States during World War II. In February 1945, before the conclusion of the war, the *Idaho Statesman,* a local newspaper, claimed that at least eight Idaho Basques had been killed in the war, and that fifteen others were missing in action. As it turned out, at least 350 Idaho Basques, both European- and American-born, served in the United States during World War II." Quoted in John and Mark Bieter, *An Enduring Legacy: The Story of Basques in Idaho* (Reno: University of Nevada Press, 2000), 96.

22. Richard Connaugton, John Pimlott, and Duncan Anderson, *The Battle for Manila: The Most Devastating Untold Story of World War II* (London: Bloomsbury Publishing Plc, 1997), 121.

23. *Enciclopedia general ilustrada,* s.v. "Filipinas," 13:480–81.

24. Ibid., 481.

CHAPTER TEN. DESCENDANTS IN PHILIPPINE SOCIETY

Epigraph: Isagani R. Cruz and Lydia B. Echauz, *1001 Reasons to Stay in the Philippines* (Manila: Aklat Pescador, 1993), 3.

1. Jon Bilbao, "Basques in the Philippine Islands," 6.

2. Uriarte, *A Basque Among the Guerillas of Negros*, 214.

3. See Ma. Lina Araneta Santiago, *Salvador Araneta—A Man Ahead of His Time* (Malabon, 1986).

4. "Dr. Salvador Z. Araneta, Educator: Molding Hearts for the Country, Souls for God," *Manila Bulletin*, 31 January 2002, B-8.

5. There is hardly any Basque descendant holding a top government position. Francis Garchitorena, is a former presiding judge of the Sandigan Bayan, a court that adjudicates corruption cases in government. Garchitorena was in the limelight recently because of the corruption charges against former President Joseph Estrada and a much publicized retirement. He was admonished by the Philippine Supreme Court because of the numerous backlogged cases under his jurisdiction.

6. "Carlos Loyzaga: Greatest Filipino Cager Ever," *Philippine Daily Inquirer* (Manila), 15 January 1999, p.B15.

7. Ibid.

8. *Enciclopedia General Ilustrada*, 13:484.

9. Ibid.

10. Carlos G. Novenario, "A Legacy from Euskadi," *Philippine Graphics*, 11 March 1994, 44.

11. José María Fernandez, "José María Aranzibia: Una leyenda de la cesta," *Kezka*, 6 época (1994).

12. According to Rodney Gallop, the Basque family traditionally regards the house as more important than its occupants. They will be assimilated in it and perforce be named after it. Even if the house may have fallen into ruin, the site will retain its ancient name. Robert Gallop, *A Book of the Basques*, 61. The Txarton Torre of the Aboitiz family still stands proudly today in Lekeitio, Bizkaia.

13. *The Story of Aboitiz & Company, Inc. and the Men Behind It* (Cebu City: Aboitiz & Company, 1973), 7.

14. Ibid.

15. Ibid., 9.

16. Mojares, *Aboitiz*, 33.

17. Ibid., 12.

18. Michael G. Say, ed., *The VIPs of Philippine Business* (Manila: Mahal Kong Pilipinas Charitable Foundation, 1987), 1.

19. Wilson Y. Lee Flores, "The Aboitizes: Family Ties that Bind," *Philippine Daily Inquirer* (Manila), 6 March 2000, p. C1.

20. Eduardo Lachica, *Ayala: The Philippines' Oldest Business House* (Makati: Filipinas Heritage Foundation, 1984), 35.

21. Ma. Teresa Colayco, *A Tradition of Leadership: Bank of the Philippine Islands* (Makati: BPI, 1984), 162–63.

22. For detailed information of the Ayala family, see I. Santiago's "Genealogy of the De Ayala and Zobel Family of the Philippines," in Eduardo Lachica, *Ayala.*

23. Tony Antonio, "MCX Rail Project Encountering Delays," *Manila Bulletin,* 17 March 1998, pp. 1, 18.

24. Erwin Romulo, "Q & A: Jaime Zobel de Ayala," *Philippine Star* (Manila), 8 February 1997, YS-1.

25. Ibid., YS-2.

26. Say, *The VIPs of Philippine Business,* 33.

27. Romulo, "Jaime Zobel de Ayala," YS-2.

28. "The CEO as Catalyst," *World Executive Digest,* May 1996, 100.

29. Carta dated 18 January 1846, Elizondo. Fermín Inarri. Archivo de Protocolos de Navarra, folder 256, no. 10.

30. Carta dated June 1, 1847, Elizondo. Fermín Inarri. Archivo de Protocolos de Navarra, folder 257, no. 42.

31. Carta dated June 22, 1847, Elizondo. Fermín Inarri. Archivo de Protocolos de Navarra, folder 254, no. 44.

32. Valentín Vásquez Prada and Juan Bosco Amores, "La emigración de navarros y vascongados en el Nuevo Mundo," in *Los Vascos y América* (Bilbao: Fundación Banco Bilbao Vizcaya, 1989), 102.

33. Antonio Maria de Ynchausti, letter to the editor, *Business World,* 14–15 March 1997, 5.

34. R. Gonzales Fernandez, *Anuario filipino para 1877* (Manila: 1877), 309.

35. "Monumento a Legazpi y Urdaneta," *Euskal Herria* 31 (1892): 221–22. The bronze monument was made by the Agustin Querol y Subirals, a famous Catalan sculptor.

36. Amada T. Valisno, "Family Portrait: The Elizaldes," pt. 2, *Mr. & Ms.* (Manila), 22 January 1985, 33.

37. Leah Salterio Gatdula, "DZRH Reinforces Network for the New Millenium," *Philippine Daily Inquirer* (Manila), 25 August 1999, p. B7.

38. J. J. Calero, "Fred Elizalde as Filipino," *Business World* (Manila), 6 March 1997, 5.

39. Ibid.

40. Salterio Gatdula, "DZRH Reinforces Network for the New Millenium," p. B7.

41. Ibid.

42. Amada T. Valisno, "Family Portrait: The Elizaldes," pt. 1, *Mr. & Ms.* (Manila), 22 January 1985, 32.

43. Amada T. Valisno, "Family Portrait: The Elizaldes," pt. 3, *Mr.& Ms.* (Manila), 5 February 1985, 24.

44. Ibid.

45. Ibid.

46. Calero, "Fred Elizalde as Filipino," 5.

47. Ibid.

48. John Nance, *The Gentle Tasadays: A Stone Age People in the Philippine Rain Forest* (London: Victor Gollanz, 1975).

49. Calero, "Fred Elizalde as Filipino," 5.

50. EDSA is the main thoroughfare of Metro Manila where massive political, but peaceful, demonstrations are held. It was the site of the so-called People Power demonstrations in February 1986 and January 2001 that toppled Ferdinand Marcos and Joseph Estrada from the presidency.

51. Salterio Gatdula, "DZRH Reinforces Network for the New Millenium," p. B7.

52. Pedro Gorospe, "Antonio María de Ynchausti: Utiliza el Estatuto de Gernika para negociar con la guerilla mora filipina," *El País* (Madrid), 11 February 1988, p. 56.

53. Jean-Claude Larronde, *Manuel de Ynchausti (1900–1961): Un mecenas inspirado* (Bidasoa: Historia Garaikideko Erakundea, 1993), 81.

54. Antonio Maria de Ynchausti, letter to the editor, *Business Day* (Manila), 17 October 1986, pp. 5, 9.

55. *Eighty Years of Public Service: A Brief History of the Monte de Piedad and Savings Bank* (Manila, 1962).

56. Antonio Maria de Ynchausti, letter to the editor, *Business World* (Manila), 14–15 March 1997, 5.

57. *Enciclopedia general ilustrada,* s.v. "Filipinas," 13:479.

58. Antonio Maria de Ynchausti, letter to the author, 7 February 2001.

59. Ibid., 8 May 2001.

60. Jean-Claude Larronde, *Manuel de Ynchausti (1900–1961): Un mecenas inspirado* (Villefranque, France: Editions Bidasoa, 1998), 79. A more comprehensive discussion of the Ynchausti family is found in chapter 9.

61. Ibid., 118–121.

62. Koldo San Sebastián, *El exilio vasco en América: 1936–1946: La acción del gobierno: Política, organización, propaganda, economía, cultura, diplomacia* (San Sebastián: Editorial Txertoa, 1988), 37–38.

63. Antonio Maria de Ynchausti, letter to the author, 8 May 2001.

64. Ibid., 23 February 2001.

65. Ibid., 20 February 2001.

66. *Elko (Nevada) Daily Free Press,* 10 February 1986, front page.

CONCLUSION

1. Andoni F. Aboitiz, letter to the author, 2 April 2001.

2. Robert Laxalt, foreword to *Amerikanuak: Basques in the New World,* by Douglass and Bilbao.

3. Gallop, *A Book of the Basques,* 60.

4. Tony D. Parajo, "Legazi's Hometown Becomes the Philippines' Own," *Philippine Daily Inquirer* (Manila), 20 September 20, 1999, p. E6.

Bibliography

BOOKS

Actas de las Jornadas: El comercio vasco con América en el siglo XVIII, la Real Compañía Guipuzcoana de Caracas. Bilbao: Fundación Banco Bilbao Vizcaya, 1989.

Aduarte, Diego de. *Historia de la Provincia del Santo Rosario de Filipinas, Japón y China.* Vol. 1. Zaragoza: 1693.

Agoncillo, Teodoro. *History of the Filipino People.* 8th ed. Quezon City: R.P. Garcia, 1990.

Alvarez Urcelay, M., et al. *Historia de Navarra.* Donostia: Kriselu, S.A., 1990.

Alzugaray, Juan José. *Vascos universales del siglo XVI.* Madrid: Ediciones Encuentro, 1988.

Amézaga, Vicente de. *El hombre vasco.* Buenos Aires: Editorial Vasca Ekin S.R.L., 1967.

Aparicio Lopez, Teodoro. *Misioneros y colonizadores agustinos en Filipinas.* Valladolid: 1965.

Arana, J. D. *Hombre, raza, nacionalidad, universalidad: Presente y futuro del pueblo vasco.* Bilbao: Ercill-Libros, 1968.

Arana Pérez, I. *Los vascos y América: Ideas, hechos, hombres.* Madrid: Espasa-Calpe S.A., 1990.

Arteche, José. *Elcano.* Madrid: Espasa-Calpe S.A., 1972.

———. *Legazpi: Historia de la conquista de Filipinas.* San Sebastián: 1972.

———. *Urdaneta, el dominador de los espacios del Océano Pacifico.* Madrid: Espasa-Calpe S.A., 1943.

Azcárraga y Palmero, Manuel de. *La libertad del comercio en las Islas Filipinas.* Madrid: Imprenta de José Noguera, 1871.

Banco Español-Filipino: Memoria leida en la Junta General. Manila: 1882.

Bieter, John, and Mark Bieter. *An Enduring Legacy: The Story of Basques in Idaho.* Reno: University of Nevada Press, 2000.

Blair, Emma, and James Robertson. *The Philippine Islands.* 55 vols. Cleveland: Arthur Clark, 1903.

Blumentritt, Ferdinand. *Ataque de los holandeses en siglos XVI y XVII.* Madrid: 1882.

Bores y Romero, J. *La insurrección filipina: Cuatro verdades.* Madrid: 1897.

Burniol, J. *History of the Philippines.* Manila: 1912.

Buzueta, Manuel. *Diccionario geográfico, estadístico, histórico de las Islas Filipinas.* 2 vols. Madrid: 1850.

Cabezas de Herrera, J. *Apuntes históricos sobre la organización político-administrativa de Filipinas.* Manila: Ciudad Condal, 1883.

Cabrero, Leoncio. *España en el Pacífico.* Madrid: Cuadernos Historia 16, 1985.
Callanta, Cesar V. *The Limahong Invasion.* Quezon City: New Day Publishers, 1989.
Caro Baroja, Julio. *Los vascos.* 3rd ed. Madrid: Istmo, 1970.
Caro y Mora, Juan. *Ataque de Limahong a Manila en 1574.* Manila: 1894.
Carrander, R., *Carlos V y sus banqueros.* Vol. 2. Barcelona: Salvat S.A., 1986.
Catálogo Alfabético de Apellidos. (Manila, 21 de noviembre de 1849, National Archives Publication No. D-3.
Cedulario de la Insigne, Muy Noble y Siempre Leal Ciudad de Manila. Manila: Imprenta de José María Dayot, 1836.
Céspedes del Castillo, G. *América Hispánica (1492–1898).* Barcelona: Editorial Labar, 1983.
Chirino, Pedro. *Relación de las Islas Filipinas y lo que en ellas han trabajado los Padres de la Compañía de Jesús.* 2nd ed. Manila: 1890.
Clark, Robert P. *The Basques: The Franco Years and Beyond.* Reno: University of Nevada Press, 1979.
Colayco, Ma. Teresa. *A Tradition of Leadership: Bank of the Philippine Islands.* Makati: BPI, 1984.
The Colonization and Conquest of the Philippines by Spain: Some Contemporary Source Documents. Manila: Filipiniana Book Guild, 1965.
The Complete Poems and Plays of Jose Rizal. Translated by Nick Joaquin. Manila: Far Eastern University, 1976.
Comyn, Tomás. *Estado de las Islas Filipinas en 1810.* Madrid: Imprenta de República, 1820.
Concepción, Juan de la. *Historia general de Philipinas.* 14 vols. Manila: 1788–1792.
Connaugton, Richard, John Pimlott, and Duncan Anderson. *The Battle for Manila: The Most Devastating Untold Story of World War II.* London: Bloomsbury Publishing Plc., 1997.
Constitución del Euskaldun Batzokija o Centro Basko de Iloilo, Islas Filipinas. Aprobada en junta general extraordinaria celebrada el 16 de febrero de 1908. Iloilo: 1908.
Corpuz, O. D. *The Roots of the Filipino Nation.* Vols. 1 and 2. Quezon City: AKLAHI Foundation, 1989.
Costa, Horacio de la. *The Jesuits in the Philippines, 1581–1768.* Cambridge, Mass.: Harvard University Press, 1961.
———. *Readings in Philippine History.* Manila: Bookmark, 1965.
Cruz, Isagani R., and Lydia B. Echauz. *1001 Reasons to Stay in the Philippines.* Manila: Aklat Pescador, 1993.
Cushner, Nicolas. *Spain in the Philippines: From Conquest to Revolution.* Quezon City: Ateneo de Manila University Press, 1972.
Davant, Jean Louis. *Historia del pueblo vasco.* Elkar Zaraus, 1980.
Díaz Arenas, Rafael. *Memorias históricas y estadísticas de Filipinas.* Manila: 1850.
Díaz-Trechuelo, María Lourdes. *Navegantes y conquistadores vascos.* Madrid: Publicaciones Española, 1965.
———. *La Real Compañia de Filipinas.* Sevilla: Escuela de Estudios Hispano-Americanos de Sevilla, Consejo Superior de Investigaciones Científicas, 1965.

Douglass, William A., and Jon Bilbao. *Amerikanuak: Basques in the New World.* Reno: University of Nevada Press, 1975.

Douglass, William A., et al., eds. *Basque Cultural Studies.* Reno: University of Nevada, Basque Studies Program, 1999.

———. *The Basque Diaspora/La Diaspora Vasca.* Reno: University of Nevada, Basque Studies Program, 1999.

———. *Basque Politics and Nationalism on the Eve of the Millennium.* Reno: University of Nevada, Basque Studies Program, 1999.

Eighty Years of Public Service: A Brief History of the Monte Piedad and Saving Bank. Manila: 1962.

Enciclopedia general ilustrada del País Vasco. San Sebastián: Editorial Auñamendi, Estornes Lasa Hnos., 1982.

Enciclopedia universal ilustrada Europeo-Americana. Madrid: Espasa-Calpe, S.A., 1966.

Exposición de Filipinas: Collección de artículos publicados en el globo, diario ilustrado político, científico y literario. Madrid: 1870.

Exposición de la Compañía de Filipinas. Cadiz: 1813.

Fast, Jonathan, and Jim Richardson. *Roots of Dependency: Political and Economic Revolution in the 19th Century Philippines.* Quezon City: Foundation for Nationalist Studies, 1979.

Feced, Pedro [Quioquiap]. *Filipinas: Esbozos y pinceladas.* Manila: 1888.

Fernández de Navarrete, M. *Viajes y descubrimientos españoles en el Pacífico (Elcano, Magallanes, Loaysa, Saavedra).* Madrid: Ediciones Atlas, 1918.

Fernando, J. *Historia de los padres domínicos en las Islas Filipinas.* 6 vols. Madrid: 1870–1872.

Filipinas y México. Manila: 1965.

Filway's Philippine Almanac. Centennial ed. Manila: Filway, 1998.

Flynn, Dennis O., Arturo Giráldez, and James Sobredo, eds. *European Entry into the Pacific: Spain and the Acapulco-Manila Galleons.* Aldershot: Ashgate, 2001.

Gallop, Rodney. *A Book of the Basques.* Reno: University of Nevada Press, 1998.

Garay Unibaso, Francisco. *Correos Marítimos Españoles: A Filipinas, Indias Orientales de 1521 a 1884 y también a Marianas e Indochina.* Bilbao: Ediciones Mensajero, 1991.

Gonzales Fernandez, R. *Anuario filipino para 1877.* Manila: 1877.

Guerrero, Leon Ma. *The First Filipino: A Biography of Jose Rizal.* Manila: National Heroes Commission, 1963.

Historia General de España y América: Reformismo y progreso en América (1804–1905). Vol. 15. Madrid: Ediciones Rialp S.A., 1989.

Historical Conservation Society. *The Christianization of the Philippines.* Translated by Rafael Lopez and Alfonso Felix Jr. Manila: 1965.

Intxausti, J., ed. *Euskal Herria: Historia y sociedad.* Caja Laboral Popular Danona, Ugaldetxo-Oiartzun, 1985.

Ira, L., and Isagani Medina. *The Streets of Manila.* Quezon City: GCF Books, 1977.

Ispízua, Segundo de. *Historia de los vascos en el descubrimiento, conquista y civilización de América.* Vol. 2. Bilbao: 1915.

Jesus, Ed. C. de. *The Tobacco Monopoly in the Philippines: Bureacratic Enterprise and*

Social Change, 1766–1880. Quezon City: Ateneo de University Press, 1980.
Kintanar, Thelma B. *U.P. Cultural Dictionary for Filipinos.* Quezon City: University of the Philippines Press, 1996.
Lachica, Eduardo. *Ayala: The Philippines' Oldest Business House.* Makati: Filipinas Heritage Foundation, 1984.
Lafarga Lozano, A. *Los vascos en el descubrimiento y colonizacion de America.* Bilbao: Gran Enciclopedia Vasca, 1973.
Larkin, John A. *Sugar and the Origins of Modern Philippine Society.* Quezon City: New Day Publishers, 2001.
Larronde, Jean-Claude. *Manuel de Ynchausti (1900–1961): Un mecenas inspirado.* Villefranque, France: Editions Bidasoa, 1998.
———. *Manuel de Ynchausti (1900–1961): Un mecenas inspirado.* Bidasoa: Historia Garaikideko Erakundea, 1993.
Legarda, Benito J., Jr. *After the Galleons: Foreign Trade, Economic Change, and Entrepreneurship in the Nineteenth Century Philippines.* Quezon City: Ateneo de Manila University Press, 1999.
Lhande, Pierre. *L'Emigracion basque.* Paris: 1909.
———. *La emigración vasca.* Translated into Spanish by Ignacio Basurko Berroa. San Sebastián: Editorial Auñamendi, 1971.
Llanes, Ferdinand, ed. *Pagbabalik Sa Bayan.* Manila: Rex Bookstore, 1993.
Luzurraga, Miguel A. *Comercio y navegación de Europa y Filipinas.* Santander: 1876.
Lynch, John. *España bajo los austrias: Imperio y absolutismo 1516–1598.* Vol. 1. Translated by Joseph Maria Bernardas. Barcelona: Ediciones Peninsula, 1989.
———. *Spain Under the Habsburg.* Oxford: Basil Blackwell, 1965.
MacMicking, Robert. *Recollections of Manilla and the Philippines During 1848, 1849, and 1850.* London: 1851.
Madaria, J. R., ed. *Los vascos en la hispanidad.* Bilbao: Diputación de Vizcaya, 1964.
Mairin, Mitchell. *Elcano: The First Circumnavigator.* London: Herder, 1958.
———. *Friar Andres de Urdaneta, O.S.A.* London: Macdonalds and Evans, 1964.
Martín Artajo, Alberto. *Presencia decisiva vasconia en las empresas españolas.* Diputación Foral de Vizcaya, 1966.
Martín Palma, María Teresa. *El consulado de Manila.* Granada: Universidad de Granada, 1981.
Martínez de Zuñiga, Joaquín. *Estadismo de Filipinas.* Vol. 2. Sampaloc: 1803.
———. *Historia de las islas Philipinas.* Sampaloc: 1803.
Martínez Salazar, Alberto. *Presencia alavesa en América y Filipinas (1700–1826).* Vitoria: Diputación Foral de Alava, 1988.
Mas y Sans, Sinilbado. *Informe sobre el estado de las Islas Filipinas en 1842.* 2 vols. Madrid: 1843.
Medina, Juan de. *Historia de los sucesos de la Orden de San Agustín de estas Islas Filipinas.* Manila: 1893.
Medina, Juan Toribio. *El Tribunal del Santo Oficio de Inquisición en las Islas Filipinas.* Santiago de Chile: 1899.
Merino, M. *Agustinos evangelizadores de Filipinas (1565–1965).* Madrid: 1965.

Molina, Antonio M. *Historia de Filipinas.* Madrid: Instituto de Cooperación Iberoamericana, 1984.

Mojares, Resil B. *Aboitiz: Family and Firm in the Philippines.* Cebu City: Aboitiz & Company, 1998.

Montero y Vidal, J. *Historia general de Filipinas desde el descubrimiento de dichas islas hasta nuestros días.* 3 vols. Madrid: 1887–1895.

Morga, Antonio de. *Sucesos de las Islas Filipinas* (obra publicada en Méjico el ano de 1609 nuevamente sacada a luz y anotada por Jose Rizal). París: Librería de Garnier Hermanos, 1890.

Nesom, G. E., et al. *Manual de la industria azucarera de las Islas Filipinas.* Manila: Manila Bureau of Printing, 1912.

Ortíz Armengol, Pedro. *Intramuros de Manila de 1571 hasta su destrucción en 1945.* Madrid: Ediciones Cultura Hispánica, 1959.

Pardo de Tavera, T. H. *Una Memoria de Anda y Salazar.* Manila: 1899.

Payne, Stanley. *Basque Nationalism.* Reno: University of Nevada Press, 1975.

Pazos, Píos. *Héroes de Filipinas.* Madrid: 1985.

Phelan, John Leddy. *Hispanization of the Philippines: Spanish Aims and Filipino Responses.* Madison: University of Wisconsin Press, 1959.

Pierre, Jacques. *Historia universal, los grandes corrientes de la historia.* Vol. 2. Barcelona: Salvat S.A., 1961.

Pigafetta, Antonio. *First Voyage Around the World.* Manila: Filipiniana Book Guild, 1969.

———. *Primer viaje alrededor del mundo.* Madrid: Historia 16, 1988.

Pildain Salazar, M. P. *Ir a América: La emigración vasca a América (Guipúzcoa 1840–1870).* San Sebastián: 1984.

Querexeta, Jaime de. *Diccionario onomástico y heráldico vasco.* Bilbao: Gran Enciclopedia Vasca, 1971.

Quijano de Manila [Nick Joaquin]. *Language of the Streets and Other Essays.* Manila: National Bookstore, 1980.

Quison, Serafin. *English "Country Trade" with the Philippines, 1644–1765.* Quezon City: University of the Philippines Press, 1966.

Recur, Carlos. *Filipinas: Estudios administrativos y comerciales.* Madrid: Moreno y Rojas, 1879.

Retana, Wenceslao. *Indice biográfico de los que asistieron al descubrimiento de las Islas Filipinas.* Madrid: 1921.

———. *Indice de personas nobles y otros de calidad que han estado en Filipinas.* Madrid: 1921.

———. *Vida y escritos del Dr. Rizal.* Epilogue by Miguel de Unamuno. Madrid: 1907.

Rizal, Jose. *Noli Me Tangere.* Berlin: 1887. Translated by Leon Ma. Guerrero. London: Longmans, 1961.

———. *El Filibusterismo.* Ghent: 1891. Translated by Leon Ma. Guerrero. London: Longmans, 1961.

Robles, Eliodoro. *The Philippines in the Nineteenth Century.* Quezon City: Malaya Books, 1969.

Rodríguez Baena, María Luisa. *La sociedad económica de amigos del país de Manila en el siglo XVIII.* Sevilla: Escuela de Estudios Hispanoamericanos, 1966.

Rodríguez García, Vicente. *El gobierno de Don Gaspar Antonio de la Torre y Ayala en las Islas Filipinas.* Granada: Universidad de Granada, 1976.

Rodríguez, Isacio. *Historia de la provincia agustina del Santísimo Nombre de Jesús de Filipinas.* Manila: 1978.

Salamanca, Bonifacio. *The Filipino Reaction to American Rule, 1901–1913.* Hamden, Conn.: Shoe String Press, 1968.

San Agustín, Gaspar. *Conquista espiritual y temporal de Filipinas.* Madrid: 1698.

San Sebastión, Koldo. *El exilio vasco en América: 1936/1946 Acción del Gobierno.* San Sebastián: Editorial Txertoa, 1988.

Santiago, Ma. Lina Araneta. *Salvador Araneta—A Man Ahead of His Time.* Malabon: 1986.

Sanz Diaz, J. *Legazpi: El conquistador de Filipinas.* Barcelona: Ediciones Patria, 1940.

Satron, M. *La insurreción en Filipinas.* Madrid: 1897.

Say, Michael G., ed. *The VIPs of Philippine Business.* Manila: Mahal Kong Pilipinas Charitable Foundation, 1987.

Schurz, William. *The Manila Galleon.* Manila: Historical Conservation Society, 1985.

Sharp, Andrew. *Adventurous Armada: The Story of Legazpi's Expedition.* New Zealand: Whitcombe and Tombs, 1961.

Sitoy, T. Valentino, Jr. *A History of Christianity in the Philippines.* Vol. 1. Quezon City: New Day Publishers, 1985.

The Story of Aboitiz & Company Inc. and the Men Behind It. Cebu City: Aboitiz & Company, 1973.

Teran, M., et al. *Geografía regional de España.* Barcelona: Editorial Ariel S.A., 1987.

Uriarte, Higinio de. *A Basque Among the Guerrillas of Negros.* Bacolod City, Philippines, Editor of Civismo Week, 1962.

Los Vascos y América. Bilbao: Fundación Banco Bilbao Vizcaya, 1989.

Warren, James Francis. *The Sulu Zone, 1768–1898.* Quezon City: New Day Publishers, 1985.

Wolff, Leon. *Little Brown Brother: America's Forgotten Bid for Empire Which Cost 350,000 Lives.* Manila: Erehwon Publishing House, 1968.

Ybarra, J. *Gestas Vascongadas.* San Sebastián: Editorial Ichaparonal, 1952.

Zweig, Stefan. *Magallanes: El hombre y su gesta.* 3rd ed. Barcelona: Editorial Juventud, S.A., 1981.

PERIODICALS AND PARTS OF BOOKS

Antonio, Tony. "MCX Rail Project Encountering Delays." *Manila Bulletin,* 17 March 1998, pp. 1, 19.

"Basque Country: A Special Advertising Supplement." *Far Eastern Economic Review,* 14 December 1995.

Bernal, Rafael. "The Chinese Colony in the Philippines, 1570–1770." In *The Chinese in the Philippines, 1570–1770,* edited by Alberto Felix Jr., 40–66. Manila: Solidaridad Publishing House, 1966.

Bilbao, Jon. "Basques in the Philippine Islands." *Basque Studies Program Newsletter* no. 20 (July 1979): 3–6.

Borja, Marciano R. de. "The Basques in the Philippines." *Philippine Panorama,* 14 November 1993: 32–34

Cabrero, Leoncio. "Desarrollo de la industria agrícola filipina durante el siglo XIX." *Anuario de Estudios Americanos* 31: 105–21.

Calero, J. J. "Fred Elizalde as Filipino." *Business World* (Manila), 6 March 1997, 5.

"Carlos Loyzaga: Greatest Filipino Cager Ever." *Philippine Daily Inquirer* (Manila), 15 January 1999, p. B15.

Díaz-Trechuelo, María Lourdes. "El comercio de Filipinas durante la segunda mitad de los siglo XVIII." *Revista de Indias* (Madrid) 22 (1963): 463–85.

———. "De la Compañia Guipuzcoana de Caracas a Compañia de Filipinas." In *Los Vascos y América,* 359–85. Bilbao: Fundación Banco Bilbao Vizcaya, 1989.

———. "Defensa de Filipinas en el último quarto del siglo XVIII." *Anuario de Estudios Americanos* 21: 145–209.

———."Eighteenth-Century Philippine Economy: Commerce." In *European Entry in the Pacific: Spain and the Acapulco-Manila Galleons,* edited by Dennis O. Flynn, Arturo Giráldez, and James Sobredo, 281–307. Aldershot: Ashgate, 2001.

———. "La empresa española en Filipinas," *Revista de Estudios Americanos* 12 (1956): 27–39.

———. "Fortificaciones en las Islas Filipinas (1565–1800). In *Puertos y Fortificaciones en América y Filipinas,* 261–80. Madrid: Comisión de Estudios Históricos de Obras Públicas y Urbanismo, 1985.

———. "Manila española: Notas sobre su evolución urbana." *Estudios Americanos (Revista de Estudios Hispano Americanos)* 9, nos. 40–41 (January–February 1955): 447–63.

"Dr. Salvador Z. Araneta, educator : Molding hearts for the country, souls for God." *Manila Bulletin,* 31 January 2002, p. B8.

Duque Montenegro, A. "Los orígenes de los vascos." *Historia Antigua* 1 (1971): 271–329.

Echegaray Corta, Carmelo de. "Legazpi y Urdaneta en la colonización de Filipinas." *Euskalerrian Alde* 12, no. 235 (July 1923): 241–48.

Feced, Pedro. "¿Hay Bascongados en Filipinas?" *Euskal-Erria* 27 (1892): 106–8.

Fernández de Navarrete, E. "Documentos relativos a Juan Sebastián del Cano." *Colección de documentos inéditos para la historia de España.* Vol. 1. 1842.

Francisco, Luzviminda. "The Philippine-American War." In *The Philippine Reader,* edited by Daniel Schirmer and Stephen Rosskam Shalom, 8–19. Quezon City: KEN, 1989.

Garante Ojanguren, L. "La Real Compañia Guipuzcoana de Caracas." In *Los Vascos y América,* 290–306. Bilbao: Fundación Banco Bilbao Vizcaya, 1989.

Gatdula, Leah Salterio. "DZRH Reinforces Network for the New Millenium." *Philippine Daily Inquirer,* 25 August 1999, p. B7.

Gorostidi Guelbenze, A. "Los euskeros en la primera vuelta al mundo." *Euskal Erria* 57 (1907): 382–86.

———. "Tripulación de la Nao Victoria" *Euskal Erria* 57 (1907): 322–26.

Guerrero, Milagros C. "The Chinese in the Philippines, 1570–1770." In *The Chinese in the Philippines, 1570–1770*, edited by Alberto Felix Jr., 15–39. Manila: Solidaridad Publishing House, 1966.

Harper, Bambi. "Sociedad Económica de Amigos del País." *Philippine Daily Inquirer*, 29 May 2001, p. A7.

Hernández, José Maria. "José María Aranzibia: Una leyenda de la cesta." *Kezka* 6 época (1994): 13–16.

"Jaime Augusto Zobel de Ayala: The CEO as Catalyst." *World Executive Digest*, May 1996, 100.

Joaquin, Nick. "Culture Hero: The Santo Niño de Cebu." In *Culture and History: Occasional Notes on the Process of Philippine Becoming*, 60–69. Manila: Solar, 1988.

Laxalt, Robert. "The Indomitable Basques." *National Geographic*, July 1985, 69–71.

Lee Flores, Wilson Y. "The Aboitizes: Family Ties that Bind." *Philippine Daily Inquirer* (Manila), 6 March 2000.

Madaria, J. R. "El navegante vizcaino Guido de Labazarri." In *Los vascos en la Hispanidad*, edited by J. R. Madaria, 199–205. Bilbao: Diputación de Vizcaya, 1964.

Martínez Ruiz, J. "Catálogo general de individuos de la Real Sociedad de los Amigos del País (1765–1793)." *Boletín de la Real Sociedad de los Amigos del País XII*. San Sebastián, 1896.

Montero, Claudio. "Exploración en Mindanao." *Boletín de la Sociedad Geográfica de Madrid* 15, nos. 1 and 2 (July/August 1883): 115–33.

"Honra á Euskaría: Monumento a Legazpi y Urdaneta." *Euskal-Erria* 27 (1892): 221–22.

Novenario, Carlos G. "A Legacy from Euskadi." *Philippine Graphics*, 11 March 1994, p. 44.

Parajo, Tony D. "Legazpi's Hometown Becomes the Philippines' Own." *Philippine Daily Inquirer* (Manila), 20 September 1999, p. E6.

Personazz, D. "Les Basques aux Philippines." *Archipel* (Paris), 31 (1986).

Quirino, Carlos. "El primer mexicano en Filipinas." In *Filipinas y México*, 61–69. Manila: Comité del Año de Amistad Filipino-Mexicana, 1965.

Rodao, Florentino. "The Falange in the Philippines, 1935–1945." In *Pagbabalik sa Bayan* (Return to homeland), edited by Fernando Llanes, 126–54. Manila: Rex Bookstore, 1993.

Romulo, Erwin. "Q & A: Jaime Zobel de Ayala." *Philippine Star* (Manila), 8 February 1997, pp. YS1–3.

Sola, V. M. de. "Juan Sebastián Elcano." In *Los vascos en la hispanidad*, edited by J. R. Madaria, 175–85. Bilbao: Diputación de Vizcaya, 1964.

Ubillos, G. "La evangelización de Mindanao por San Francisco Javier." *Principe de Viana*, no. 18 (1945): 160–64.

Urritia, Eduardo de. "Biografía: Antonio Urbiztondo." *Euskalerrianen Alde* 19 (September 1923): 352–54.

Valisno, Amada T. "Family Portrait: The Elizaldes." Three parts in *Mr. & Ms.* (part 1, 22 January 1985; part 2, 29 January 1985; part 3, 5 February 1985).

Vásquez de Prada, Valentín, and Juan Bosco Amores. "La emigración de navarros y vascongados en el Nuevo Mundo y su repercusión en las comunidades de origen." In *Los Vascos y América*, 98–105. Madrid: Gela: Espasa-Calpe/Argantonio.

Ynchausti, Antonio Maria de. "Quelques Basques qui ont contribué au developpement des Philippines." *Gurre Herria* 31 (1959): 122–28.

———. Letter to the editor. *Business Day* (Manila), 17 October 1986, pp. 5, 9.

———. Letter to the editor. *Business World* (Manila), 14–15 March 1997, 5.

UNPUBLISHED MATERIALS

Bilbao, Jon. "Philippine Islands (1830–1910)." Unpublished monograph. Basque Emigration Studies, Working Papers 1. Reno: Basque Studies Program, University of Nevada, 1979. Photocopy.

Borja Ramos, Marciano de. "Los vascos en Filipinas." Master's thesis, Universidad de Navarra, Pamplona, 1992.

Escobedo Mancilla, Ronald. "El americanismo en el País Vasco: La emigración al nuevo mundo." Universidad del País Vasco, Vitoria, 1990.

INTERNET SOURCES

www.basque.unr.edu

www.euskadi.net

Index